American State Legislatures

AMERICAN
STATE
LEGISLATURES

Report of the
Committee on American Legislatures
AMERICAN POLITICAL SCIENCE ASSOCIATION

BELLE ZELLER, *Editor*
Professor of Political Science
Brooklyn College

New York - 1954
THOMAS Y. CROWELL COMPANY

Preface

Modernization of the American state legislatures is considered by many to be the most important piece of unfinished business in the area of government reorganization. Some view with alarm the expansion of federal power, lament the loss of states' rights, and urge the reascendency of the state legislatures. Despite federal expansion, the importance of the state legislatures has grown enormously during the past decades.

This report of the Committee on American Legislatures of the American Political Science Association presents the results of a four-year study of the state legislatures. It is, perhaps, not without significance that its appearance coincides with the establishment by Congress of a Commission on Intergovernmental Relations to re-examine the relationships among the federal, state, and local governments. The conclusion is clear that the state legislatures are poorly equipped to serve as policy-making agencies in mid-twentieth-century America. In fact, the skepticism concerning the proper role of the legislature in a complex and technological world calls for an intensive philosophical and practical examination that will reaffirm the democratic way of life.

The Committee, composed of professors of political science in American colleges and universities and of professional personnel attached to the American state legislatures and the Congress, believes that the state legislatures can—and should—function as dynamic, coordinate, efficient policy-formulating bodies.

In undertaking its assignment, the Committee on American Legislatures made a number of basic decisions regarding the nature and scope of its work:

v

1. To collect a body of factual data upon which to base conclusions and recommendations for reorganization that will meet the needs of the states or will serve as a basis for adaptation for specific legislatures.

2. To encourage the study of the state legislative processes, particularly in college undergraduate and graduate courses of political science and law.

3. To stimulate the appropriation of more generous state funds for study of individual state legislatures by their own research agencies.

4. To enlist the aid of government officials, The Council of State Governments, and civic organizations in encouraging state legislative reform.

5. To encourage the establishment of a citizens' clearing house, aided by the mass media of communication to keep alive interest in state legislative reform as a continuing process.

6. To stimulate broader research in the legislative process with the assistance of foundation and government funds.

This report is, then, only a first step in achieving these objectives. The Committee hopes that all cooperating groups will study not only the informational data presented in this report but especially the recommendations at the close of the chapters.

The Committee wishes to thank the executive council, officers, and staff of the American Political Science Association for their sympathetic cooperation. The Committee deeply appreciates the assistance rendered by the staffs of the Bureau of Public Administration of Boston University, The Council of State Governments, the Legislative Reference Service of the Library of Congress, the state legislative libraries and councils, the National Municipal League, and the library of Brooklyn College.

Grateful acknowledgement is also due Winston W. Crouch of the University of California at Los Angeles, George B. Galloway of the Library of Congress, Edward H. Litchfield of Cornell University, Lloyd M. Short of the University of Minnesota, Harvey Walker of the Ohio State University, and Herbert L. Wiltsee of The Council of State Governments. The Committee records with sorrow the death of its esteemed member, Professor Joseph P. Chamberlain of Columbia University.

BELLE ZELLER

December, 1953

Contents

American State Legislatures at Mid-Century

THE STORY of the rise of popular government over the centuries has been of the slow and halting and painful increase in the percentage of the population having the right of representation—the right to be consulted through their popularly elected representatives on questions of public policy. In the United States today this fight has been largely won. We have achieved not only universal manhood suffrage, but by the adoption of the Nineteenth Amendment early in the twentieth century, virtually universal suffrage.

The legislative system of the American states was derived, to a large extent, from two sources—British experience in the development of institutions of representative government and colonial experience under the Crown and trading company charters. As the latter followed rather closely English thinking and English precedents, the prevailing influence at the end of the colonial period was the legislative concept that had evolved during the rise of Parliament. Thus American legislatures were originally based on inherited principles and practices. Moreover, for the better part of the more than 300 years that legislatures have existed on this continent, these basic concepts have remained unchanged and largely unquestioned. Not until a generation or two ago did the impact of changing conditions on the legislative system prompt any serious rethinking of long-standing procedures.

1

GROWTH IN IMPORTANCE OF STATE LEGISLATURES

There was a time—not so long ago—when state legislative bodies played a relatively minor role in government, although practically all authority came through their consent. Effective power too frequently resided elsewhere; life itself was far less complicated than it is today; and government did not do very many things and frequently did not do them well. The state legislators were able to meet for limited sessions of thirty or forty or sixty days every two years, pass a few laws and the necessary appropriations, and go home. The people— and the members of the legislatures—heaved a sigh of relief when the sessions were over, and proceeded to forget about legislation and legislative problems for the next eighteen months or more.

Those days are no more, and it is wholly unrealistic to expect that they will ever return. The increase in the number and scope and complexity of government services at all three levels of government— national, state, and local—has imposed vast new burdens and responsibilities upon legislatures that are bound by old and traditional concepts of organization and procedure.

During the first half of the twentieth century the growth of state functions, especially in the important areas of education, public works (highways), health, and welfare, has been enormous.[1] Although these burdens are sometimes shared with local communities, their extent may be roughly indicated by the growth in the number of state civil employees and in total state expenditures. State employment rolls have expanded during the last generation from tens of thousands to almost a million in 1949.[2] In 1913 the total cost of operating the forty-eight states amounted to only $378 million; by 1940 total state expenditures had reached $5.1 billion. In the fiscal decade 1940-49 the figure soared to $11.6 billion, an increase of 127 per cent in this ten-year period alone. Similarly the increases in state revenues have been spectacular, rising from $345 million collected in 1913 to $6.1 billion in 1943 and $11.0 billion in 1949. Thus in

---

[1] See symposium on the governments of the states at mid-century, *State Government,* June, 1950, entire issue.

[2] U. S. Bureau of the Census, *Public Employment in April, 1949,* Government Employment Series (Washington: July, 1949).

1949 the states collected thirty-one times the amount collected in 1913.[3]

The legislatures of the states are faced—to a lesser degree, to be sure—with the same types of problems that all but overwhelm the Congress. Legislative committees must inquire into and evaluate programs of far-reaching scope and importance. They must analyze and pass upon huge budget requests and be responsible for the proper surveillance of the executive agencies that spend the money.

In addition to expanded state services, the interrelationships of governments under our federal system have also increased the burdens confronting state legislatures. Many a federal program requires not only cooperation on the part of the state administrative officers concerned but legislative action as well. For example, nearly all grants-in-aid programs prescribe legislative approval as a prerequisite of state participation,[4] and numerous other types of programs may call for supporting legislation. At the other end of the governmental scale legislative action may be required as a basis for the development of various types of programs at the local level and for cooperation across state lines by means of interstate compacts.

Present-day legislative responsibilities are of such complexity, such magnitude, that they cannot be met adequately by the old-fashioned, time-consuming legislative procedures, antiquated organization, inadequate and incompetent staff services. Committee systems are archaic, not having been changed in most states in any important respect for fifty or a hundred years—or more. Rules of procedure that antedate the invention of the printing press still prevail in many jurisdictions. Some legislative bodies still continue to consume from one fourth to one third of their session time in roll calls. If the legislatures are to meet the challenge that now confronts them—their responsibility to the people of the states—these conditions cannot continue.

---

[3] U. S. Bureau of the Census, *Compendium of State Government Finances in 1949* (Washington: 1950), and *Historical Statistics of the United States. 1789-1945* (Washington: 1949), pp. 314-17.

[4] Exceptions are found in the U. S. Public Health Service and Children's Bureau programs.

PRE–WORLD WAR II STEPS TOWARD LEGISLATIVE REORGANIZATION

Although a number of important steps have been taken in the twentieth century in the direction of improving state legislative organization and procedure, little or nothing was done before World War I. However, the legislative reference services, now existing in some form in nearly all states, did begin their significant services to the legislatures late in the nineteenth century; the New York State Library led the way in 1890 and was followed by the Massachusetts State Library in 1892. The idea was expanded and developed in Wisconsin beginning in 1901, under the leadership of Charles McCarthy, and the Wisconsin Legislative Reference Bureau celebrated its fiftieth anniversary in 1951. The original twofold purpose of supplying information to members and rendering assistance in the drafting of bills still holds in many jurisdictions, although the tendency in late years has been in the direction of separate agencies for reference and for bill-drafting work.

The split session, with which a number of states have experimented —in some cases by constitutional provision, in others by legislative practice—has been in use in California since 1911. It was subsequently adopted constitutionally, and later abandoned, in West Virginia and New Mexico. The split session was an effort to reduce confusion during the session and give members a better opportunity to study, and obtain constituents' reaction to, pending legislation. The same purpose can be achieved—and has been in some states—merely through agreement to adjourn until some specified date. Whichever the method used, however, careful students of the results indicate a good deal of doubt that the objectives have actually been attained.

Prominent among the developments of the post-World War I period was the first appearance in 1921 of the *Model State Constitution,* whose important recommendations relating to state legislatures are considered on page 10.

The early 1930's witnessed some further advances. The state legislative councils, now existing in more than two-thirds of the states, owe their origin to the precedent established in Kansas in 1933. The council plan achieves the objectives of closer coordination between the executive and legislative branches and provision of machinery for legislative planning. The members of the council committees and the research staff work in close cooperation with the appropriate representatives of the executive branch while developing important pieces of legislation, and the work of developing the program for the next legislative session begins as soon as the preceding one has been concluded.

In 1934 Nebraska, under the leadership of the late Senator George W. Norris, adopted its present unicameral legislative system. This new system has functioned successfully since January, 1937. The action of the voters of Nebraska was the more significant in view of the numerous unsuccessful attempts made in other states some years earlier to adopt the unicameral system.

REORGANIZATION OF CONGRESS

The events leading up to World War II gave added impetus to the movement for legislative reform. The rise of the dictators Mussolini and Hitler provided a clear challenge to the efficiency and effectiveness of representative legislative institutions. As Mussolini made secure his control over Italy, as Hitler extended his power from country to country across Europe, one disturbing fact became clear: when representative legislative assemblies collapsed, dictatorship moved in.

Under the leadership of the late Dr. Benjamin B. Wallace the American Political Science Association established in 1941 its Committee on Congress under the chairmanship of Dr. George B. Galloway. The report of this committee stressed problems of internal organization and operation as well as of external relationships. The committee's findings included a list of eight influences believed to handicap the Congress as an institution in the performance of its proper functions and a list of ten suggested means of reducing—if not eliminating—these handicaps. Publication of this excellent report in 1945 aroused a widespread interest in the subject of congressional reorganization, both in the Congress and throughout the country.[5] Also published in 1945 was the so-called Heller Report,

---

[5] *The Reorganization of Congress:* A Report of the Committee on Congress of the American Political Science Association (Washington: Public Affairs Press, 1945).

Strengthening the Congress, which went through three printings within a period of four months.[6]

Congress itself in 1945 established the Joint Committee on the Organization of Congress headed by former Senator Robert M. La Follette, Jr., and Senator (then Representative) A. S. Mike Monroney. Dr. Galloway was appointed staff director. Extensive hearings were held and further studies were made.[7] In its final report the committee made recommendations on the following matters: committee structure and operation, majority and minority policy committees, research and staff facilities, legislative fiscal control, the more efficient use of congressional time, the registration of organized groups, congressional pay and retirement, and other recommendations of a miscellaneous nature. Finally, in 1946, the Congress passed and the President signed the La Follette-Monroney bill, known as the Legislative Reorganization Act of 1946.

Instrumental in securing passage of the Legislative Reorganization Act of 1946 was the National Committee for the Strengthening of Congress. This citizen organization, originally established to publicize the Heller Report and to further the national campaign for the modernization of Congress, has continued in existence for the purpose of studying the operation of the act and making recommendations for its improvement. These recommendations have taken the form of an annual appraisal of the functioning of the Congress as related to the matters covered by the act.

In addition a Senate committee has twice examined the administration of the Legislative Reorganization Act as a whole, and a House

---

[6] Planning Pamphlet No. 39 (Washington: National Planning Association, 1945).

[7] Joint Committee on the Organization of Congress, *Hearings,* 4 parts (a *Summary* of these *Hearings* was published, also an *Index*). The committee issued two reports: *First Progress Report* (S. Doc. No. 36, 79th Cong., 1st sess., 1945) and a final *Report* (S. Doc. No. 1011, 79th Cong., 2d sess., 1946). See also its *Suggestions for Strengthening Congress by Members of Congress and Others* (Joint Committee Print, 79th Cong., 2d sess., 1946) and William R. Tansill, *A Select, Annotated Bibliography on the Organization, Procedure, and Reorganization of Congress* (Joint Committee Print, 79th Cong., 1st sess., 1945).

regard to related subject matter, equalization of work, and cooperation between legislative houses.

Committee meetings should be scheduled and announced so as to prevent conflicting duties for committee members, and a permanent and public record of committee action should be kept.

6. *Legislative Committees—Public Hearings.* Provision should be made for public hearings on all major bills and advance notice of hearings should be published and made readily available, giving time and place of hearing and subject matter of legislation to be heard and, whereever possible, indicating the number and title of bills. Rules of procedure by committees governing hearings should likewise be published and made readily available.

7. *Legislative Councils and Interim Committees.* Provision for legislative councils or interim committees with adequate clerical and research facilities deserves serious consideration. These facilities can be provided most readily and effectively through a legislative reference bureau.

8. *Reference, Research, Bill-Drafting, and Statutory Revision Services.* Legislative reference, research, bill-drafting, and statutory revision services should be reviewed in each state, and strengthened wherever necessary by improved organization and more adequate staffing and appropriations.

9. *Introduction and Printing of Legislation.* Consideration should be given to limiting by rule the period during a legislative session when new bills may be introduced. Provision should be made for the drafting, filing, and printing of bills before the opening of the session. All bills and important amendments introduced during a session should be printed promptly after introduction and whenever possible they should be inspected, before printing, by bill drafters or revision clerks. Careful consideration should be given in order to avoid indiscriminate insertion of emergency or immediate-effect clauses in pending legislation.

Publication of manuals covering the form, style, and grammatical construction of bills is suggested.

Adequate provision should be made for printing statutes and making them generally available at the earliest possible time after final enactment.

10. *Legislative Rules.* The rules of legislative houses should be reviewed and revised wherever necessary to expedite legislative procedure, with due regard for adequate deliberation on measures and fairness to minority parties.

Permanent standing committees or a joint committee on legislative organization, rules, and procedure should be established in some form by each legislature.

11. *Legislative Finance.* The legislature should provide for a budget adequate to meet all probable expenditures during a fiscal period. Provision for a fiscal officer responsible for the centralized custody of legislative personnel, payroll, and expenditure records of each house, and the supervision of legislative expenditures should be considered.

12. *Local and Special Legislation.* Consideration and settlement of claims against the state should be delegated to judicial or administrative agencies, and general, optional, or home rule legislation should provide positive substitutes for special legislation affecting cities, counties, and other political subdivisions of the states, particularly in matters of purely local concern.

Constitutional Revision and Legislative Reform

The *Model State Constitution* has gone through a number of revisions, the last (Fifth Edition) appearing in 1948. Framed by the National Municipal League's Committee on State Government, the model constitution has had a constantly growing influence and usefulness. It proposes (1) the establishment of a legislative council to collect information and submit measures for action by the legislature; (2) a closer relationship and greater harmony between the governor and the legislature; (3) a continuous legislative process; (4) improvements in committee procedure; (5) a general grant of power to the legislature, accompanied by safeguards to protect that body from unfavorable judicial decisions on questions involving the delegation of legislative powers. Although a unicameral system continues to be advocated in this document, the fact that many states may not be willing to go this far is recognized and the general proposals are applicable also to bicameral legislatures.

Since 1938 there has been a growing interest in problems of constitutional revision among the states, revised constitutions having been adopted in Georgia, Missouri, New Jersey, and New York and more or less active campaigns for revision undertaken in approximately one third of the states. High on the list of problems raised in constitutional revision, which are both numerous and broad in scope, are those relating to the legislature. These problems include not only legislative organization and procedure, but also the exceedingly difficult question of apportionment. The experience of New Jersey in this connection is significant. The New Jersey convention did an outstanding job of revising the state's constitution, more than a century old, but the convention itself and the resulting constitution were obtained only at the price of an iron-bound agreement that no change would be made in the provisions relating to legislative apportionment. These provisions, in New Jersey as in most other states, are most inequitable and operate to prevent the selection of a legislative body truly representative of the people of the state. The New Jersey incident serves not only to underscore the importance of the apportionment problem, but to illustrate the intimate relationship existing between apportionment and constitutional revision—and legislative reform.

"Little Hoover Commissions" and Other Committees

Encouraged by the establishment in 1947 of the Federal Commission on Organization of the Executive Branch of Government (popularly known as the Hoover Commission), well over half of the states and two territories had set up "little Hoover commissions" by 1952. Most of these commissions were concerned with setting in order state administrative houses, but some—for example, the Connecticut commission—did recognize that "all roads lead to or from the General Assembly" and that greater efficiency in state government involves not only stronger management in the executive branch but also a strengthening of the legislature. Although the Connecticut report, published in February, 1950, was largely devoted to recommendations for the executive and administrative agencies of the state, it did treat the legislative problems of apportionment, size, greater independence for individual members, more collective authority, and better internal management.[11]

---

[11] Commission on State Government Organization, *The Report to the General Assembly and Governor of Connecticut* (Hartford: February, 1950), pp. 50-60. Of the 33 states and 2 territories that authorized reorganization studies, 4 included studies of all three branches of government, and in 5 others attention was given to both the legislative and executive branches.

Many states are attacking these important questions of reorganization by still another means—legislative committees and commissions on legislative organization and procedure. Even under existing constitutional provisions much can be accomplished in this way. For example, many of the recommendations of The Council of State Governments' Committee on Legislative Processes and Procedures have been adopted in the various states. It is to be expected that constitutional revision, state investigating bodies, and the influence of the council's committee may be productive of many further improvements in the months and years ahead.

Legislative Service Conference

Prior to World War II there had been a number of informal conferences of persons engaged in legislative reference work. There had also been a rapid increase in the number of state agencies functioning in this field—a fact that prompted The Council of State Governments in 1947 to call a conference of the professional personnel engaged in providing staff services for state legislatures and legislative committees. This conference authorized the appointment of an organizing committee whose report was presented and accepted at another similar meeting the following year. At this 1948 meeting the Legislative Service Conference was formally organized. Its membership includes state, federal and territorial professional personnel engaged in legislative reference work, legislative research, bill drafting, statutory or code revision services, and budgetary and fiscal analysis, as well as the directing staffs of legislative councils. The conference's membership has been extended to include state legislators who are officers of legislative service agencies, clerks of the legislative chambers, and a very few academicians designated by the conference because of their close connection with legislative research.

The early meetings were devoted largely to instructional talks by some of the ablest and most experienced men in the field and to the exchange of information regarding work methods and problems, although some attention was given to the exchange of information on research completed or in progress. Although these problems still find a place in the program, members of the conference have, in recent years, been thinking more in terms of help on specific current legislative problems, and in terms of long-range planning for more effective service to the legislatures of their respective states. Consequently, attention is being given to the means of (1) obtaining accurate information promptly on current questions; (2) avoiding duplication of effort in research work and making the results of research done in one state available to research workers in all the states; (3) developing a sound structural organization, making provision for each of the several types of legislative service necessary in a well-rounded program—that is, reference, research, bill drafting, statutory revision and codification, and budgetary and fiscal analysis.[12]

THE AMERICAN POLITICAL SCIENCE ASSOCIATION COMMITTEE

The American Political Science Association, still mindful of the indispensability of strong representative institutions to the preservation of free government, has continued its legislative committee—which was established as the Committee on Congress—under the new title Committee on American Legislatures and expanded its functions to include state legislatures as well as the Congress. Believing that there was need for a comprehensive survey of existing practices of legislative organization and procedure at the state level, this committee undertook the assignment and presents its findings and recommendations herewith. The work has been carried on over a four-year period and has entailed numerous conferences with state legislators, legislative professional personnel, and others, as well as conferences at meetings of professional associations and a vast amount of correspondence. It is hoped that the results of the committee's work as presented in this report may be found useful to the states, to the public, and to the members of the profession.

The business of legislation today has taken on new proportions and a new importance. As a people we talk, often boastfully, about the superiority of our democratic system. We are even willing to expend substantial sums to export it to other peoples—peoples who are watch-

---

[12] See *The Book of the States, 1950-51* (Chicago: The Council of State Governments), p. 18, and *1952-53,* pp. 16-17.

ing us closely, matching our actual performance against our claims. We cannot afford, from any point of view, to fail to make good. At the same time, there is serious danger that we will not succeed unless we strengthen our representative legislative bodies, modernizing their organization and adapting their procedures to meet the exacting requirements imposed upon them by the conditions of a complex twentieth-century civilization.

2

Constitutional Basis of State Legislatures

AMERICAN STATE LEGISLATURES rest squarely on the legislative provisions of the several state constitutions, which provide for their establishment and define their powers and procedures. This constitutional basis of our legislative bodies appears to be little understood. The restrictive—if not obsolete—character of many of these provisions, some of which have no proper place in a constitution anyway, imposes serious obstacles to the efficient conduct of legislative business.

It is the established practice for the people of each state to frame and adopt an instrument of government known as a constitution. A constitution is—or should be—a body of *fundamental* law. Established for the purpose of providing a set of governmental machinery on the one hand, and of protecting citizens from an unfair or improper use of governmental authority on the other, a constitution must contain four essential elements: (1) a bill of rights; (2) provision for the framework of government; (3) delegation of powers or the establishment of some basic principle for determining what powers the government may exercise and under what conditions; (4) provision for orderly change through a workable amending procedure.[1]

---

[1] For a discussion of the essential elements of a state constitution, see W. Brooke Graves, *American State Government* (4th ed., Heath, 1953), pp. 49-54.

NORMAL LAWMAKING PROCEDURES

As the blueprint of the framework of government the constitution must provide for the organization and powers of the three branches of government—legislative, executive, and judicial. Although there is a separate article relating to each branch, the article relating to the legislature ordinarily contains but a small portion of the provisions affecting that body, restrictive provisions being scattered throughout the remainder of the document. Moreover, the detail in the rest of the document is frequently more important than the legislative article in determining the area within which the legislature may act.

These facts, so familiar to the student of constitutional law, are frequently not at all clear to the layman. The state legislature is a repository of the residual powers of the people. Unless restricted by provisions in the state constitution itself, it can do anything that has not been delegated to the national government or expressly or impliedly denied to the states by the federal Constitution. Grants of power to the federal government operate as restrictions upon the otherwise plenary powers of the state legislature, even though stated not in terms of limitation. In addition a doctrine of implied limitation applied by the courts in the interpretation of state constitutions removes from legislative judgment and decision many matters of governmental organization and powers that were fixed in the constitution in an earlier period in the history of the state and that now require constitutional amendment to effect needed changes.

The constitutional basis for the legislature, consequently, cannot be understood without careful examination of the provisions of all of the other articles of the constitution: the structure of the executive department and the judicial department; provisions as to local government, education, taxation, budget procedure, and other aspects of finance; and limitations in the bill of rights and specific prohibitions against the abuse of legislative power. The more detailed these articles, the more the legislature will be restricted in its ability to meet future problems in these fields.

In all constitutions or constitutional amendments adopted by 1850, and for more than fifty years thereafter, the emotional basis upon which the constitutional provisions rested was primarily one of distrust of state legislatures. Constitution makers gave expression to this attitude by increasing the rigid limitations within which the legislature must be confined or by writing into the constitution large numbers of specific provisions that were primarily legislative in character.

The legislative article itself must always contain provisions for the structure, size, composition, election, sessions, and procedure of the legislative body. Structure is concerned with the number of chambers. Shall there be one or two? Although there was some experimentation with unicameralism in the late colonial and early national periods, the American system, for exactly 100 years beginning in 1836, uniformly provided for a bicameral legislature with fairly large membership. Nebraska's unicameral plan did not become effective until January, 1937, and although several states have considered it since, none have adopted it.

Because many of our legislative bodies are much too large, and the compensation of members is seriously inadequate, the trend of current thinking is toward smaller size and more adequate compensation—the latter in the form of annual salary rather than on a per diem basis.[2] Members are nominated in most states under the direct primary and elected by the people for terms of two years in the lower house, or four years in the upper. In practice, this procedure has been found to produce a surprisingly accurate cross-section of the body politic. In all but ten states the legislature is prevented from meeting more often than once in two years (unless special sessions are called), and then under strict limitations regarding the length of the session. Such limitation is accomplished by specifying the number of calendar days or legislative days, or through imposing a limitation on the number of days for which per diem compensation may be drawn by members. Legislative procedure is governed by the rules adopted by the two houses, joint sessions by the joint rules, but in every case the rules are based upon and are an elaboration of the constitutional provisions governing legislative organization and the procedure to be followed in the enactment of laws.

---

[2] This should be determined legislatively, not by a rigid constitutional mandate.

Legislative Sessions

The problems of modern government are so numerous and of such great complexity that it is almost futile to try to deal with them in severely limited biennial sessions.   As we think now of enlarging the responsibilities of the states through needed adjustments in federal-state relations, the urgency of longer and more frequent sessions seems likely to be increased.   There is already apparent a trend in the direction of annual sessions, even though such sessions have sometimes been based upon the unrealistic assumption that fiscal matters and policy matters can be sharply differentiated and dealt with in separate sessions held at different times.   The authorization of annual sessions diminishes the need for special sessions, which have been more and more necessary in recent years.

For 100 years the trend was to place the responsibility for the calling of special sessions upon the governor, and even to give him power to restrict the session to items that he enumerated in the call. As an effort is now being made to restore the legislature to its proper place in the governmental system, there is a tendency to favor permitting the legislature to reconvene itself.   Such a procedure, which does not infringe in any way upon the power of the governor, merely authorizes the legislature to reconvene upon its own motion—upon the signed request of a specified percentage of the membership.   This procedure, which applies after adjournment, is to be distinguished from reconvening after a recess, as for instance, under the split-session plan, and is entirely within the powers of the legislature itself to determine.

The *Model State Constitution* advocates a continuous legislature with quarterly sessions, and with the recommendation that the work on the floor and in committee be planned to eliminate present congestion in the presentation of bills, particularly at the end of the legislative session.   On this point Frederic H. Guild has written:

The periodic piling high of the legislative hopper, the waste of legislative time waiting for committees to digest hundreds of bills, and the frantic congestion of the closing days of the session, all because legislation must come only once in two years, has long been noted as a grave evil. The holding of four to seven regular sessions over a period of twenty-four months need not mean a total length of session much in excess of the number of days many legislatures now sit in regular session. Indeed, the growing practice of recessing and the increased frequency of special sessions have already been responsible for many more legislative days in the biennium in some states without removing the evils inherent in the present single, regular session.

The process of legislation is in fact continuous. The need for legislation does not arise once in two years, or from January to March of each year. Normal legislative problems should be faced when the need arises as a regular process, not in periodic spasms nor as emergencies for special sessions. Moreover, legislative problems require study for solution. Research and discussion in advance of a legislative session are fundamentally as much a part of the legislative process as the actual session of the legislature itself. With a legislative council constantly at work preparing material for future sessions and with improved procedure for committees and committee hearings, the preliminary, preparatory aspects of legislation would be continuous. When material necessary for proper consideration was ready, the subject would come before the next regular session whenever it occurred. Legislative consideration would then be timed and informed, not periodic and unsystematic.[3]

Problem of Apportionment

One serious defect of legislative composition has been the failure of the legislature to reapportion the membership at regular intervals, as required by most constitutions. The practical difficulty of securing redistricting at the hands of the legislature, many of whose members benefit by the *status quo,* is recognized, but the present trend is to advocate a change in the constitutional base that would permit automatic reapportionment without legislative action. Some states now vest power to apportion in a board that can be mandamused.

The *Model State Constitution* proposes that the legislature fix the district boundaries, but that from five to seven members be elected in each district, with the number of members for each district determined automatically every ten years. This proposal does not change

---

[3] National Municipal League, *Model State Constitution,* with Explanatory Articles (5th ed., New York, 1948), pp. 27-28.

the fundamental constitutional basis of the legislature as originally intended in the earlier editions of the model constitution, but merely attempts to implement that provision so that it will operate, as it is failing rather completely to do in the modern period.

This question of reapportionment has been a stumbling block in various constitutional conventions in past years, but recommendations for more fundamental changes in the principle of representation are still largely in the academic stage, as they are not understood by the layman and are opposed by overrepresented districts that would undoubtedly lose representation on the basis of any change that might be made. Even where reapportionment takes place in accordance with the constitutional mandate, the existence of constitutional requirements with regard to minimum representation for counties may prevent representation of the people on a fair and equitable basis.

Effect of Restrictive Provisions

Most of the present state constitutions were framed in an era of fear and distrust of state legislatures, and past history provided much evidence for this distrust on a rational basis. The modern legislature, however, requires an entirely different psychological approach, aimed at freeing the legislature from the numerous limitations of most constitutions, indicated in Chapter 1, and permitting more discretion in the light of the very different history of most state legislatures in the last fifty years.

Considerable research is desirable to present concrete evidence of the effect of restrictions, or to demonstrate that legislative power is not abused in states lacking such restrictions, in order to develop a general awareness of the reasons why the students in this particular field do feel confident that a shift in the present constitutional basis would be wise and sound. Some monographs do exist, but the variations in the forty-eight state jurisdictions are so great that much more specific work needs to be done within each jurisdiction; also needed are complete cross references to other states for comparative purposes on the basis of somewhat similar studies. To the student it seems clear that the present constitutional restrictions have handicapped the states to a serious extent in meeting present-day needs as promptly and efficiently as they should.

It has even been argued that one reason for the increasing concentration of power in the federal government has been the fact that these basic restrictions in state constitutions have prevented decisive action by state governments in dealing with modern problems. The vital question in modernizing state constitutions can be simply stated: how much discretion shall be left with the legislature itself and how much shall be put beyond its reach? The general tendency in modern discussion is to remove as many shackles as possible from the legislature, especially those relating to procedural matters.

ADMINISTRATIVE PROCEDURE ACTS

The growth in the number and complexity of governmental services has brought with it important changes in legislative practice. Whereas in times past legislative enactments were comprehensive in that they included in some detail provisions covering all contingencies that could be foreseen, it is now thought that legislation should be confined largely to policy declarations, leaving to the enforcing agency in the executive department the responsibility for drafting and promulgating supplementary rules and regulations. These rules and regulations may include interpretation of the statute, procedural matters, and instructions as to whom the statute applies, in what manner, and under what conditions.

Any executive agency, therefore, in the discharge of its duties and responsibilities, may employ the rule-making power delegated to it by statute or by subdelegation from a higher echelon within the department or agency of which it is a part. The resulting administrative legislation seeks to implement, interpret, and particularize the legislative purpose, as expressed in the statute. The breadth of this power to regulate gives to administrative agencies an important legislative role, affecting private individuals and all kinds of groups and organizations.

The tremendous increase in the use of the rule-making power and of administrative procedures generally produced widespread criticism and resentment on the part of legislators who objected to what they regarded as an executive encroachment upon the legislative prerogative. The fact that instances of carelessness—or worse—regarding the rights of citizens became more or less prevalent in the decade of the thirties intensified this criticism. Lawyers and the bar associations were particularly prone to object to what they regarded as short cuts to established judicial procedures, to the failure to observe those time-honored rights that are a part of the birthright of citizens of English-speaking countries. The situation was definitely one requiring legislative consideration and action. After prolonged discussion and debate, the Congress passed and the President vetoed the highly controversial Walter-Logan bill in 1940. In 1946, however, the Federal Administrative Procedure Act was placed on the statute books.

While this discussion was taking place and federal legislation was under consideration, many of the states were likewise engaged in an effort to establish minimum standards in the field of administrative procedure. The same criticisms that were directed against federal administrative procedures prior to 1946 were also voiced in the states, in which somewhat parallel attempts were made to determine through surveys and reports the essential qualities of a desirable procedure. Notable among these studies was the so-called Benjamin Report in New York in 1942.[4]

Between 1940 and 1943 the National Conference of Commissioners on Uniform State Laws had a committee at work on the drafting of a Model State Administrative Procedure Act.[5] Dean E. Blythe Stason of the University of Michigan Law School, who served as chairman of the committee, emphasized the fact that this proposed act "deals primarily with major principles, not with minor matters of procedural detail." The following "basic principles of common sense, justice, and fair play are deemed to be an irreducible minimum, and as such are embodied in the provisions of the measure":

---

[4] Robert M. Benjamin, *Administrative Adjudication in the State of New York* (Albany, 1942).

[5] For brief discussion of the activities of this organization, see *The Book of the States, 1952-53* (Chicago: The Council of State Governments, 1952), pp. 135-39.

1. Assurance of proper publicity for administrative rules that affect the public.

2. Provisions for advance determinations, or "declaratory judgments," on the validity of administrative rules, and provision for "declaratory rulings" affording advance understanding of the application of administrative rules to particular cases.

3. Guarantees of fundamental fairness in administrative hearings, particularly in regard to rules of evidence and the giving of official notice in quasi-judicial proceedings.

4. Provisions assuring personal familiarity on the part of the responsible agency heads, with the evidence in quasi-judicial cases decided by them.

5. Assurances of proper scope of judicial review of administrative orders to guarantee correction of administrative errors.[6]

Between 1939, when North Carolina adopted a uniform procedure act and 1947, when Indiana adopted the model act, no less than eleven states adopted laws dealing more or less comprehensively with administrative procedure. Four of these cover substantially all the subjects suggested in the model act. Several of them provide for some kind of supervisory or enforcement agency. The nature and scope of this legislation are shown in the accompanying table; although there were no further enactments through sessions of 1952, others may be expected during the next few years.

STATE ADMINISTRATIVE PROCEDURE ACTS[7]

1939 *North Carolina*—Laws 1939, ch. 218; amended Laws 1943, sec. 150-1–150-8.

Provides a uniform procedure in the revocation of certain types of licenses, including prior notice, hearing, appearance by counsel, written findings of fact, right to subpoenas, and judicial appeal.

---

[6] *Handbook of the National Conference of Commissioners on Uniform State Laws, 1943* (Baltimore: Lord Baltimore Press, 1944), p. 228.

[7] From W. Brooke Graves, *Public Administration in a Democratic Society* (Heath, 1950), pp. 593-94. Data compiled from a number of different sources; for discussion of the problems involved, see Chapter 29 of this volume. See also Ferrel Heady, *Administrative Procedure Legislation in the United States* (University of Michigan Press, 1952).

1941   *North Dakota*—Laws 1941, ch. 240.

Enacted the Administrative Agencies Uniform Practice Act, somewhat along the lines of the Model Act. The first of the general remedial acts, its provides for basic procedures both for rule making and for adjudication.

1943   *Ohio*—Laws 1943, 120 v. 358; amended Laws 1945, 121 v. 378.

The act prescribes procedure for licensing agencies only, although the term "licensing" is broadly defined. Provides for public notice and hearings, with right to appear by counsel and to subpoena witnesses, etc.

Wisconsin—Laws 1943, ch. 375.

Wisconsin adopted the Model Act.

1944   *Virginia*—Laws 1944, ch. 160.

This act provides for notice of proposals to change or amend rules, specifies hearing procedures, including notice, evidence, appeals, etc.

1945   *California*—Laws 1945, chs. 867, 868, 869.

The first of these three related acts provides for the procedure in administrative adjudications and gives the right of judicial review; the second provides procedure for judicial review by mandamus; and the third for a staff of qualified hearing officers, to be assigned to the various boards upon request.

Illinois—Laws 1945, p. 1144.

The Administrative Review Act concerns itself with the judicial review of administrative decisions.

Minnesota—Laws 1945, ch. 452.

This act deals with the method of procedure in making rules, providing that no new rules are to be promulgated without hearing, and notice thereof being sent in advance to trade groups and others interested, by the Secretary of State. Interested persons may ask for reconsideration of any rule and in such case a public hearing is to be granted.

Pennsylvania—Laws 1945, P. L. 1388.

This enactment is based largely upon the Model Act, providing for publication of all administrative rules and regulations.

1946   *Missouri*—Laws 1946, S. B. 196.

This enactment is essentially an adaptation of the Model Act.

1947   *Indiana*—Laws 1947, ch. 365.

This enactment is very similar to the Model Act.

INITIATIVE AND REFERENDUM

The initiative and referendum are authorized in the constitutions of a little more than one third of the states.[8]   These two devices were developed from earlier practices involving the right of petition and were given their current forms by the Progressive movement in the earlier part of the twentieth century.   There has been no further adoption of these devices since World War I, although several states have made intensive use of them in the past decade or two.

The initiative and the referendum were originally conceived as checks upon the legislature to be applied only in extreme instances when that elected body strayed badly from its mandate.   In many instances in recent years, however, the initiative has been put to uses not originally intended, uses that, if successful, would take from the legislature its rightful role.   The referendum, on the other hand, remains in most states "a stick behind the door" to be used only upon infrequent occasions to demand a popular vote upon a measure that has passed the legislature and has been signed by the governor in the face of strong opposition.

The Direct Initiative

The initiative is of two types, direct and indirect.   The direct type, authorized in eleven states, permits the circulation of a petition to propose a measure to be placed upon the ballot directly without legislative action.   In the indirect type, used in six states, the initiated measure proposed by petition goes to the legislature, which must act

---

[8] The following states have the initiative for constitutional amendments and legislation: Arizona, Arkansas, Colorado, Massachusetts, Michigan, Missouri, Nebraska, Nevada, North Dakota, Ohio, Oklahoma, and Oregon.   The following states use the initiative for ordinary legislation only: Idaho, Maine, Montana, South Dakota, Utah, and Washington.   Montana and New Mexico have the referendum only and not the initiative.

upon it within a reasonable period of time.   If the initiated measure is passed unchanged and signed by the governor, it becomes law in the usual fashion.   If it is amended, or if it is not acted upon within the specified period of time, it must be placed before the electorate at the next general election.   Normally, the legislature may also submit a competing or alternative proposal at the same election.   California and Washington have both the direct and indirect types of initiative.

Greatest criticism of any of the direct legislation measures has been levied at the direct initiative, because it has tended to encroach upon the legitimate province of the legislature.   In a number of states, however, some very excellent measures, including a state civil service law, a permanent registration of voters law, and other similar improvements, have been brought in by the direct initiative.   In the judgment of some persons a direct initiative offers an opportunity to present a complete draft of legislation for acceptance or rejection in toto.   In those instances in which the two houses of the legislature are chosen in such a manner as to represent different constituencies and thereby be committed to a deadlock on certain issues, the direct initiative has proven useful when used sparingly.   Use of the direct initiative in recent years for old-age pension plans, tax measures, and a number of panacea legislative proposals has tended to reduce confidence in this device.

The Referendum

The referendum is a different type of operation from the initiative and is primarily an instrument to suspend legislation that has been passed by the two houses of the legislature and approved by the governor.   There are four types of referendum.   That used with greatest frequency among the states is known as the compulsory referendum. Measures such as constitutional amendments and, in many states, bond issues proposed by the legislature must be placed before the voters and approved by a majority of those voting on each proposition.   This does not require any petition.   The petition referendum is the type more generally identified in public thinking with the term referendum.   It may be invoked against an act of the legislature if a specified number of registered voters sign a petition demanding a referendum.   In most states, this suspends operation of that particular statute until the next state general election, unless a special election is called before.   Most states having the referendum exempt certain types of measures, such as appropriation statutes for the regular support of the state government and those that are deemed to be emergent, from the operation of the referendum.

The third type of referendum is a vote upon public policy.   It is deemed largely an advisory referendum not binding upon the legislature.   The fourth type comes into being through the exercise of legislative discretion.   Theoretically, it is a deferential gesture by the legislature in permitting the voters to decide.   Actually, in practice, it is usually a buck-passing device by means of which the members of the legislature avoid the unpleasant task of committing themselves and making a firm decision on a controversial subject.

In most states that have adopted the petition referendum, a statute adopted by the legislature and approved by the governor does not go into effect until a specified time, usually sixty or ninety days after signature by the governor.   During that time a referendum petition may be circulated, and if it achieves the required percentage of signatures within the period of time that the statute is suspended, the measure remains suspended until the next election.   Constitutional requirements usually specify that the legislature may adopt emergency legislation if it obtains an extraordinary majority in both houses of the legislature and if an emergency clause is attached to the legislation. Some states, for example Oklahoma, merely require the legislature to declare that in its judgment the measure is emergent.   Other states, such as Washington and California, require the legislature to give an explanation of the reasons for declaring the measure emergent.   In Washington, particularly, the state supreme court has accepted jurisdiction in cases to investigate the face validity of the emergency clause, and in some instances where it felt that the reasons were clearly not valid, has set aside the emergency clause and permitted the circulation of a referendum petition against the particular statute. Normally, a statute with an emergency clause goes into effect immediately after passage and signature and is exempt from the referendum.

The petition referendum is a safety valve for easing discontent and widespread opposition to measures that may have sufficient strength to pass the legislature. When used sparingly, the petition referendum tends to aid the legislative process rather than to interfere with it or undermine the principle of a responsible representative legislative assembly. All such devices, however, should be surrounded by protective legislation designed to make the use thereof as responsible as possible.

The Indirect Initiative

The indirect initiative fits readily into a pattern of responsible legislation. It gives an opportunity to groups that may wish to do so to present a completely drafted item of legislation to the legislature for its consideration. The legislature then has the opportunity either to accept the proposal or to submit its own alternate. In this way, minorities or other groups that may from time to time feel thwarted in dealing with the normal legislative process may have an opportunity to participate in formal fashion and thereby reduce their feeling of irritation and lack of confidence in the legislative process. It has been found wise, in using both the direct and indirect initiative, to require that a descriptive circulation title for a proposed measure be prepared by the state attorney general or some similar duly qualified official independent from the group circulating the initiative petition.[9]

RECOMMENDATIONS

Restrictions that prevent the legislature from exercising its complete power as a representative body of a sovereign people should be removed from the state constitution.

1. Sections of the constitution designated as "statutory" prescribing major policy or details of administration should be repealed and all such powers should be delegated with proper safeguards to the legislature or to the executive department. The principle of separation of powers has been implemented in some cases by carrying it

---

[9] See Winston W. Crouch, *The Initiative and Referendum in California* (Los Angeles: Haynes Foundation, 1950).

to an unfortunate extreme. Nevertheless, the legislature should be so strengthened that it can perform effectively as an equal and coordinate branch of the government.

2. The initiative and referendum should be retained where they now exist, but only as weapons of popular control when representative action appears to be blocked. Anything more than this, by way of direct legislation, tends to undermine the responsibility of the legislature for representative action.

3. The legislature should be organized to formulate major public policy. To this end:

(a) Details of policy and sublegislation should be delegated to administrative agencies in keeping with state administrative procedure acts. Constitutional instructions to the courts should serve to provide against too narrow an interpretation of delegated authority.

(b) A larger measure of power over county, city, and other local matters should be vested in local units of government through general state law. Many state legislatures are heavily loaded with problems of a purely local nature. Extension of the principle of local home rule would be in the public interest when consistent with minimum and uniform standards of statewide application.

3

Representation and Apportionment

IN THEIR REPRESENTATIVE ARRANGEMENTS, our state legislatures reflect conflicting theories. Although representation of wealth in landed property as such has disappeared, the rural portions of many states continue to be overrepresented. This rural dominance is one reason why the states have not always been able to cope with the greater problems of an urbanized society, such as housing, metropolitan transportation fares, price control on foods, social insurance, and community planning beyond city limits. Bicameralism frequently adds confusion to rather than providing a solution for the rural-urban cleavage. Conservatism prevails in matters of representation, making accepted theories and long-established arrangements, however inequitable, hard to change. Under such conditions periodic reapportionment of state legislatures to reflect urban growth is difficult to assure.

CONSTITUTIONAL PROVISION

Although there are various interpretations, some provision for legislative reapportionment is made in every state. The two elements —(1) reapportioning (allocation of seats to districts) and (2) redistricting (redrafting of district lines)—are written into many constitutions in one form or other. In our federal system "apportionment" for Congress is the concern of national authorities, and redistricting is a matter for the states. However, in some states both functions for their own legislative houses are performed by the legislatures themselves. In some states the terms "apportionment" and "districting" are used interchangeably; for example, the California constitution uses the term "apportionment" for the creation of single-member districts. Frequently both the legislatures and the courts refer to establishment of districts as "apportionment acts."

In any consideration of reapportionment of the state legislature— the allocation of seats—the question arises, what should be the basis of representation? Should it be all the people, or only the citizens? Or would it be better to consider only qualified voters or only those who bother to vote? The state constitution makers are not in total agreement regarding the solution to this problem, but "population" and "area" are the most commonly accepted criteria. Area is less discernible because it is usually in combination with population. Population is by far the most used criterion and, contrary to general opinion, it serves as the basis for distribution of seats in more state senates than houses of representatives. Twenty-four state constitutions specifically provide population as a basis of representation for the senate, although in five of these states—Alabama, Florida, Iowa, Pennsylvania, and West Virginia—the provision is almost nullified by the limit placed upon the number of senators a district may have.[1] Nine other states limit the application of this criterion slightly by

---

[1] The references are to articles and sections of the state constitutions: Arkansas, VIII, 1-5; Colorado, V, 45-49; Connecticut, III, 3, 4; Georgia, III, 2 (Par. ii, iii), 3 (Par. i); Illinois, IV, 6, 7, 8; Kansas, II, 2; X, 1-3; Kentucky, 33; Louisiana, II, 2, 5, 6; Michigan, V, 2-4; Missouri, III, 2-11; Nevada, I, 13, XVII, 6; New Mexico, IV, 42; North Dakota, II, 29, 35; XVIII, 214; Ohio, XI, 1-11; Oklahoma, V, 9-16 (b); Utah, IX, 2, 4; Vermont, II, 13, 18, 37; Virginia, IV, 43; Wyoming, III, 3, III-A, 2-4. Five others give population as the basis but limit its effectiveness, viz: Alabama, IV, 50, IX, 198-203; Florida, VII, 3, 4; and Iowa, III, 34, 35, which limits any county to no more than one senator; West Virginia, VI, 4-10, 50, which limits any county to two senators; and Pennsylvania, II, 16-18, which limits a city or county to no more than one-sixth of the members of the senate. See *The Book of the States, 1950-51* (Chicago: The Council of State Governments, 1950), pp. 121-24, for the best summary. See also Lashley G. Harvey, "Reapportionment of State Legislatures—Legal Requirements," *Law and Contemporary Problems,* 17 (Spring, 1952), 364-76.

excluding Indians not taxed, aliens, and military personnel;[2] Indiana specifies adult males as the population base;[3] and Oregon limits population to white population.[4] The remaining states have variations of these limitations, a progressive formula; or an apportionment of one senator to each county.[5]

Population is also the principal basis for representation in the lower chambers, although many state constitutions contain provisions that make reapportionment very difficult. Twenty-one state constitutions specify population as the basis of apportionment,[6] and nine others limit this factor by excluding aliens, Indians not taxed, or military personnel.[7] One restricts "population" to white population,[8] and one limits "population" to adult males.[9] Twelve other states either permanently prescribe the distribution of representatives or provide inelastic formulas for reapportionment in their constitutions.[10] Mas-

---

[2] California, IV, 6; Maine, IV, pt. 1, 2, 3; IV, pt. II, 1, 2; Minnesota, IV, 2, 23, 24, sched. 10, 12; Nebraska, III, 5; New York, III, 3-5; North Carolina, II, 4-6; Washington, II, 3, 6, XXII, 1, 2; Wisconsin, IV, 3-5. Military personnel are excluded from population in Washington and South Dakota, III, 5, XIX, 2.

[3] Indiana, IV, 4-6. This was made ineffective by the 19th Amendment to the Constitution of the United States.

[4] Oregon, IV, 6, 7. This is, of course, obsolete because of the 15th Amendment.

[5] See in particular Idaho, III, 2, 4, 5, XIX, 1, 2; Montana, V, 4, VI, 3-6; New Jersey, IV, ii, 1, IV, iii, 1; South Carolina, 1, 2, III, 3-6.

[6] Alabama, IX, 198-203; Arkansas, VIII, 1-5; Colorado, V, 45-49; Illinois, IV, 6, 7, 8; Kentucky, 33; Louisiana, III, 2, 5, 6; Michigan, V, 2-4; Missouri, III, 2-11; Montana, V, 4, VI, 2-6; Nevada, XVII, 6; New Hampshire, pt. II, 9, 11, 26; New Jersey, IV, iii, 1; New Mexico, IV (42); North Dakota, XVIII, 214; Ohio, XI, 1-11; Pennsylvania, II, 16-18; South Carolina, I, 2, III, 3-6; Utah, IX, 2-4; Virginia, IV, 43; West Virginia, VI, 4-10, 50; Wyoming, III-A, 2-4.

[7] California, IV, 6; Maine, IV, pt. II, 1, 2; Minnesota, IV, 2, 23, 24, scheds. 10, 12; Nebraska, III, 5; New York, III, 3-5; North Carolina, II, 4-6; South Dakota, XIX, 2; Washington, XXII, 1, 2; Wisconsin, IV, 3-5.

[8] Oregon, IV, 6, 7. Made obsolete by the 15th Amendment.

[9] Indiana, IV, 4, 5, 6. Made obsolete by the 19th Amendment.

[10] Connecticut, III, 3, 4, amdts. II, XV, XVIII, XXXI; Delaware, II, 2; Florida, VII, 3, 4; Georgia, III, 2, pt. ii, iii, pt. i, 3; Idaho, XIX, 1, 2; Iowa, III, 34, 35; Maryland, III, 2, 5; Mississippi, XIII, 254-256; Oklahoma, V, 9-16 (b); Rhode Island, XIII, amdt. XIX; Texas, III, 25-26a, 28; Vermont, II, 13, 18, 37.

sachusetts and Tennessee base their apportionment upon legal voters, a formula that is somewhat restrictive but less rigid.[11] Arizona uses "votes cast for governor" at the last preceding election with the limitation that there may not be a reduction of any district below its quota based on the 1930 election.[12]

Many constitutions contain provisions against gerrymandering by requiring that the district be "composed of contiguous territory" and that all districts "be equal in population as nearly as may be." However, the provision for equality is subordinated to other qualifications that in a number of states result in an overrepresentation of rural elements. Twenty-six states have some such constitutional provision: nineteen guarantee at least one representative to each county,[13] and seven specifically limit the more populous areas. For example, Connecticut assures representation to the towns; Delaware permanently specifies the apportionment in its constitution; Maine limits any town to seven representatives. Maryland fixes a maximum of six from any county; Rhode Island assures each town one representative and limits any town to one fourth of the total of the lower house; Vermont assures every town representation; New York fixes one third of the total in the senate as the limit for any county.

Several states base legislative representation on the privilege of the suffrage. Thus Massachusetts determines by a special process the total number of legal voters in that state, as does Tennessee; in each case both houses of the legislature in question are covered by this rule. Texas bases representation in her senate on the number of qualified electors. The vote for members of Congress is the standard for representation in the legislative body in Idaho. In Kansas, the lower house must have one member from each county in which at least 250 legal votes were cast for any candidate at the last preceding election. Arizona uses the official canvas of votes cast for all candidates for governor at the last election as the basis for the apportion-

---

[11] Massachusetts, pt. II, ch. I, sec. III, art. I, amdt. LXXI; Tennessee, II, 4, 6.

[12] Arizona, IV, 2, 1 (1).

[13] Alabama, Arizona, Arkansas, Florida, Georgia, Indiana, Iowa, Kansas, Louisiana, Mississippi, Missouri, New Jersey, New York, North Carolina, Ohio, Pennsylvania, South Carolina, Utah, Wyoming.

ment for her lower house, although the senatorial distribution is prescribed by the constitution of that state.

Maryland, Montana, New Jersey, and South Carolina define membership in their senates by requiring the representation of their counties as governmental units. Connecticut, Rhode Island, Vermont, and to a certain extent New Hampshire, use their cities and towns as legislative districts. Connecticut, New Hampshire, and Vermont use towns as a basis for representation in the lower chamber, and Rhode Island uses them for election of senators.

Although state constitutions usually specify a reapportionment after each federal census, the legislatures frequently fail to take any action. In Minnesota failure to reapportion and to redistrict the state has resulted in such wide disparities as one representative for a district containing 7,254 people and only two representatives for another district with a population of 128,501.[14] In Texas, on the basis of the 1940 census, eleven metropolitan cities are entitled to one half the representation in the senate, but actually they elect slightly over one third of the senators.[15] In California, Los Angeles County, with a population of 2,785,643 (1940 census), has one senator, whereas the district consisting of Inyo and Mono counties, with 9,923 people, is entitled to the same representation in the upper chamber.[16] In Alabama, where the population of the northern cities has shown a marked increase in the last twenty years, one district with 140,420 people has one senator, whereas another district with only 58,621 is also entitled to one senator.[17] Fulton County, which includes

[14] Louis C. Dorweiler, Jr., "Minnesota Farmers Rule Cities," *National Municipal Review,* 35 (March, 1946), 116.

[15] Stuart A. MacCorkle, "Texas Reapportionment Problem," *National Municipal Review,* 34 (December, 1945), 540-43.

[16] Dean E. McHenry, "Urban v. Rural in California," *National Municipal Review,* 35 (July, 1946), 350-54.

[17] Hallie Farmer, "Legislative Apportionment," *Bureau of Public Administration Bulletin,* University of Alabama, 1944, p. 10. See Douglas H. MacNeil, "Urban Representation in State Legislatures," *State Government,* 18 (April, 1945), 59-61. The United States Conference of Mayors in a study conducted in 1949, *Government of the People, by the People, for the People,* indicated that whereas urban peoples constitute 59 per cent of the population, they have only 41 per cent of the legislators. The study cites further discrepancies: Detroit, with 40 per cent of the population of Michigan, has only 27 per cent of the representation; Oklahoma City, with 244,000 people, has seven repre-

Atlanta, pays one fourth of Georgia's taxes, has one eighth of the state's population, but has only three of 205 representatives in the lower house of the legislature.

Forty-two states place full responsibility for reapportionment upon the legislature itself. If the legislature should fail to act, the courts treat the matter as a political question and not subject to review.[18] However, if the legislature reapportions, a subsequent districting can be challenged in the courts on such constitutional requirements as the stipulation that "counties or towns may not be divided," and such discretionary requirements as the rule that "districts must be equal" and "compact." The courts have shown a willingness to protect the people from arbitrary and obviously capricious action of districting agencies—usually county commissioners or city councils.

PROPOSALS FOR NEW BASES OF REPRESENTATION

If bicameralism is retained by our states and if it is to have any vital significance, the two chambers should have fundamentally different representative bases or they serve no useful purpose as a check on each other. The democratic ideal of equal representation and our traditional acceptance of bicameralism are in conflict. It may be necessary to abandon the second if the first is accepted. If we are to retain and invigorate bicameralism, there may have to be a modification or rethinking of the theory of popular representation.

What are the possibilities for a different basis of representation for the second chamber? A number of diverse bases have been sug-

---

sentatives, whereas seven rural counties with a total of 57,000 have equal representation; Chicago, with 51 per cent of the population, has 37 per cent of the representation in the Illinois legislature; Hartford, with 166,000 people, has two representatives, whereas Colebrook, with only 547 people, has the same number of representatives in the Connecticut lower chamber. These are some of the glaring examples of inequity indicated in the study.

[18] See *Colegrove, et al.* v *Green, et al.*, 66 Sup. Ct. Reports, 1198 (June 10, 1946) discussed by Franklin L. Burdette in "The Illinois Congressional Redistricting Case," *American Political Science Review*, 40 (October, 1946), 958-62. See also Lloyd M. Short, "States That Have Not Met Their Constitutional Requirements," and Hugh A. Bone, "States Attempting to Comply with Reapportionment Requirements," *Law and Contemporary Problems*, 17 (Spring, 1952), 377-416.

gested.   Among these are land, property, political or governmental units, political parties upon some type of proportional representation, occupational or functional representation, and suffrage and voting performances and behavior rather than the relatively inert basis of population.

Area as a Criterion

No one seriously desires to represent land *qua* land, and the present contention that acreage is favored in many of our state legislatures at the expense of the people serves but to highlight difficulties inherent in popular representation and its realization.   The day is past, and properly so, when any purely property or taxpaying basis could be rendered acceptable or effective for the upper chamber in order to make it different from the popular lower chamber.   Hence it might be safely concluded that land and property should be eliminated as feasible alternative bases of representation.

Political Units

Political units, although more acceptable than land or wealth as a basis for representation in senates, pose puzzling and difficult problems that render inadvisable their use as representative areas.   The unitary character of the American state governments would seem to render unnecessary the representation of units of local government as such.   Moreover, counties and towns as units of local government have largely lost the significance they once had and are no longer vital rural communities with independent and distinctive interests of their own.   Of much greater importance are the larger areas or sections of our states.

At present local governmental units are used in three principal ways for purposes of representation in state legislatures: (1) equal representation of counties, especially in the senate; (2) unequal representation of counties in the senate according to population (several states also follow the same proportionate distribution for their lower chambers, as in the case of Florida and Georgia); (3) representation based upon towns, as in some New England states, ranging from little regard for the population factor in Connecticut to increased representation according to population based upon a formula in New Hampshire. However, the local government unit has not proved satisfactory as a basis of representation, perhaps because it tends to accentuate rivalries, and make the state assembly the arena for local disputes. Representation based on local units of government starts with the concept that state government is a federation of local governments—an assumption not uncommon in New England. The practice of assuring representation to each county can lead to many complications. For example, in Kansas the house of representatives is limited to 125 members. With each of the 105 counties guaranteed one representative only twenty seats are available for distribution upon the basis of population, yet the constitution requires reapportionment every five years. Reapportionment of the entire state according to population is impossible. Small counties are always overrepresented and large ones underrepresented.

The use of local government as a basis for representation in the state legislatures has declined greatly in the past hundred years. Whenever local units are not stipulated as legislative districts by constitution or statute, the legislature is empowered to divide the state into legislative districts; usually the dissection is restricted not only by a prohibition against gerrymandering, but also by specific instructions for drawing district lines. The drafting of district lines is quite a technical problem, but its political aspects presented as a contest for power always receive publicity. The party out of power is ever eager to object to any deviation from old district boundaries as an example of gerrymandering. In some states this comes with such frequency that those voters desiring peace at any price can be misled into thinking that the district system is at fault and that a return to local units of government would prevent friction and gerrymandering. Actually abuses in redrafting district lines are a negligible evil in comparison with the silent gerrymandering of constitutional allocation of seats to local units, through which depopulated rural local governmental areas retain representation they do not deserve. In too many instances, moreover, such undeserved power has been used against the newer and more populous urban communities.

Turning to the technical aspects of redrafting district boundaries, where legislative districts consist of combinations of counties, and where no counties may be cut across in the laying off of such districts, the problem often arises of what should be done with fractional remainders of representative population over and above the average constituency for the state. These remainders may have to be disregarded, or they may be combined into large flotorial districts as in Texas or cared for by other devices. The problem presents complexities, sometimes highly mathematical, if districts of reasonably equal population are to be assured. Another problem arises when a populous county is assigned more than one representative. Shall these representatives be elected at large within the county? Shall each seat be voted for within the county as "place number one," "place number two," and so on? Or shall the county be divided into districts if the constitution of the state permits? If so, upon what basis? Perhaps some system of proportional representation could be adopted for such counties if the evils of microscopic gerrymandering are to be avoided.

Legislative Districts

The political unit has not proved satisfactory. It tends to strengthen the importance of local government as against the unifying influence of the state. The political unit as a basis of representation has been abandoned in the newer state constitutions in favor of districts having boundaries drawn with a view to convenience, utility, and equity. The problem, of course, is to find a device that can operate to keep the allocation of members to districts abreast of population shifts. The National Municipal League's *Model State Constitution* proposes that large legislative districts with variable numbers of members be chosen by proportional representation. However, states prefer to allocate seats to districts on some formula consisting of a division of the number of the total population by the available seats in the house of representatives. The quota thus established, it becomes the task of the legislature or some administrative agency to draw the district lines in recognition of it. Some states follow the practice of making the districts large enough to permit election of two or three representatives. They feel that the large district will more likely reflect a state instead of a purely local interest.

Large multi-member districts, however, might be considered for the election of senators or house members in a bicameral legislature to provide the contrast between the senate and the house alluded to above.   They should be of equal population, but so laid off as to take into account distinctive economic regions of a state.   A system of voting for specific places could be employed, or proportional representation could be used in the election within each district.   Thus could be combined the advantages of a modified functionalism and proportional representation with a population basis of representation. For a senate of thirty members, five or six such districts might be suggested.

Functional and Proportional Representation

Possibilities for improvement of representation may lie in a shift to either occupational (or functional) representation, or to various types of proportional representation.   The first of these is predicated upon the assumption that the various interests of mankind within the modern state deserve to be reflected within the major policy-determining agencies of government in terms of economic or social functions or occupational enterprises or status; proportional representation rests upon the assumption that every political faction or party should have the same percentage of membership in the assembly as the faction or party has in total membership throughout the state.

Functional representation has been somewhat discredited by its association with Mussolini's fascism.   Difficulties also inhere in its application: minuteness of functional specializations would vitally affect the size of chambers; overlapping of interests on the part of individuals would dull its acuteness and tarnish its equity.   In addition, conflicts would arise as to the degree of virtue implicit in certain occupations or interests; granted that barbers and bean growers and beauticians have interest in government and its activities because of their occupations, what of bookies and racketeers?   Functional representation might be more effective on the level of larger categories, but the problem of reapportionment of seats among constantly changing functional constituencies would seem to be insuperable. In fact, the gerrymandering of functional representation could surpass anything we have seen and would not be acceptable. Moreover, any form of functional representation may require abandonment of the principles of populational representation and of "one man, one vote." Finally, it must be emphasized that a citizen's interest in politics is not confined exclusively to matters that involve his occupation or business concerns; this, perhaps, is the most telling argument against functional representation.

Proportional representation systems, applied to all seats in one house or both, would seem at least worthy of consideration, despite the very limited popularity of such schemes in the United States. Cumulative voting for state representatives in Illinois is the nearest thing to proportional representation at the state level in this country, although it is not a perfect example. It shares the objective of proportional representation in that it aims to provide representation for the minority party. The Illinois voter is allowed three votes, which he may cast for a single candidate or divide between two or three candidates. This system serves the purpose of the minority party quite well but does not give splinter parties their proportionate representation. Constitutional impediments to proportional representation exist in a number of states, and it would appear that an extensive program of education would have to be undertaken in most states to prepare the way for the consideration of any form of proportional or minority representation. There are many arguments against proportional representation that would have to be overcome, even if some may be considered of questionable validity. One is that it is ill-adapted for use under a two-party system that favors majority or plurality choices. Again, its unfortunate results in some European countries have given it a decided setback. Also, the emphasis it has placed on minority interests in American cities where it has been used to elect city councils and its consequent abandonment in several cities[19] have not contributed to its popularity. Finally, it is little

<hr>

[19] See Belle Zeller and Hugh A. Bone, "The Repeal of P.R. in New York City—Ten Years in Retrospect," *American Political Science Review,* 42 (December, 1948), 1127-48. For cumulative voting in Illinois, see C. S. Hyneman and J. D. Morgan, "Cumulative Voting in Illinois," *Illinois Law Review,* 32 (May, 1937), 12-31, and George S. Blair, "Cumulative Voting in Illinois," *National Municipal Review,* 42 (September, 1953), 410-14.

understood by most Americans and is regarded as an alien system, as well as one subject to freak results and to manipulation on the part of those who count the votes.[20]

THE APPORTIONING AGENCY

Many contend that most representative ills could be cured if reapportionment could become automatic and removed from partisan influence. The nearest approach to an automatic system may be found in Arizona where the secretary of state is required to certify the number of members of the house who are to be chosen from each county at the next succeeding election. Apportionment is made on the following basis: one member is allotted to a county for each 2,500 votes or major fraction thereof cast in that county for all gubernatorial candidates at the last general election, subject to the proviso that at no time may this number be less than that allotted upon the effective date of this constitutional amendment in 1930. Thus in Arizona an automatic reapportionment occurs every second year upon the basis of the vote cast for governor. True, this is not the instantaneous type of apportionment that occurs under most systems of outright proportional representation, but it is a more responsive and current type of apportionment than exists in most states. Attention could well be directed to this feature of Arizona practice and an appraisal made of the results, as well as consideration given to the possibility of further employment of this device of allotting legislative seats upon the basis of votes cast. By this system the bottleneck of the apportioning agent is broken by removing legislative control entirely, and in effect by resting the apportioning function with the electors themselves.[21]

Forty-two states specifically provide in their constitutions that the legislature shall be the apportioning agency. Thirty-nine of these

---

[20] For an excellent list of references on reapportionment methods see Guthrie S. Birkhead, "Legislatures Continue to Be Unrepresentative," *National Municipal Review,* 41 (November, 1952), 523-25, and "Researchers Probe Legislative Problems," 42 (May, 1953), 254.

[21] See Bone, *op. cit.,* for a discussion of the automatic features in Missouri, Ohio, and Massachusetts.

states make the legislature the sole agency. Oregon directs that the number of members of her legislature be fixed by law, and Tennessee simply says that the personnel of her legislature shall be apportioned. Idaho and Nevada make specific enumerations of the number of districts and legislators in their constitutions, which allocations may not be changed except by law. In New York and Oklahoma the authority to apportion rests with the legislature subject to review in the courts at the suit of any citizen. Delaware alone of all the states retains actual constitutional apportionment.

A member of states utilize special agencies to accomplish their actual apportionments. California has a reapportionment commission consisting of the lieutenant governor, the attorney general, the secretary of state, the controller, and the state superintendent of education. This body must complete the apportionment in the event that the legislature fails to do so. Similarly empowered bodies with differing personnel are found in South Dakota and Texas. In other states the actual apportionment is made by a special body. Ohio uses a commission composed of the governor, the secretary of state, and the state auditor; action by this agency is supposed to follow each federal census and may be taken by any two of these officials. Arkansas created a special board of apportionment in 1936 consisting of the governor, secretary of state, and the attorney-general.

Missouri devised a widely proclaimed method of apportionment in her new constitution of 1945. In that year she provided for an apportionment commission of ten members to reapportion senate seats. This body was to be selected from lists of ten nominees proposed to the governor by the state committee of each of the two major political parties casting the highest vote for governor at the last preceding election for that post. This commission must complete its apportionment and file a report within six months after it is called into action, or the selection of the entire senate, now numbering 34, reverts to general election from the state at large. For the house the secretary of state is charged with the responsibility of apportionment in accordance with a formula set in the constitution. Thus Missouri has recognized that reapportionment for both houses is a task that lies outside the legislature itself.

The presumed frequency of reapportionment varies considerably among the states, both in law and in practice. In most states reapportionment does not comes more often than every ten years, although Kansas provides a minimum of five years and Indiana a minimum of six years between reapportionments. In some states it is not to take place more often than once in ten years, and in others there is a specific constitutional mandate to reapportion once every ten years. States vary, too, in the use of the federal census as the basis for reapportionment; a few prefer their own census. Reapportionment should be required soon after the census figures are made available, but some states do not insist on this point.[22]

In summary, constitutional provisions charge the legislatures themselves with the responsibility for reapportionment in forty-two states. Only Arizona, Arkansas, Missouri, and Ohio provide some other agency for this function. No provision is made at all in Delaware, since legislative districts are fixed in the constitution. California,

---

[22] Although reapportionment is required every five years in Kansas, no real reapportionment has been made since 1909. Florida, Illinois, Kentucky, Michigan, Ohio, Tennessee, and Virginia specifically require a lapse of ten years between apportionments. Alabama, Arkansas, Georgia, New Jersey, Pennsylvania, South Carolina, Texas, West Virginia, and Wisconsin require an apportionment after each federal census. Nebraska applies this rule with the reservation that such revisions of the distribution of legislative seats shall not be made oftener than once in ten years.

A number of states requiring ten-year reapportionments also enjoin that reapportionments be made at the first session of the legislature after the completion of the federal census. These states are California, Louisiana, Mississippi, New York, North Carolina, and Connecticut. South Dakota provides that reapportionment is to be made at the first regular session of the legislature after each enumeration by the United States or by the state itself.

Massachusetts requires a reapportionment after each decennial state census on the basis of the number of qualified electors. In Oklahoma reapportionments are to be made after each decennial census of the United States unless the legislature directs otherwise. Maine provides for reapportionment after each state census. Oregon specifies that apportionment shall follow any enumeration, state or federal, and that it be done at the next legislative session. New Hampshire distributes the seats in her house of representatives after the last general census of the state, whether carried out under her own authority or that of the United States. Rearrangement of the senate of New Hampshire may come from time to time. Seats in the lower house of Rhode Island are redistributed after each new census taken by either the national or state government; her senate may be reapportioned after any presidential election. Colorado, Iowa, Montana, North Dakota, Utah, Washington, and Wyoming call for reapportionments after any decennial census by any government.

South Dakota, and Texas provide for reapportionment by an ex officio committee when the legislature fails to carry out its function. A special session may be called in Florida by the governor, and legislative reapportionment is subject to review by the courts in New York. However, these are legal provisions more often observed in the breach, especially in those states where the legislature is the reapportioning and redistricting agency. Specifically it may be said at this point that reapportionment is a mere mathematical computation easily assigned to administrative bodies, for there is little possibility for discretion. Redistricting is the application of the formula to a geographical area, and discretion may be kept to a minimum by adequate standards. Certainly reapportionment should not be a matter for the legislators who may wish to protect their own interests; it should be recognized as an administrative function that would become more or less automatic, as in the case of reapportionment for the lower chamber of Congress. Because of legislative control of this function, the legislatures of Alabama and Illinois have not been reapportioned since 1901.[23] Although these are extreme cases, failure to reapportion fully after a census is the rule and not the exception for too many of our states. Twenty-six states reapportioned one or both houses to some extent after the census of 1940 (see Table 1). By September, 1953, six additional states made substantial or minor changes based upon the 1950 census.[24] The remaining sixteen have legislatures that they call "representative bodies," with representation based upon census figures of twenty, thirty, and in some cases more than forty years ago. If our state legislatures had been reapportioned periodically and systematically, direct legislation would not be so necessary. It is not surprising that in many of the states where there has been a definite reluctance to reapportion, each election ballot is cluttered with initiated and

---

[23] A constitutional amendment (pending in 1953) provides for a commission appointed by the Illinois governor to apportion if the legislature fails to act.

[24] The states that reapportioned one or both houses after both the 1940 and 1950 censuses were Arkansas, California, Connecticut, Georgia, Idaho, Maine, Michigan, Missouri, Nevada, New Hampshire, Oklahoma, South Carolina, South Dakota, Virginia, and West Virginia. In November, 1953, New York approved a new apportionment bill. In 1950 Maryland froze the number of members of the lower chamber at 123 by a constitutional amendment.

TABLE 1

States That Reapportioned One or Both Houses after the
1940 and 1950 Census

State	Year of Reapportionment Based on 1950 Census	Year of Reapportionment Based on 1940 Census	State	Year of Reapportionment Based on 1950 Census	Year of Reapportionment Based on 1940 Census
Arizona	1952		Nevada	1951	1947
Arkansas	1951	1941	New Hampshire	1951	1943
California	1951	1941	New Jersey		1941
Colorado	1953		New York		1944
Connecticut	1953	1941	North Carolina		1941
Florida		1945	Ohio	1953	
Georgia	1950	1940	Oklahoma	1951	1941
Idaho	1951	1941	Pennsylvania	1953	
Kansas		1945[H]	Rhode Island		1940
		1947[S]	South Carolina	1952	1942
Kentucky		1942	South Dakota	1951	1947
Maine	1951	1941	Tennessee		1945
Maryland		1943	Texas	1951	
Massachusetts		1947	Virginia	1952	1942
Michigan	1953	1943	West Virginia	1950	1940
Missouri	1951	1946	Wisconsin	1953	
Montana		1943			

Source: Preliminary Report, *American State Legislatures: Structure and Procedures* (Chicago: The Council of State Governments, September, 1953).

referred measures—apparently the only course open to the under-represented populous and urban areas for securing needed services and social legislation.

CONCLUSIONS AND RECOMMENDATIONS

From this discussion it may be seen that our states present many variations with respect to representation in their legislatures. Many anomalous situations exist, and inequities are common. Since constituencies of equal population and periodic and fair reapportionments of seats seem most consistent with our democratic tradition, it would be well for all states to adjust their representative arrangements to comply with these fundamental principles. New forms of representation, such as proportional representation, may be matters of controversy, but they may well be considered in any reorganization of the representative system. The following four recommendations would seem to follow the discussion in this chapter:

1. The state should be divided into districts for the election of members to the legislature. For bicameral bodies, districts serving as the basis for election to the upper chamber should be larger than for the lower chamber. The controlling factors in drawing district lines should be: equal numbers of population in each district; no gerrymandering; district lines drawn to permit a wide representation of interests.

2. Provision for reapportionment of seats in both houses following each decennial federal census by a special administrative agency outside the legislature, which reapportionment shall go into effect either automatically or in case the legislature fails to act promptly.

3. Disregard of counties and other areas of local government in laying off representative districts insofar as is consistent with efficient election administration.

4. If bicameralism is to be retained, the use of different bases of representation for each house not inconsistent with the principle of equal population constituencies might be proposed to produce a more vital bicameralism. It is suggested that if single-member districts are retained for the lower house, the senate might be elected from multi-member districts laid off with regard to important economic regions with or without proportional representation for each district. Or such a plan might be used for the lower rather than the upper house, for both houses, or for a unicameral legislature.

4

One House or Two?

THE FIRST LEGISLATIVE BODIES in some of the American colonies, following the practice of trading company organization, were essentially unicameral in form. Thus the elected representatives of the colonists sat with the governor and his appointed council of assistants in "general court" to consider the enactment of laws, to vote taxes, and to transact other important business. Differing interests and points of view soon developed, however, with the result that long before the end of the seventeenth century the council members as a rule sat separately in order more effectively to exercise a veto over the assembly's enactments and because the members of the latter objected to their presence.

EARLY BICAMERALISM IN AMERICA

By the late colonial period all the colonies except Pennsylvania and Delaware had two houses, the governor and council forming the upper house. The latter body, representing the Crown, the ruling oligarchy, and the larger propertied classes, exercised important executive and judicial functions and shared the legislative function with the lower house. With the passing of time the representative chambers had gained more powers over finance and the initiation of legislation, and legislatures in general had come to look upon themselves as small-scale models of the English Parliament, the structure and functions of which had become more clearly defined after its protracted struggle with the Crown.

Early State Legislatures

Bicameralism thus firmly established was perpetuated in all the Revolutionary state constitutions except those of Georgia, Pennsylvania, and Vermont. Governors' councils were transformed into senates and stripped of most of their executive and judicial powers, but the need for upper houses was more strongly emphasized than ever before in order to represent and to protect the interests of property. These upper houses were also needed for advice and to defeat the ill-considered measures that, it was assumed, would inevitably originate in the more democratically constituted lower houses. Fear of concentrating all legislative power in a single house was expressed by John Adams, who wrote that "a single assembly is apt to grow ambitious, and after a time to vote itself perpetual." For these reasons and because of a tendency to imitate the legislatures of older states and the bicameral Congress established in 1789, all the new states later admitted into the Union adopted two-house legislatures.[1]

Perhaps the strongest consideration in creating an upper house was the belief that the lower house, popularly elected on the basis of population, would be a radical body, likely to encroach on the rights of property. A second chamber, representing the interest of the wealthy and well to do, was to be elected in a different manner, with higher property qualifications for both voters and members. In this way, it was believed, the excesses of a popularly elected lower house could be avoided. In England the upper house consisted of the nobility, who also constituted, for the most part, the landowning and wealthy class; in America, where there was no nobility, the provisions governing the upper house were designed to insure protection to the wealthy and large landholding class. In New York, for example, only voters having a freehold worth £100 or more were permitted to vote for members of the senate. According to the census of 1790 only 1,209 persons out of a population of 30,000 could qualify. Massachusetts restricted membership in the senate to those owning

---

[1] For a brief summary of the history and theory of bicameralism see O. Douglas Weeks, *Two Legislative Houses or One* (Dallas, Texas: Arnold Foundation Studies, vol. VI, Winter, 1938), p. 26.

property worth £600 or more, whereas South Carolina required ownership of property worth £2,000. The requirements for the lower house were considerably less.[2]

Unicameral Legislatures

It is significant that three states—Pennsylvania, Georgia, and Vermont—for varying periods of time operated with unicameral legislatures, although each had a council of censors that in some respects resembled a second house. The functions of the censors were to investigate the operation of the government, to make recommendations for change, and, if need be, to call for a constitutional convention. Georgia abandoned its unicameral plan in 1790, apparently largely influenced by the pattern of the national Congress. Pennsylvania did likewise in 1789, apparently largely because of dissatisfaction with her council of censors and with the executive council, which acted as a plural executive. The new constitution created a second house of the legislature, abolished the council of censors, and established a single executive.

The longest experience of any American state with a unicameral legislature was that of Vermont from 1777 until 1836, a period of over 59 years. This experience has been the subject of a careful historical study by Professor Daniel B. Carroll, who found that prior to 1835 the unicameral state legislature was well regarded by the people of the state.[3] After a legislative deadlock that year in the election for governor (no candidate having received a majority of the preceding general election) the recommendation of the council of censors for the adoption of a bicameral legislature was approved by a close vote. Professor Carroll found that the merits claimed for the bicameral system were not realized, and that, as far as can be judged from historical evidence, the previous unicameral legislature worked as well as, if not better than, the succeeding bicameral legislature.

---

[2] Charles A. Beard, *An Economic Interpretation of the Constitution* (Macmillan, 1913), pp. 67-68.

[3] Daniel B. Carroll, *The Unicameral Legislature of Vermont* (Montpelier, Vermont: Vermont Historical Society, 1933).

DEMOCRATIZATION OF LEGISLATURES—THE MOVEMENT FOR UNICAMERALISM

Later Experience with Bicameralism

With the spread of manhood suffrage in the nineteenth century and the consequent abandonment of property qualifications for voting and membership in both houses of the state legislatures, the basic reason for having an upper house to protect property disappeared.   Beginning in the Jacksonian age the two houses came in many states to be almost equally representative of the people, except that the state senates were smaller in size and members were usually elected for longer and staggered terms.   Although in many states representation in the lower house was based on population, place representation continued to characterize state senates, resulting in serious underrepresentation for the larger cities.   This situation has remained and, with the growth of large urban populations in many states, the problem has become even more acute.   These remaining differences have maintained in a measure the abler personnel and greater prestige of the upper houses, and, in some states, their more conservative character.   Although state senates have not infrequently blocked progressive legislation originating in lower houses, the reverse has often been true.   Lower houses are usually more democratically constituted; yet because of their larger size they can be more easily controlled by frequently conservative legislative oligarchies, and because of the smaller constituencies of their members can be more readily dominated by localism, which often makes them resistant to the broader needs of the state as a whole.   In any event, both houses may respond simultaneously to powerful, well-organized pressures, whether conservative or liberal.   It cannot be stated as a generalization, therefore, that senates have uniformly filled the more conservative role that their creators intended them to assume.[4]

---

[4] In a recent study of four successive Ohio legislatures it was discovered that the house of representatives never passed as many as two thirds of the proposals received from the senate, whereas the latter body passed three out of four house bills.—Mona Fletcher, *A Decade of Bicameralism in Ohio with Special Reference to the 1930's* (Abstracts of Doctoral Dissertations, No. 59, Ohio State University Press, 1950).

Unicameralism in the Twentieth Century

During the last thirty years or more widespread discussion of the unicameral legislature has taken place, and many proposals for its adoption have been made, the most noteworthy being that of the National Municipal League in its *Model State Constitution.* Constitutional amendments providing for the establishment of a single house have been proposed at one time or another in more than half of the states, but where submitted to the voters, they have been rejected in all states except Nebraska.[5] After the creation of a one-house legislature in that state in 1934, the movement toward unicameralism took on new life for a few years but has lagged for the past decade. The Nebraska experiment, however, has been watched with interest, and, on the whole, has proved to be successful. Thus it is quite probable that other states may sometime be won over to unicameralism. Certainly all states contemplating reorganization of their legislatures will do well to examine Nebraska's experience with a unicameral legislature and to reconsider fully the arguments both for and against bicameralism and unicameralism.

MERITS CLAIMED FOR A BICAMERAL LEGISLATURE

Claim 1. A bicameral legislature prevents hasty and careless legislation.

The case for a two-house legislature was well stated by Justice Story in his *Commentaries on the Constitution of the United States*[6] as follows:

The utility of a subdivision of legislative power into different branches, having a negative on each other, is . . . admitted by most persons of sound reflection. . . . There is scarcely in the whole science of politics a more important maxim, and one which bears with greater influence upon the practical operation of politics. . . . It forms a great check upon undue, hasty, and oppressive legislation. Public bodies, like pri-

---

[5] For an account of the movement for unicameral legislatures, see Alvin Johnson, *The Unicameral Legislature* (University of Minnesota Press, 1937); and John P. Senning, *The One House Legislature* (McGraw-Hill, 1937).

[6] 5th ed., Little Brown, 1891, p. 407.

vate persons, are occasionally under the domination of strong passions and excitements; and are impatient, irritable, and impetuous. . . . Measures are often introduced in a hurry, and debated with little care, and examined with less caution. . . . If it feels no check but its own will, it rarely has the firmness to insist on holding a question long enough under its own view, to see and mark it in all its bearings and relations on society.

Justice Story's observations reflect the deep distrust of legislative bodies characteristic of his time. The experience of most states over a period of many years, however, indicates that the bicameral system has not prevented hasty and ill-considered action, but, on the contrary, many state legislatures enact a large amount of legislation in the last few days of the session, when careful consideration is out of the question. Although limitations upon the length of sessions are in part responsible, the complex structure and procedure of a bicameral legislature are important contributing factors to this situation.

The widely accepted belief that the second house provides an additional independent and thorough review of bills passed by the other house has been disproved in numerous instances. Many bills passed by one house are received by the second house so late in the session that it is quite out of the question for the latter to give them more than perfunctory consideration. Often bills are passed without much consideration by the first house on the assumption that they will be given careful consideration in the second house—an expectation not always realized. On the other hand, noncontroversial bills that have passed one house are seldom given careful consideration by the other house, and in many instances are enacted without adequate consideration by either house. It should be noted in fairness, however, that the device of introducing companion bills in both houses somewhat obviates the delays produced by two houses. Even so, a reading of the veto messages of the governors will reveal that many of the bills passed by both houses are ill-considered, poorly drawn, inconsistent, and badly designed to carry out their objectives, which indicates that neither house has given them careful attention. These failings would seem to show that there are other and better means than a bicameral system to safeguard against hasty and ill-considered legislation.

The Nebraska unicameral legislature has demonstrated that careful and deliberate consideration can be secured in a single house.[7]   The rules of this legislature (which, contrary to the practice in many other states, are not suspended as a means of expediting legislation near the end of the session) provide for a series of steps that assure full and careful consideration of every measure before it is enacted.   All bills are considered by one of eleven standing committees, and no bill may be reported out by a committee until after an opportunity has been provided for a public hearing, which must be scheduled five days in advance.   Careful consideration in full committee is made possible by the rule that no member may serve on more than two committees, and committee meetings are scheduled so as to avoid conflicts.   The legislature as a whole gives two separate considerations to a pending bill, one when it is considered under General File and is at the amendment stage, and a second time under Select File. After a bill has been passed on General File, it is referred to the committee on enrollment and revision, where a staff of attorneys who are experts in bill drafting reviews and may revise or rewrite the bill if necessary.   The bill then goes back to the legislature for consideration on the Select File, and if it passes a second debate, it is advanced to third reading and passed.   A competent observer describing the operation of the Nebraska legislature has stated: "Twice as much time is devoted to consideration of legislation as was possible under the bicameral operation.   The observer is impressed . . . with the orderliness which has been substituted for the chaos and haste of the old days, with the seriousness which the members take considering proposed measures, and the care taken to avoid mistakes."[8]   The unicameral legislature of Nebraska has been criticized not for its haste, but rather because it takes much longer to get a bill through the legislature than under the old system.   Despite the absence of a second house and the fact that only about half as many bills are introduced as formerly, the sessions have become longer.   It is probably true to state that today no other legislature gives consistently more

---

[7] The Nebraska experience in unicameralism is more fully described in Appendix A.   See also shorter description by Richard C. Spencer, "Nebraska Idea 15 Years Old," *National Municipal Review,* 39 (February, 1950), 83-86.

[8] Harry T. Dobbins of the Nebraska State Journal, "Nebraska's One-House Legislature," *National Municipal Review,* 30 (September, 1941), 511-15.

thorough consideration to measures that it enacts than that of Nebraska.

Claim 2. A second chamber serves as a check against popular passions and impulses.

Another argument for a two-house legislature was well stated by John Adams, who said:

A single assembly is liable to all the vices, follies, and frailties of an individual; subject to fits of humor, starts of passion, flights of enthusiasm, partialities or prejudice, and consequently productive of hasty results and absurd judgments.

This statement was written at a time when there was great fear of the excesses of democracy, when the committee system as it now operates in legislatures was unknown, and before the veto power of the governor was generally used. Then it was greatly feared that a popularly elected assembly would be irresponsible and would ride roughshod over the rights of the wealthy and well to do. Subsequent experience in this country has indicated, however, that legislative bodies usually consist of persons who are more inclined to avoid action on important issues than to rush into untried solutions, and who are usually not unduly influenced by popular passions and impulses. This situation has been in part the result, no doubt, of the general character of our party system and our practical policies. Certainly the extensive use of the executive veto in most of our states has proved to be a powerful restraining factor upon legislative excesses. Facts demonstrate that it is often a more effective check than that of two houses.

Claim 3. There is danger that a single legislative body will usurp the powers of other branches and invade the rights of the people.

The argument that a single legislative body might usurp the powers of the other branches was made at a time when the legislature was virtually supreme in the state governments, overshadowing the other branches. Today the three branches of government are coordinate, and legislative acts are subject to extensive constitutional restraints, judicial review, executive veto, and in some states to popular referendum. At the time this argument was advanced the primary consideration was to safeguard the public against encroachment by the government itself, and the doctrine that the least government is the best was generally accepted. Today the establishment of a government that is able to cope effectively with the pressing problems of an industrialized and urbanized society has become a primary consideration, and no longer are eighteenth-century conceptions of *laissez faire* accepted.

Claim 4. A bicameral legislature provides protection against corruption and the control of the legislature by special interest lobbies.

It has been argued that unscrupulous men might corrupt one house to secure the passage of legislation that they desire, but they would be unable to corrupt both houses. On the other hand, the principal argument used by the late Senator George W. Norris in his advocacy of the one-house legislature in Nebraska was that it would curb the power of lobbyists and make it much more difficult to corrupt the legislature. Senator Norris pointed out that most special-interest lobbies desire to defeat rather than to promote legislation, and that the bicameral system offers the lobbyists many points at which a bill may be blocked. The lobbyist does not need to control the entire legislature, or even one house, in order to block a pending measure; all that he needs is to control the votes of one or two members of key committees, or of the conference committee. Observers of the Nebraska unicameral legislature agree that the lobby is still present and still powerful; some believe, however, that it is forced to work more in the open, and that the members whom it controls find greater difficulty in escaping responsibility. Certainly in eliminating the need for conference committees the unicameral legislature has removed one focal point of undue influence or corruption.

Claim 5. A bicameral legislature permits the use of a different basis of representation in the two houses; for example, one house may be based strictly on population, whereas in the other house representation may be based on a formula that takes into account counties or other local units of government.

In at least half of the states the rural areas and small towns are overrepresented in one house of the legislature. This practice is defended on the ground that it safeguards the states against being dominated by the large cities with their supposedly radical and unstable populations, often controlled by corrupt political machines. In some states, however, of which Massachusetts is a notable example, representation in both houses is based strictly on the number of qualified voters.

The use of a unicameral legislature does not require that representation be based strictly on population. If desired, provision may be made that no city or county, regardless of its population, shall be entitled to more than a designated percentage of the entire membership, and a formula may also be adopted that takes into account local political subdivisions of the state. In Nebraska, it may be noted, representation in the unicameral legislature is based on population. Great care was exercised in the division of the state into legislative districts to secure a fair representation of each geographical part as well as a fair division between urban and rural areas.

The "rotten borough" system that prevails in many states for one house or the other is perhaps the greatest barrier to consideration of a unicameral system. The sections or groups within the state who believe that they benefit by the existing basis of representation oppose any change that might do away with this advantage. In Nebraska the unicameral amendment provided that the last session of the bicameral legislature should divide the state into not less than thirty nor more than fifty single-member legislative districts. A similar procedure in other states would leave the way open for compromise between those who advocate representation on the basis of population and those who favor a modification.

Claim 6. Bicameral legislatures are used by forty-seven states and the national government; they have been the traditional American form of legislature since the very beginning of our government. The unicameral legislature is an untried experiment of foreign origin, contrary to American political institutions, advocated by theoretical persons but not by experienced legislators.

Although forty-seven states and the national government use two-house legislatures, this alone is not proof that two houses are preferable to one. The bicameral form of Congress was the result of a compromise between the large states and the small states, and is so firmly a part of our constitutional system that change is highly improbable. The same is not true of the states. There are no constitutional reasons why any state may not follow the example of Nebraska and adopt a one-house legislature. Formerly many of our cities used bicameral city councils, which were often marked by corruption, bad politics, manipulation, and inefficiency. Today the unicameral city council has been adopted by practically every city in the country and is universally regarded as a great improvement over the old bicameral form.

In the British Parliament, the principal model of our bicameralism, the House of Commons has taken practically all power unto itself. Unicameral legislatures operated in colonial America before even the Cromwellian experiment with a single chamber. It proves little or nothing, therefore, to attempt to label either type as American or foreign in origin. The unicameral plan has been advocated by many leading legislators, governors, and persons with practical experience, as well as by students of government. It is now successfully operating in Nebraska.

MERITS CLAIMED FOR A UNICAMERAL LEGISLATURE

The arguments for a unicameral legislature may be briefly summarized as follows:

Claim 1. Membership in a single chamber carries greater prestige, dignity, and opportunity for public service than membership in a bicameral legislature, and hence attracts more outstanding and representative citizens.

Claim 2. A single chamber operates more efficiently than two, and is able to give more thorough consideration to proposed legislation than two chambers. By the adoption of suitable rules of procedure and the establishment of an effective committee system, it can assure that every measure is carefully reviewed before it is acted upon, with adequate safeguards to prevent hasty action, and thus avoid the serious evils of the closing rush that obtains in many states.

Claim 3. The jealousy, friction, and rivalry between the two houses, which often result in deadlocks and the defeat of needed legislation, will be eliminated.

Claim 4. Responsibility can be more definitely fixed upon a single legislative body, and upon individual members, than is possible under a bicameral system.

Claim 5. A single house facilitates the development of essential leadership within the legislature by concentrating such leadership in one place.

Claim 6. The single house permits closer and more effective relations between the governor and the executive departments and the legislature—a prime need of state legislatures today—because it substitutes one set of legislative leaders for two.

Claim 7. Some observers of the Nebraska legislature claim that a single-chambered lawmaking body reduces the power of special interest groups and lobbies to defeat needed legislation and at the same time makes it easier for groups of citizens who are interested in pending legislation to present their recommendations openly and aboveboard to the legislature.

Claim 8. The unicameral legislature does away with the need for conference committees, employed by a number of bicameral legislatures, which frequently meet in closed session and secretly decide upon the most important legislative issues, sometimes under the influence of undercover and irresponsible forces.

Claim 9. The unicameral legislature facilitates public reporting of the work of the legislature and the issues before it and enables the public to keep informed on the course of legislation, which should serve to increase public confidence in the legislative body.

Claim 10. A unicameral legislature results in substantial economies. The cost of the legislature itself is reduced because the number of members and the size of the legislative staff are reduced.

SUMMARY

A one-house legislature has many advantages over a bicameral system. No business organization, or organization in any field, whatever its size or however complex its problems, would consider utilizing two boards of directors. A dual legislative body has little to commend it, other than to serve as an impediment in the way of legislative decision and leadership. It defeats that prime requisite in the management of all affairs, public and private—the establishment of definite responsibility. The change from a bicameral system to a one-house legislature is not the radical change that it is sometimes represented to be, nor is there any evidence to support the contention that two houses prevent ill-considered action more effectively than one. The experience of Nebraska indicates that conservatives, as well as liberals, have no reason to fear the adoption of a unicameral legislature. Professor Lancaster has pointed out that the Nebraska legislature has continued to be conservative, perhaps even more so, because its present membership has more political experience than was formerly true, at least of the lower house, and can therefore be considered of somewhat higher caliber.[9]

On the other hand, it may be contended that a bicameral legislature, if all other matters are properly ordered, may be as satisfactory as a unicameral lawmaking assembly. The long-standing high reputation of the Massachusetts General Court and the Wisconsin Legislature attest to the fact that good work can be accomplished in spite of bicameralism. Factors of prime importance in the success of any legislature are the election of the right kind of representatives, the assurance of proper leadership, and the maintenance of sound and effective traditions and practices in the conduct of legislative business. Perhaps the outstanding feature of the unicameral legislature is that it affords a better setting in which to effect other legislative reforms.

RECOMMENDATIONS

1. States with bicameral legislatures might well re-examine the traditional arguments and claims for bicameralism in the light of the facts of its actual operation. It may be found that some of the original justifications for two houses are now obsolete and that many of the supposed advantages cannot be demonstrated in practice. Many of the supposed checks and safeguards provided by a bifurcated legis-

---

[9] *Kansas City Law Review,* 11 (December, 1942), 24-30.

lature are more or less illusory. Other checks, notably the executive veto, judicial review, and public opinion, are more effective. Most of the reasons for maintaining a bicameral Congress are not applicable to the state legislatures.

2. Unicameralism has proved to be successful in Nebraska, has improved the legislative process there, and has developed none of the evils anticipated for a one-house legislature. Moreover, unicameral city councils have been an important factor during the last half-century in improving municipal government.

3. Although unicameralism is not a panacea for legislative ills, and although numerous improvements can be instituted that will remove many of the practical objections to the bicameral form without abandoning it, a single house seems a more logical framework upon which to hang these changes. It facilitates in many respects the effectiveness and responsibility of the legislature as the "board of directors" of state government.

5

Membership

STATES STAND MIDWAY between the local community and the national government. As control agencies over local affairs and as channels through which the federal government usually operates in its relationships with regional and local communities, the states have an importance far out of proportion to their total budgets and size of personnel staff. The state legislature as a public policy-forming agency plays a crucial role in the entire governmental system —although frequently not to the satisfaction of either Main Street or Washington. State policy is usually the controlling one over such intimate services affecting the citizen as public education, roads, public health, and welfare. States have much to say about local expenditures, forms of local government, elections, and in fact most matters vital to the operation of democracy at the local level.

SIZE OF STATE LEGISLATIVE HOUSES

What sort of boards of directors are these legislatures for the forty-eight holding companies for local governments? Approximately 7,600 persons are members of the 95 separate state legislative chambers. Except for Nebraska the general pattern is bicameral with a wide range in total membership. For example, for the forty-seven state senates the size ranges from 17 in Delaware and Nevada to 67 in Minnesota, with an average of 39.8. Florida and Kentucky each have 38 in their upper houses. Nebraska's unicameral legislature has 43 members, all of whom are called senators. The range of the lower chambers is much greater than that of the senates—from 35 in Delaware to 399 in New Hampshire. Here the median is 100, the number in no less than eight states, although the arithmetical mean is 120 members for the house of representatives.[1]

There seems to be no generally accepted numerical ratio in terms of a proportionate number of representatives to each state senator. California, Indiana, and Oregon each provide a 2 to 1 ratio with a senate exactly half the size of their lower chambers. Illinois and Tennessee hit the 3 to 1 ratio exactly with houses of representatives three times as large as their senates. Virginia has a 40 to 100 span between the two chambers, and the same ratio exists in Florida with a 38 to 95 range. Massachusetts has a 6 to 1 relationship between the two chambers. These are the precise ratios that are determinable. In many states there are approximations of ratios, with 1 to 3 being more general. There is evidence of premeditation in these arrangements in some states, notably in Illinois, which uses her senatorial districts as the electoral units for three representatives per district. In fact the determination of the number of legislative seats to over-all totals and to the interrelation between individual chambers in the great majority of American states is not coincidental nor the result of sheer accident; it is often a way of assuring an overbalance of area in the senate as against population as a basis of representation in the house.

The tendency is toward the reduction of the total number of legislators. New Jersey has only 81, Oregon 90, and California 120 legislators, yet all three legislatures transact much above the average load of legislative business. Whether a reduction in the size of most legislatures is possible depends much upon the local concept of the basis of representation. In New England, where for so many years legislators represented towns that were definite social or community entities, there is great reluctance to reduce oversized legislative bodies. Strangely enough, in some states there is a strong faith in the large

---

[1] See *The Book of the States, 1952-53* (Chicago: The Council of State Governments, 1952), for comparisons between states.

unwieldy legislature as a means of keeping the volume of legislation to a minimum.   Some feel that the larger bodies are better protection against pressure groups that might find it difficult to influence all or even the majority of legislators.   The larger assemblies have not demonstrated these virtues, for because of their size they are likely either to be controlled by a few leaders or to be stampeded into unwise action.

ELECTIONS AND VACANCIES

In a democratic society formal qualifications for office-holding are supposed to be held at a minimum, and the electorate is left with the responsibility of separating the wheat from the chaff in the election process.   Citizenship, ability to qualify as a voter, residence in the state and district from which elected, and sometimes an age greater than 21 constitute the usual requirements for membership in a state legislative assembly.   These qualifications are subject to interpretation by legislative bodies themselves in their control over membership, they are not rigid legal standards that may be challenged in the courts, but standards upon which the legislature is usually the final judge, the courts being loath to review them because of their political nature.

Popular election from single-member districts is the prevailing method by which individual legislators are chosen to fill actual legislative seats.   Within the United States legislators are elected on a long and over-burdened ballot, and in all states except Minnesota and Nebraska, where election is nonpartisan, are selected upon a partisan basis.   Although there is little basis for it in state government, state senators serve for a longer term than do representatives. In thirty-two states the term for the senator is four years, and in forty-three the term for representatives is two years.   This difference of terms between the two houses, obviously a reflection of the congressional practice of recognizing two distinct factors as the basis of representation (equality of states in the Senate and population in the House) has little meaning when applied to state legislatures.   In nine states the term of the senate is longer than the governor's term, which greatly weakens his leadership.[2]

It might be said that Anglo-American experience indicates that vacancies in our state legislative bodies ought to be filled somehow by election. The theory is clear enough, but the practice presents virtually insoluble difficulties. There are three different types of provisions for filling legislative vacancies. These are (1) election by popular vote at either a special or regular election, (2) appointment by the governor, and (3) action by some local agency such as the county or the county party committee. Kansas changed to appointment by the governor as a means of filling legislative vacancies in 1946; since that date there have been 3 such interim appointments, whereas in the previous seventeen years 30 vacancies occurred. In North Dakota vacancies in the house are not ordinarily filled, because of the two-year term limitation, and special writs are issued only in the case of senate vacancies. During the past twenty years in New Jersey there have been 13 elections to fill vacancies in the legislature. The record for Wisconsin for the same period of time shows 51 vacancies, only 11 of which have been filled and all by special election. Vacancies in the legislature of Ohio are filled by a special election that must be called by the governor. However, there have been no such special elections called during the past twenty years by any Ohio governor. Vacancies in Vermont occurring between regular sessions are filled by the governor. Since 1935 there have been 60 vacancies in Oregon and all of them have been filled by the county courts. Nebraska uses gubernatorial appointment as a means of filling legislative vacancies, with 25 such appointments during the past twenty years. Nevada and Washington empower their county commissions to fill legislative vacancies. By gubernatorial appointment Maryland filled the 54 vacancies that have occurred during the last thirteen years.

[2] The gubernatorial term is two years and the senate four years in Arkansas, Colorado, Iowa, Kansas, Maine, New Mexico, North Dakota, Texas, and Wisconsin. In 1953 California initiated a constitutional amendment to increase the terms of senate members from four to six years and of house members from two to four years; a similar step was taken in Ohio to increase senate and house terms from two to four years. Ten other states rejected proposals to lengthen legislative terms for one or both houses during 1952 and 1953.

Some of the more populous states prefer elections for the purpose of filling vacancies in the legislature. During the past twenty years New York has filled 29 senate vacancies—19 at regular elections and 10 at special. In Massachusetts there have been a total of 108 house vacancies during the period of review, and 43 of them have been filled by election. Indiana has had 12 vacancies in the same twenty-year period, and half of them have been filled by election.

Infrequency of sessions and the limitations upon their length in some states might seem to require a method of filling vacancies less time-consuming than that of special elections. Even so, appointment by governors appears to be contrary to the principle of separation of powers. Selection by county boards has the merit of preserving action at the local level and in a way in which a certain measure of local responsibility can be felt and enforced, although it does emphasize the local area as the basis of representation. In view of these difficulties, and the fact that the trend of American state legis-latures is toward annual or more frequent sessions, selection of re-placements at so-called by-elections would seem to be the ideal method of filling legislative vacancies. However, it is difficult to generalize on this point. The more sparsely settled states may not fill vacancies even if by-elections are permitted. In many states today vacancies are not filled because of the cost of holding elections.

TENURE AND TURNOVER

The British often speak of members of Parliament as amateurs in government and of their career administrators as experts. Although it is doubtful that a similar concept prevails in regard to our American legislators, it is nevertheless a fact that most of them would qualify as amateurs because of their lack of experience. However, many have had experience in governmental service at the lower levels and would readily admit their ineptness as beginners in their new func-tion as legislators. Over half of the state legislators are new at each session, the lower chamber having a greater percentage of new mem-bers than the senate. It is difficult to obtain exact figures on turnover in these bodies, and when obtained they have little significance if

TABLE 2

Length of Service of Members of Legislatures Meeting in 1950

TERMS OF SERVICE

State	One		Two		Three		Four		Five to Nine		Ten or More	
	S	H	S	H	S	H	S	H	S	H	S	H
Alabama	31	61	2	34	2	7	0	4	0	0	0	0
Arizona	1	32	8	17	3	10	2	5	5	8	0	0
Arkansas	6	47	8	25	9	12	4	6	7	8	2	2
California	6	21	4	17	1	7	2	17	21	15	6	3
Colorado	9	38	5	12	5	5	4	3	12	7	0	0
Connecticut	10	121	9	70	8	31	3	22	6	20	0	3
Delaware	17	25	0	6	0	3	0	1	0	0	0	0
Florida	6	37	3	23	6	13	5	10	17	11	1	1
Georgia	26	101	7	57	6	12	7	10	6	19	1	1
Idaho	19	22	16	17	6	1	2	5	1	8	0	0
Illinois	7	31	8	23	5	16	11	11	16	53	4	19
Indiana	17	64	10	11	4	4	7	7	11	14	0	0
Iowa	6	35	11	32	5	19	5	10	22	11	2	12
Kansas	10	60	5	27	6	15	4	17	15	6	0	0
Kentucky	11	50	11	20	6	18	4	9	5	3	1	0
Louisiana	3	6	17	49	0	0	11	26	8	19	0	0
Maine	4	76	3	40	7	16	7	12	12	7	0	0
Maryland	16	67	11	33	0	13	1	8	1	2	0	0
Massachusetts	8	67	12	45	5	30	5	38	7	54	3	6
Michigan	7	20	10	35	3	14	2	14	8	16	0	1
Minnesota	2	33	11	26	2	19	9	14	31	35	12	4
Mississippi	1	2	26	73	8	37	10	6	2	20	2	2
Missouri	7	65	5	54	7	28	6	10	8	17	1	9
Montana	11	35	10	26	7	10	7	4	18	13	3	2

only one particular year is selected. Thus because of these handicaps the accompanying figures were compiled for the legislatures in 1950 with no attempt to plot a trend or to measure in larger numbers for a period of ten or more years. It would be well to compare these statistics with those compiled by Professor Charles S. Hyneman in 1938.[3]

---

[3] "Tenure and Turnover of Legislative Personnel," *The Annals* of the American Academy of Political and Social Science, 195 (January, 1938), 21-31.

TABLE 2—*continued*

Length of Service of Members of Legislatures Meeting in 1950

State	One		Two		Three		Four		Five to Nine		Ten or More	
	S	H	S	H	S	H	S	H	S	H	S	H
Nebraska	14	0	9	0	9	0	6	0	5	0	0	0
Nevada	3	20	3	6	5	5	0	7	6	3	0	2
New Hampshire	6	175	1	85	5	46	2	28	10	55	0	10
New Jersey	0	4	0	20	3	1	7	10	5	19	6	6
New Mexico	10	27	0	13	7	5	4	1	3	3	0	0
New York	9	2	4	29	7	4	1	22	15	45	20	48
North Carolina	18	60	13	24	6	12	4	7	9	16	0	1
North Dakota	12	36	11	21	3	18	6	11	15	26	12	1
Ohio	33	44	26	33	9	26	6	9	5	6	1	5
Oklahoma	7	60	7	31	8	16	8	5	13	6	1	0
Oregon	12	29	5	5	5	4	3	11	5	11	0	0
Pennsylvania	9	55	5	47	4	28	4	26	26	48	2	4
Rhode Island	6	15	14	27	7	7	2	6	14	36	1	9
South Carolina	8	54	9	59	0	0	9	32	10	19	18	14
South Dakota	9	27	9	15	6	13	4	8	7	10	0	2
Tennessee	10	58	9	25	4	8	7	5	3	3	0	0
Texas	6	62	4	52	4	12	5	7	13	20	0	1
Utah	7	30	10	16	2	6	2	1	1	5	1	1
Vermont	17	131	9	55	4	36	0	12	0	11	0	1
Virginia	3	25	10	31	2	9	13	11	9	22	3	2
Washington	12	40	11	18	6	11	11	10	6	19	0	1
West Virginia	32	16	18	8	10	10	8	5	4	3	10	13
Wisconsin	4	28	6	28	6	12	2	6	13	22	2	3
Wyoming	5	27	0	0	1	9	0	0	12	14	9	6

Source: Questionnaires sent to clerks of house and senate, state librarians, and scholars in the field.

The figures in Table 2, "Length of Service of Members of Legis-latures Meeting in 1950," indicate a lack of legislative experience on the part of most members. More adequate pay may account for the greater percentage of experienced legislators in California, New York, Illinois, New Jersey, Pennsylvania, and Wisconsin, but does not account for the strong position of Minnesota, which pays its

TABLE 3

Legislative Experience of Committee Chairmen in State Legislatures, 1950

| | | | | | | TERMS OF SERVICE | | | | | |
| | One | | Two | | Three | | Four | | Five to Nine | | Ten or More | |
State	S	H	S	H	S	H	S	H	S	H	S	H
Alabama	23	14	5	0	2	0	0	0	0	0	0	0
Arizona			22[a]	16[a]								
Arkansas	6	23	8	11	9	5	5	6	7	8	3	1
California	0	0	0	5	1	5	1	7	13	7	6	1
Colorado	7	9	1	8	1	4	3	2	7	4	0	0
Connecticut[b]	11	0	7	13	8	7	0	6	7	7	0	0
Delaware	9	10	0	6	0	1	0	0	0	0	0	0
Florida	6	0	3	5	6	12	5	6	17	5	1	1
Georgia	16	2	5	26	2	11	7	6	4	15	0	0
Idaho			14[a]	36[a]								
Indiana	1	24	9	6	1	0	6	3	7	4	0	0
Illinois	2	0	5	0	5	3	4	0	9	18	3	5
Iowa	0	4	5	11	4	10	3	7	22	6	2	1
Kansas	3	0	4	14	5	11	2	12	16	6	0	0
Kentucky	19	59	8	8	5	2	3	1	2	0	0	0
Louisiana	2	6	8	0	0	18	12	14	8	0	0	0
Maine[b]	1	1	3	7	7	10	6	6	9	4	0	0
Maryland	13	7	2	7	3	6	0	1	0	0	0	0
Massachusetts[b]	2	0	1	1	0	0	0	1	1	3	0	1
Minnesota	0	0	0	0	0	0	7	13	21	24	8	1
Michigan	2	10	5	12	2	7	4	8	6	8	0	1
Mississippi	0	0	22	14	6	13	8	2	2	15	3	2
Missouri	5	5	3	14	3	18	0	3	7	6	1	0
Montana	8	20	7	6	5	2	5	2	22	6	0	0

legislators only $2,000 for a term of two years (raised to $3,000 in 1951), or Florida, which pays a mere $10 per day of service. In Massachusetts, where the annual salary is $4,500 plus subsistence and travel and where—until 1952—legislators had one of the best pension systems for state legislators, one must regard an equally balanced two-party system as the explanation for lack of experience among its legislators, for the Democrats rose suddenly after World War II to dislodge the more experienced Republicans. One-party states, such as Missis-

TABLE 3—continued

Legislative Experience of Committee Chairmen in State Legislatures, 1950

| | TERMS OF SERVICE | | | | | | | | | | | |
| | One | | Two | | Three | | Four | | Five to Nine | | Ten or More | |
State	S	H	S	H	S	H	S	H	S	H	S	H
Nebraska[c]	1		11		5		2		5		0	
Nevada	2	10	2	3	2	3	0	2	5	3	0	0
New Hampshire	6	5	4	6	0	4	1	1	3	7	0	0
New Jersey	0	0	0	15	1	8	4	15	4	15	4	2
New York	0	0	2	0	3	0	1	0	9	16	12	20
New Mexico	8	8	0	0	5	3	2	0	3	3	0	0
North Carolina	17	1	10	17	8	8	5	3	10	11	0	0
North Dakota	1	0	0	2	1	2	5	1	7	8	0	1
Ohio	All with previous experience											
Oregon	12	0	6	4	5	3	3	9	5	9	0	0
Oklahoma	1	0	6	14	3	10	7	3	11	3	0	0
Pennsylvania	0	0	1	1	0	1	6	2	24	7	2	1
Rhode Island	0	0	0	1	2	0	0	0	9	7	1	5
South Carolina	2	1	5	5	1	0	10	2	10	0	6	0
South Dakota	7	1	7	7	5	11	3	5	7	7	0	2
Tennessee	10	19	9	15	4	7	6	2	3	3	0	0
Texas	6	1	5	22	4	7	6	3	18	9	1	0
Utah	3	18	8	10	1	2	0	1	3	4	0	0
Vermont	6	8	7	3	0	2	0	0	1	0	0	0
Virginia	7	15	10	14	1	2	2	3	2	0	0	0
Washington	5	6	10	10	3	5	8	5	3	10	0	1
West Virginia	4	1	3	1	6	0	7	0	4	0	4	0
Wisconsin	0	0	0	4	1	8	2	2	7	9	1	2
Wyoming	3	1	0	0	0	8	0	0	10	7	7	4

Source: Questionnaires sent to house and senate clerks, state librarians, and scholars in the field.

[a] Reported two terms or more.

[b] Joint Committees.

[c] Chairmen listed under senate for unicameral legislature.

sippi, Louisiana, and Florida, seem to return the same group of legislators year after year, as do strong Republican states, such as Iowa and Connecticut. A study of experience of committee chairmen in the state legislatures reveals a similar pattern, with states that tend to re-elect their legislators showing the highest degree of experienced chairmen. As might be expected, therefore, Table 3, "Legislative Experience of Committee Chairmen in State Legislatures," closely parallels Table 2. Any generalization from these statistics, however, may prove dangerous. The marked turnover in state legislators may indicate, at the state level, the general political instability of our time.

Permanency of legislative members is considered a virtue by many. For example, Professor Charles S. Hyneman, in his exhaustive study of tenure and turnover in state legislatures, says: "It is my own assumption that a state legislature will not function effectively unless its members have acquired several sessions of experience in lawmaking."[4] As most legislators contend that it takes one term to become acquainted with the legislative process, Professor Hyneman would have ample support from the legislators themselves. However, the legislative task is not just getting things done—it is also representing the people. The tables indicate that the turnover is not ordinarily so great in the larger, more commercially and industrially developed states as in the predominantly rural ones. Is this because the salaries are higher and the stakes greater, or does it reflect the greater effectiveness of the urban political organization? Usually we think of the more industrial states as less stable. The wealthier and more populous states have more experienced legislators. All things being equal these legislatures should be relatively better operated and controlled, but local political cross currents make stability extremely difficult.

OCCUPATIONS OF LEGISLATORS

Upon the basis of a questionnaire compiled for this study certain interesting facts were disclosed in regard to the occupational background of members of the forty-eight legislatures in 1949.[5] Although a great number of lawyers and farmers continue to serve in our legis-

---

[4] *Ibid.*
[5] See pioneer study on state legislative personnel by Samuel P. Orth, "Our State Legislatures," *Atlantic Monthly,* 94 (December, 1904), 728-29.

latures, businessmen predominate. For example, of the 7,475 members, 1,063 were listed as merchants, 311 as engaged in insurance, 212 as dealers in real estate, and 142 as bankers and investors—a total of 1,728 gave some form of business as their occupation. To these should be added 40 undertakers. The lawyers constituted the next largest group of legislators, with a total of 1,674; 1,468 were classed as farmers. Not only do businessmen constitute the largest group in our state legislatures at mid-century, but lawyers are more likely to represent business interests than any other, even though many come from small towns and reflect a rural point of view. Moreover, many of the 327 legislators who list no occupation, preferring to be classed as retired, must be recognized as having had business interests. That they are not generally retired farmers is indicated by the facts that 176 of the 327 are to be found in New England, 76 in New Hampshire alone, where in most cases they were former residents of New York and Boston, and that such agricultural states as Iowa, Kansas, and Illinois had only 4, 10, and 3 respectively.

TABLE 4

Occupations of State Legislators, 1949

Occupation	House	Senate	Total
Lawyers	1078	596	1674
Farmers	1110	358	1468
Merchants	795	268	1063
Insurance	236	75	311
Banks and trusts	101	41	142
Real estate	174	38	212
Doctors	46	34	80
Teachers	155	33	188
Laborers	129	16	145
Craftsmen	191	31	222
Undertakers	31	9	40
Retired	286	41	327
Other	1318	285	1603
GRAND TOTALS	5650	1825	7475

Source: Occupations listed by legislators in state manuals.

Those states that because of their climate could be assumed to attract a retired group included very few persons in the legislature who were retired from their former business or professional activities. California had 3, Florida 1, Arizona 2, and Colorado 6. Except for the lawyers few legislators were drawn from the professions in 1949. There were 188 teachers, and an additional 80 were engaged in the practice of some form of medicine or dentistry.

Only 367 members of the legislatures in 1949 gave "laborer" or "craftsman" as their occupation. This total includes labor leaders, but the majority of the 222 craftsmen, such as carpenters, plumbers, and barbers are hardly qualified to speak for the mass of organized unskilled labor. The greatest number of "laborers" was found in the Rhode Island legislature, with 46 members so classified; Minnesota had 29, Connecticut 28, Pennsylvania 25, and Indiana 22. In such traditionally industrial states as Massachusetts, Michigan, New York, and New Jersey representatives of labor were so few that in numerical terms they were of little consequence, although in these states there were more labor leaders. Thus state legislatures are likely to reflect a conservative economic point of view; few legislators can be counted upon to voice the views of organized labor.

Many studies of the occupations of legislators tend to overemphasize the influence of occupation on the vote of the legislator. Any careful analysis will show that farmers do not always support farm programs, businessmen do not all vote to protect the interest of business, and that laborers do not see only the interest of labor. The controlling factor in the mind of the legislator must always be the important interests of his constituency. A lawyer may represent a rural community and a farmer an urban community. Occupation under such circumstances must give way to other considerations. Occupational interest is most frequently reflected in committee assignment. Lawyers predominate on the judiciary committee and farmers on such committees as agriculture, roads, county government, and the state agricultural college. The occupations listed in Table 4 indicate more of a social than an occupational interest. The legislators are drawn largely from the middle income group whether urban

or rural.   Actually their occupations may have little to do with their
ability as legislators.

TRAINING AND ORIENTATION OF THE NEW MEMBER

As in the past, so today, in many legislatures new members are
compelled to "learn the ropes" on their own initiative.   Recently,
however, some effort has been made in a number of states to give
new members some sort of training or assistance in preparing them
for their duties.   On the basis of inquiry made among legislative
clerks and secretaries regarding the orientation of new members for
the legislative sessions of 1949 the state legislatures fall into three
categories (no answer was received from a few states): (1) those
that undertake a program of active orientation and training; (2) those
that furnish each new member with copies of the rules, legislative
manuals, or other handbooks; and (3) those that make no effort to
help new members.

For example, it was found that in California the members receive
the *Legislative Handbook,* which contains a chapter of material
relevant to the new member, and a leaflet containing information on
the California legislature.   Connecticut had a short biennial presession training conference for members of the General Assembly.
Florida, Idaho, Iowa, and Massachusetts offered officially sponsored
presession conferences, variously programmed, but in each instance
designed primarily for the instruction and orientation of the new
members of the legislature.   Massachusetts arranged a class that
any interested member might attend, and Illinois gave instruction to
the chairmen of legislative committees.   In Michigan an outside
organization provided an orientation dinner.   In Minnesota and
New Hampshire classes were arranged for the instruction of the new
member in the mechanics of legislation, experienced teachers being
called in to help in the administration of the New Hampshire program.

Developments in orienting the new member are shown in Table 5.
The legislative council in Oklahoma has undertaken a training course
for both legislative employees and lawmakers.   Early in the session
of 1952 the University of Mississippi conducted a course primarily for

TABLE 5

States Holding Orientation Conferences for Legislators

State	When Orientation Conferences Are Held		Length of Conference	Conferences Arranged by—			
	Prior to Session	Early in Session		Legislative Leaders	Legislative Clerks	Legislative Service Agencies	Other
Arizona	X		1 day		X	X[a]	University law school[a]
Arkansas	X		2 days			X	
California		[b]					
Florida	X		2-3 days	X			
Idaho		X	1-2 hours	X	X		
Illinois		X	6 sessions[c]	X	X		A legislator[e]
Kansas		X	2-3 hours	X			
Kentucky	X		3 days[d]				Governor
Louisiana	X		1 day[e]	X			
Maine		X			X[e]		
Massachusetts		X	12 hours[f]				Division of University Extension, Department of Education
Minnesota		X					
Mississippi		X	[g]	X			
Nebraska	X		½ day		X		University
New Hampshire		X	½ day				Bureau of Government, University of N. H.
New Mexico	X		2 days			X	

74

State				Secretary of state
New York		X		
North Carolina		X	[h] [i]	
Oklahoma	X		2 days	University[a]
Pensylvania		[j]		
Rhode Island		[j]		
South Carolina		X	Few hours	X
South Dakota		X	½ day	
Texas		X	[k]	X University law school
Washington	X	[l]		
West Virginia		[b]		X
Wisconsin	X		1 day	
Wyoming	X		½ day	X

Source: Preliminary Report, *American State Legislatures: Structure and Procedures* (The Council of State Governments, September, 1953).

[a] Arkansas, Oklahoma: Joint sponsorship.

[b] California, West Virginia: Informal, unofficial meetings have been held.

[c] Illinois: Weekly evening sessions during first part of session, a total of about six sessions. One legislator has taken primary responsibility for the conferences.

[d] Kentucky: House and Senate meet in separate sessions, each three days long.

[e] Maine: In 1953 Clerk gave informal instruction in parliamentary procedures.

[f] Massachusetts: Twelve one-hour sessions.

[g] Mississippi: Meetings over a period of several days.

[h] New York: Over a two-week period, beginning second week of session.

[i] North Carolina: Daily 20-minute meetings over period of five days, beginning second week of session.

[j] Pennsylvania, Rhode Island: Conferences are held as a matter of political party practice.

[k] Texas: Meeting held over a three-day period in 1953.

[l] Washington: Just prior to session and may continue through first week of session.

the benefit of new legislators. Table 5 indicates that by 1954 twenty-eight states held orientation conferences; in seventeen of these states the conferences took place early in the session, and in eleven prior to the session. Thus it may be seen that notable progress has been made in the training of new members by several of the states. However, more detailed information is needed with respect to the nature and the effectiveness of these programs.[6]

SALARIES

Although being a state legislator is not considered a career, the American people have from the beginning accepted the principle that state legislators should be paid something for their services to offset the sacrifices entailed by absence from business and the costs of living away from home. Nevertheless, salaries have been inadequate in most cases, and few men have been able to afford the sacrifice for many sessions. Various ways of adjusting regular salaries have been employed, such as increased transportation gratuities, recess commissions with ample budgets for use of the members, and the practice of recruiting a member of a legislator's family to the legislative secretarial staff. Half the states have fixed salaries by constitutional provision, assuming that the legislators should not have power to raise their own salaries, although they might appropriate public funds for everything else.

Since World War I regular sessions of the legislatures have lengthened and special sessions have become more frequent, in part because of the increased legislative problems resulting from depression, war, and reconstruction.[7] How much the automobile has contributed to the lengthening of sessions has not been determined, but it has become common practice in all states for legislators to return to their homes each week, and many commute daily. Mileage is more easily provided than most other expense allowances. Oddly enough, for many

---

[6] See *State Government*, 25 (April, 1952), for discussion of Massachusetts' two-decade experience with a school for legislators and the newer Mississippi program.

[7] During a postwar biennium (1947-1948) nineteen states held thirty-seven special sessions in addition to their regular sessions. Under the system of quadrennial regular sessions between 1901 and 1943 eleven special sessions were held in Alabama in addition to the eleven regular sessions.

a legislator compensation for mileage has been greater than his constitutional salary. For example, Connecticut, which pays legislators $600 per biennium, allows ten cents a mile for travel; Kentucky, which pays $25 per day in general and special sessions, allows fifteen cents a mile; New Hampshire, which pays legislators $200 per term, provides a rate-distance ratio ranging from ten cents to five cents per mile; and Vermont, which pays its legislators $1,250 for a biennium, allows twenty cents a mile; Massachusetts, which pays its legislators a much more generous $4,500 per year, also allows $400 a year for general expenses and seven cents a mile per day, with an additional $38.50 per week for expenses, for members living beyond forty miles. Only New Jersey retains the outmoded practice of free state railroad passes in addition to the $3,000 annual salary. All of these states are small enough to allow great numbers to commute daily.

Legislators also receive allowances for expenses other than travel, in part to offset the extra cost of living in the state capital city. In Pennsylvania, where each legislator receives a salary of $6,000 for the biennium, an additional $3,600 is granted to cover cost of living for the biennium. Arizona, which pays its legislators only $8 per day, gives them each $17 per day during a session in addition to travel allowance. California provides additional expense allowance during session of $12 per day with another per diem allowance of $15 for service on interim committees; Alabama and North Dakota grant $10; Kansas $7; and Florida $7.50 per day above mileage. Michigan makes an allowance of $500 per year. Although the above are examples of states that provide extra compensation to offset some of the sacrifice made by legislators, nineteen states grant no expense allowances beyond travel, and in far too many instances the total compensation remains inadequate.

Since the reorganization of Congress in 1946 and the accompanying increase in congressional salaries, twenty-five states have raised the salaries of their legislators. However, in 1953 nineteen states still fixed the legislator's specific salary in their constitutions, although it should be noted that states are rapidly introducing greater flexibility by permitting the legislators to fix their own salaries.

Thirty-two states now provide an annual salary for legislators, but sixteen continue the practice of per diem payments for regular sessions. Twenty, most of which pay on an annual basis, make no provision for extra payments during special sessions. Salaries range from $5,000 per annum in New York and Illinois and $4,500 per annum in Massachusetts to $200 for a term of two years in New Hampshire. North Dakota and Rhode Island pay $5 per day. In 1953 Tennessee raised its legislators' salaries to $10 per day plus $5 per day for living expenses. In many states the president of the senate and speaker of the house receive larger per diem payments than do other members. Per diem payment is by and large very unsatisfactory. There are still three states (Montana, North Dakota, Rhode Island) that have not changed their legislators' compensation during the past half century.[8]

It is difficult to determine the amount a legislator should receive. Living costs vary from family to family and community to community. What might attract one good legislator might prove totally inadequate for another. Whether or not the legislative product would improve with the raising of salaries is a debatable question, for there is little correlation between high salaries and superior laws. Robert Luce, a veteran legislator, some years ago ventured the following criterion for the payment of legislators: "The pay of a state legislator ought not to be large enough to make it a material factor in candidacies for the position. It ought not to be so small as to impose real hardship on a man without resources."[9] The larger and more populous states seem to require more legislation and thus more time from the legislator. The more continuous the legislative session, the less the time remaining for a legislator to devote to his private business and the more he becomes dependent upon his legislative salary.

Some feel that state legislators should receive salaries comparable

---

[8] The following fourteen states in their 1952 or 1953 legislative sessions either adopted or initiated amendments providing for increased compensation for legislators to take effect between 1952 and 1955: Arkansas, Colorado, Florida, Indiana, Louisiana, Maine, Massachusetts, Minnesota, New Mexico, Oregon, South Carolina, Texas, Vermont, and West Virginia.

[9] *Legislative Assemblies* (Houghton, Mifflin, 1924), p. 553.

to those of councilmen in our larger cities. A recent study by the American Municipal Association disclosed that councilmen's salaries in thirteen of the largest cities in the United States averaged $4,408 a year, ranging from $8,000 in Pittsburgh to $1,800 in St. Louis,[10] an average much above that of the salaries of our state legislators. However, a city council performs a role quite different from that of a state legislature; a council is much more involved in the details of administration. Although it enacts ordinances within certain restrictions of charter and statute, in many cities the council sits as an administrative board to the mayor; has a hand in granting abatements upon assessments, letting of contracts, and surveying expenditures; acts as a court of review on zoning regulations; and handles numerous other administrative matters—even to the point of being a regulatory body on matters of business practices within the city. The work of a councilman in a city of over 500,000 is likely to require his full time. Proposals to reorganize legislatures so that they would sit in more or less continuous session to conduct the business of the state could mean more legislative supervision of administration.[11] If state legislatures were organized to permit legislative oversight of administration, along the lines contemplated for Congress under the provisions of the Legislative Reorganization Act of 1946, they might be better equipped for such a role.

The modern faith in strong executive leadership underlies the administrative reorganization movement at both federal and state levels and the council-manager movement in our cities. If legislatures would allow governors a free hand in the management of state administration, and if they would delegate control over local matters to local bodies, the work of legislators would be greatly reduced, and

---

[10] *News Bulletin,* Public Administration Clearing House, Release No. 5, April 29, 1949. See Henry W. Toll's "Today's Legislatures," and also Charles S. Hyneman's "Tenure and Turnover of Legislative Personnel," *The Annals* of the American Academy of Political and Social Science, 195 (January, 1938), 21-31, for a discussion on this point.

[11] See Hyneman, *op. cit.,* p. 30, and Leonard White's views on legislative interference, "Legislative Responsibility for the Public Service," in *New Horizons in Public Administration* (University of Alabama Press, 1945).

less time would be required for legislation. Thus the legislature could devote more time to the broader problems of the state.

RETIREMENT FOR LEGISLATORS

Retirement pensions for legislators are a new development, so new that no textbook on the legislative process published prior to 1946 made reference to them. Since Congress set the example in 1946 by establishing a retirement system for its members, sixteen states have extended retirement benefits to legislators. Abuse of the system in Massachusetts brought its repeal in 1952, and in 1953 the attorney general of Nevada ruled that legislators were not eligible for the state retirement system, although they had been admitted since 1949.[12]

Retirement benefits are provided in the form of annuity payments from funds accumulated by deductions from the legislator's salary plus a similar contribution by the state. The amount of annual retirement payment depends upon a number of factors, such as the amount of the accumulated fund (including interest), years of service, and the age of the recipient. Payments are usually distributed according to a previously determined actuarial plan.

Except in Illinois and California, state legislators receive retirement benefits by being incorporated into retirement systems for regular civil service employees. Although these state retirement plans were originally designed to remove from administrative posts those employees who because of old age had become ineffective and inefficient, the additional security and income derived from a retirement plan appealed to elective administrative officials as well as to civil service employees. Elected officials brought pressure for their inclusion in the system during the twenties and thirties, and state retirement systems were gradually extended to include both state and local elected officials. Legislators, as elected officials, have claimed the benefits of state retirement systems in Florida, Maryland, Montana, New

---

[12] The table in Appendix C gives the details of the plans in operation in the remaining fourteen states. See also Betty J. Echternach, *Retirement Systems for Legislators,* University of Hawaii, Legislative Reference Bureau, Report No. 5 (1949).

Jersey, New Mexico, Nevada, Ohio, and Washington. However, in Louisiana, Massachusetts, Pennsylvania, Rhode Island, and South Carolina the term public "employee" was actually redefined to include all "persons whose regular compensation is paid" by the state, and the New York statute specifically extends the benefit of the state's retirement system to legislators, instead of covering them as "elected officials" or "employees." Illinois and California have gone farther than any other states to provide retirement benefits for their legislators through a system designed to meet their peculiar needs. Stated in simple terms, the California and Illinois plans provide for retirement and payment to a beneficiary in case of death. They prescribe "service in the legislature" as the basis for payment instead of allowing service in the capacity of an elected state or local official to apply. Although the plan is administered in California by the state retirement system, it is a separate plan. In Illinois the plan is administered as a separate system. By not having the legislative retirement system a part of the employees' retirement plan, which is built for a career service, certain complex provisions are avoided, such as disability through injury, mandatory age for retirement, special death benefits, and the whole question of "accredited service," including service not otherwise covered by a pension system. Legislators hesitate to insist that these provisions be inserted in their special plan. Such provisions are subject to abuse in the states that do not separate the two plans.

The general provisions and variations of retirement systems may be briefly summarized:

1. Retirement plans are optional on the part of the legislator, requiring either an application for membership, as is the case in California, Florida, Maryland, Mississippi, Montana, New Mexico, Ohio, Pennsylvania, Rhode Island, and New Jersey, or a positive action against becoming a member, as in South Carolina and Illinois.

2. Except in Illinois, at the time of their inclusion in the system legislators may count all previous public service—legislative or otherwise—toward retirement, provided they make all back payments on contributions. However, South Carolina gives credit for all legislative service prior to 1945 without cost to the members.

3. There is no compulsory retirement age for legislators, as there is for public employees, and most systems specifically exempt legislators from the compulsory retirement age requirement.

4. Except for Nevada and New York, where a legislator may be retired at fifty-five, New Mexico and Mississippi, where retirement is at sixty-five, and California, where it is at sixty-three, sixty is the retirement age. Additional accumulations beyond that age are permitted if the legislator wishes to remain in service.

5. Many states have minimum service requirements for retirement benefits: for example, Ohio, five years; Illinois, eight years; Florida, Montana, and South Carolina, ten years; New Mexico, fifteen years; New York, twenty years.

6. All plans are contributory, ranging from 1.5 per cent in Mississippi to 7 per cent in Illinois. State contributions vary from actuarial needs to a fixed sum as high as 7.2 per cent in California. State contributions are invariably met by annual state appropriations.

7. In all states legislators may withdraw their own contributions, but not those of the state, when they leave legislative service. Except for Florida, Rhode Island, and Illinois, where no interest upon contributions may be withdrawn, legislators may receive interest on contributions upon withdrawal. New Jersey, Pennsylvania, and South Carolina allow as much as 4 per cent interest upon the legislator's contributions.

A. A. Weinberg has well summarized the purpose served by retirement plans for civil service employees: retirement systems aim primarily "to provide an income during old age." The principal provision of the plan, therefore, is the superannuation retirement benefit, which should be viewed as a benefit for old age and not as a bonus or reward for services rendered. The employer's contributions to this benefit are in the nature of additional salary, the payment of which is deferred until the employee has reached a state of old-age inefficiency.[13] However, retirement of state legislators

---

[13] "Retirement Planning for Public Employees," *State Government,* 20 (January, 1947), 11. This idea has been written into the Iowa statute providing retirement for civil servants; see Iowa Old-Age and Survivor Insurance, *Code of Iowa,* 97.2 (G. A. ch. 91, sec. 2).

according to the established plans obviously do not have as its purpose the removal from service of older members, for in every state plan legislators are exempted from compulsory retirement at the usual age for civil servants. It is recognized that a man may not efficiently perform the routine of administrative tasks after seventy, but that he may be very valuable in the councils of the state as an "elder statesman."[14] Retirement benefits for legislators, then, may be considered only as deferred additional compensation for service to the public to offset the personal losses incurred. Nevertheless the practice as it is applied to legislators contains an element of reward differing from the objectives of retirement plans for civil servants formulated by A. A. Weinberg. For example, reward must have been uppermost in the mind of the Pennsylvania legislators in 1949 when they extended the benefits of retirement to all former members of the legislature.[15] It must also have prompted the South Carolina legislators when they gave credit for all service prior to 1945 to all legislators without the requirement that they contribute. It must have been a principal consideration for making the plans retroactive to include previous service in all other states.

Including state legislators under the regular retirement systems for civil service employees raises a number of questions. In most states time spent in a military organization or as an elected or appointed official is accumulated creditable service for retirement. This may mean retirement after a very few years in the legislature, and it may develop into a perpetual practice in favor of legislators who have been in the armed services.

The major question, however, is whether a retirement system for legislators should be separate from that provided for public employees. Certain administrative and financial gains result from having all retirement funds consolidated and administered as one. On the other

---

[14] See "What Congress Pensions Mean: Chance for Younger Leaderships," *United States News,* September 6, 1946, pp. 26-27; George B. Galloway, *Congress at the Crossroads* (Crowell, 1946), p. 330. In an address at Cornell University February 15, 1949, Congressman Mike Monroney said that retirement provisions had not resulted in the older leaders seeking retirement. They preferred the more active role as legislators.

[15] Pennsylvania, House 121, Session 949, Senate reprint, Printer's No. 752.

hand, some features of retirement plans for public employees should be carefully examined; for example, many state retirement plans provide disability and death benefits.   Should this feature be available to legislators?

It is difficult to determine in a general way what legislators may expect from retirement plans, for much depends upon the funds accumulated and the actuarial plan established.   In Illinois a legislator will receive 25 per cent of his final salary after ten years service, or $750 (based on present salaries), and 50 per cent of his final salary at the end of twenty years service, or $1500, upon reaching the retirement age of sixty.   After having six years' minimum service in the legislature and reaching the age of fifty-five a Massachusetts legislator, before repeal of the act in 1952, could have received retirement benefits of $1200 per year or $3000 annually after twenty years of public service, not all of which needed to be in the legislature.[16] Although these payments seem sizable, retirement benefits in states that follow the practice of per diem payments are of little consequence because of the small opportunity to build an annuity fund.   For example, both Montana and Florida extend retirement benefits to legislators, but they do not think it worth while to apply.

The impact of retirement plans upon the tenure of legislators has not yet been measured.   Inasmuch as legislators serve for noticeably longer terms in the states that pay more adequate salaries, provisions for retirement *should* act as a further inducement, but there are other implications.   For example, a study conducted in Illinois in 1948 revealed that of the 204 members of the legislature 190 had elected

---

[16] *The Boston Herald,* September 1, 1949, p. 6.   Present salary is $4500 per year.   Repealed by Chapter 634 Acts of 1952.   The repeal was the result of a struggle between Governor Dever and the legislature.   The act was not repealed solely upon its faults, but was one phase of a conflict between a Democratic Governor and a group of Republican legislators.   This group of legislators sought to abolish former Mayor (of Boston) Curley's pension.   In support of Curley, Governor Dever tried to punish the legislators by the abolition of their pensions.   Many interests rallied to his assistance, particularly the Federation of Taxpayers Associations.   However, in the election year of 1952 this proved to be poor political judgment for he failed re-election.   There were many reasons for his defeat, but repeal of pensions was no doubt an important one.

to join the retirement system. The average age of this group was 54.6, the mean 55. The average service was ten years. In 1948 half of the members of the Illinois legislature were eligible for retirement in terms of service and would meet the age requirment within three years and be entitled to $750 annually.[17] Will these legislators prefer to retire to their businesses on a pension or continue longer as legislators with the possibility of larger pensions? Moreover, retirement plans may have a different effect upon legislators than upon civil service employees. Retirement benefits are held out to young civil servants to justify low salaries and to induce them to remain in government employment in order to build up substantial benefits. A much higher percentage of legislators than of civil service employees is within five years of the retirement age. Thus pensions may act as a special inducement for older men to campaign for the legislature. It will be some time before it can be determined whether provisions for retirement will serve to attract capable young men to legislative halls.

The question of retirement of legislators is one that deeply concerns the citizen. Any increase in compensation either by a raise in salary or by provisions for retirement must be considered in terms of the role expected of the legislature and the representative nature of the popular assembly.[18]

The extension of federal Social Security[19] to state and local government employees and officials in 1950 suggested to some legislatures that their members might be included. Idaho and Wisconsin in adopting the federal act in 1951 specifically included legislators,[20] and in Tennessee the inclusion of "legislative officials elected by the General Assembly" has been interpreted to include legislators.[21]

---

[17] "First Annual Statement of the Board of Trustees," General Assembly Retirement System of Illinois, June 30, 1948.

[18] See Joseph P. Harris, "Modernizing the Legislature," *National Municipal Review,* vol 36, March, 1947.

[19] 49 U. S. Stat. 629, ch. 531 (1935).

[20] *Wisconsin Laws,* 1951, ch. 60, sec. 66.99(4a); letter to L. G. Harvey from Idaho clerk of house of representatives, July 22, 1953.

[21] Letter from acting director, legislative council committee, to L. G. Harvey, August 6, 1953.

The question of eligibility of legislators for federal Social Security benefits has arisen in Arizona and Nebraska, although in Oregon the legislature specifically excluded its members from Social Security.[22]

The issue of including state legislators in federal Old Age and Survivors Insurance (Social Security) raises some nice questions of constitutional interpretations of our federal system. There seems to be no question that the federal government may subsidize a state activity, such as highways or welfare, through grants-in-aid even to the point of paying a part of the salary of a state or local employee. However, a legislator is neither an employee, in the strictest sense, even though many participate in retirement plans for employees, nor is he an elected officer. Although elected, he is not an "officer," the term being reserved for executives and administrators.[23] The federal government has left interpretation of eligibility to Social Security in this matter to state definition, but it is a question whether the original intent of the law was to subsidize state lawmakers. If our federal system means anything, it means complete independence of state legislators and state judges from federal control. A grant for retirement is a subsidy, although the control is mild. Both the grant and control are subject to increase. Although there is little constitutional justification for extension of federal Social Security to state legislators, there is some justification upon the basis of fair play. It would be unfortunate indeed if a person were deprived of Social Security benefits just because he was a member of the state legislature during the last years before seeking retirement. It is conceivable that hardship cases could arise. Since Social Security still does not reach everyone, the fault lies in the present system, which permits the designation of the "occupation"—state legislator—supposed to be independent of federal control, for federal financial assistance in old age. Even considering the questions raised previously, it would be better for the state to have its own retirement plan for legislators free from federal subsidy than to cover them into Social Security.

---

[22] *Oregon Laws,* ch. 193 (1953).

[23] See James Hart, *Introduction to Administrative Law* (2nd ed., Appleton-Century-Crofts, 1950), ch. V, especially pp. 111-118.

A CODE OF ETHICS FOR LEGISLATORS

It would seem that after more than one hundred and fifty years of experimentation with state legislatures we should give some consideration to a code of ethics for legislators. A proposed code of ethics for the state legislators in New Mexico was drafted by a committee of the legislative council in that state in 1952 and was published in *The National Municipal Review* with some very penetrating comments by the editor of the *Review*. It was indicated in these remarks that "There is no opportunity for an unethical legislator where there is no conniving private or special interest or an individual or group ready to buy favors in the black market."[24] Because of these pressures it is imperative that the rules of ethical conduct be well understood by the legislator and all persons concerned—including citizens.

Certainly we have developed very elementary notions regarding the ethical basis of a legislator's relations with his fellow legislators, his constituency, and the people as a whole on matters of additional compensation or aid to campaign funds. Is compensation adequate or are the costs of being a legislator too great for the average man? This is a vital question. A code of ethics would clarify the responsibilities of the legislator and pave the way for popular demands for restraint upon interests seeking special favors. The citizen is vitally interested in such a statement and its development should not be left to legislators themselves.

RECOMMENDATIONS

1. State legislatures need not be so large as they are in most states. They should be small enough to permit deliberation, but large enough to provide adequate personnel for committee work. A unicameral legislature or the lower house of a bicameral legislature should not have fewer than forty members. A ratio of one senator to three representatives is desirable.

---

[24] *National Municipal Review*, 41 (November, 1952), 488-489. See also Paul H. Douglas, *Ethics in Government* (Harvard University Press, 1952).

2. Any qualified voter should be eligible for election to either house of the legislature.

3. The legislative term should be long enough to permit a legislator to participate in two or more sessions. The term of the governor should equal the maximum term for members of either house.

4. Vacancies should be filled by special elections.

5. Elections should not be scheduled in presidential election years, or years when the mayors of large cities are elected.

6. The seating of a legislator in the case of a contested or disputed election should be the prerogative of the house concerned, but should follow an investigation of the law and facts by either the courts or a special tribunal for that purpose.

7. Orientation and training programs for newly elected legislators should be the rule. This task might well be assigned to the legislative councils wherever they exist.

8. Legislators should receive salaries at least sufficient to offset personal sacrifice as measured by average income. The amount should be determined by statute and not by the constitution. Extra compensation by way of appropriate expense allowances should be provided for the presiding officers, floor leaders, members of the legislative council, and members of interim or recess committees to encourage year-round continuity of services of recognized leaders.

9. Retirement payments should be made available to legislators under a system separate from that of state employees. Such a retirement system should take into account the nature of the legislative office, and the legislator should contribute while in office. Payments to retired legislators should be based upon the fund accumulated during the time in the legislature.

10. A special commission should be created consisting of legislators and leaders in government and other walks of life to develop a code of ethics for legislators.

6

Legislative Sessions and Organization

WHEN STATE GOVERNMENTS were first formed, annual sessions of the legislature were the rule. In fact, it was a common assumption of Revolutionary political philosophy that the representatives of the people should meet every year. The Massachusetts constitution of 1780 contained these interesting instructions: "The legislature ought frequently to assemble for redress of grievances, for correcting, strengthening, and confirming the laws, and for making new laws, as the common good may require." During the nineteenth century, however, the state legislature fell into disrepute, and the people lost confidence in it. It was frequently asserted that "the common good" did not require such an annual "grist of bad laws" and that the people would be better off if the legislature met less often. The widespread corruption of state legislatures and the expense of annual sessions were additional reasons for the abandonment of annual regular sessions.

LIMITED LEGISLATIVE SESSIONS

Recoiling from the earlier faith in the ability of representatives to shape the laws of the state, forty-three states had by 1900 abandoned annual sessions. Even today only ten states—Arizona, California, Colorado, Maryland, Massachusetts, Michigan, New Jersey, New

York, Rhode Island, and South Carolina—provide for annual sessions.[1] California, Colorado, and Maryland limit the purpose of the sessions in the even-numbered years to budgetary, revenue, financial, and urgent matters.

Most states have adopted a pattern of biennial sessions, and many have specific constitutional provisions limiting the number of days a legislature may sit in regular session. Alabama restricts its legislature to 36 legislative days. Regular sessions in Wyoming are confined to 40 days; in Arkansas, Florida, Louisiana, Montana, Nevada, New Mexico, South Dakota, Utah, and Washington to 60 days; in Kentucky and North Dakota to 60 legislative days; in Indiana to 61 days; in Georgia to an aggregate of 70 days in two years; in Maryland and Minnesota to 90 days; and in California to 120 days. In several other states limitations upon legislative sessions are stated in terms of days for which legislators may be paid: Arizona and Idaho (60 days), Rhode Island (60 legislative days), Tennessee (75 days), North Carolina (90 days), and Colorado (120 days). Texas reduces the per diem for a regular session from $10 to $5 after the first 120 days.

Efforts to Counteract Limitation

Special Sessions. Biennial regular sessions and limitations upon their length, the normal demands of increased legislative business, and the requirements of depression, war, and national emergency have necessitated the calling of many special sessions during the last twenty-odd years. From 1927 to 1940 no less than 280 such sessions were convened, with 46 meeting in 1936 alone. Since 1940 extraordinary sessions have been numerous. Thirty-three states summoned their

---

[1] As recently as 1950 Arizona and Colorado provided for annual sessions. Michigan adopted the same plan in 1951. In Kansas, New Mexico, Pennsylvania, and West Virginia constitutional amendments providing for annual sessions were pending in 1953. Annual sessions may be held in states that place no constitutional limitation on the duration of sessions by taking a recess rather than adjournment *sine die*. In Idaho, where the regular session is constitutionally limited, the legislature in 1949 made appropriations for only one year, necessitating a special session, called by the governor, in 1950. When Ohio, adopted a new constitution in 1851 changing from annual to biennial sessions, annual adjourned sessions continued to 1895.

legislatures in 1944 to enact absent-voting laws for the armed services. In 1950, 28 special sessions were held in seventeen states, Alabama topping the list with 5.

Special sessions are frequently convened immediately after regular sessions and sometimes after special sessions themselves in states where time limits are placed upon both types of sessions. Nineteen states place limitations upon the length of special sessions: Alabama restricts them to 36 legislative days, twelve states to a period of from 15 to 60 calendar days,[2] and six cut off legislative pay after 15 to 60 days.[3]

In addition to the restrictions upon the number of days the legislature may sit in special session, most states leave the calling of special sessions entirely to the governor. The need of such sessions is a matter that the legislature as well as the governor should be competent to determine. Only in Arizona, Massachusetts, and New Hampshire, however, may the legislature itself provide for special sessions without petitioning the governor. Although the governor may be forced to call a special session when presented with a petition, which in Georgia must be signed by three fifths of the members of the legislature and in Louisiana, Nebraska, Virginia, and West Virginia by two thirds of the members, in all other states legislatures are dependent entirely upon the initiative of the governor. In general, governors look with disfavor upon lengthy sessions at any time and are loath to call assemblies unless they confine their deliberations to certain specified matters. In only twenty states are legislatures considered competent to determine their agenda.[4]

Time-Saving Devices. Legislators faced with the tremendous pressures of modern governmental problems are thwarted on every side

---

[2] Arkansas—15 days; Florida, Idaho, Nevada, Oregon—20 days; Louisiana, Maryland, Texas, Utah, and Virginia—30 days; Indiana—40 days; Missouri—60 days.

[3] New Hampshire—15 days; Arizona, Tennessee—20 days; North Carolina—25 days; Delaware—30 days; Montana—60 days.

[4] Alabama, Arizona, Connecticut, Delaware, Florida, Indiana, Kansas, Maine, Massachusetts, Minnesota, New Hampshire, New Jersey, North Carolina, Oregon, South Carolina, South Dakota, Vermont, Virginia, Washington, and Wyoming. See *The Book of the States, 1950-51* (Chicago: The Council of State Governments, 1950), p. 109.

by shortsighted restrictions of time and are forced to circumvent them by such childlike maneuvers as stopping the clock. Such tactics seem beneath the dignity of responsible representative assemblies.[5] Such devices for averting overcrowding at the end of the session as executive and adjourned sessions have not been effective. Certainly the states that have experimented with the "split session" have not achieved in practice the advantages claimed for it, particularly with respect to the early introduction of bills with substance and the elimination of the rush at the end of the session. However, in California, with some 5,000 bills introduced in the first 16 days of a 120-day session, the period of recess (which may last as long as six weeks) is used to advantage by the office of legislative counsel to prepare short digests and a subject-matter index of the introduced bills.[6]

Twenty-one states now recognize that mechanical systems of recording legislative votes save substantial time. It is reported that in New Jersey's assembly, with sixty members, it takes from thirty to sixty seconds for a quorum call or to pass a bill instead of the former three-minute minimum. Thirty-nine states have lower houses with larger memberships than New Jersey. Electrical roll call systems are in operation in both houses of the legislature in Indiana, Louisiana, Minnesota, Missouri, North Dakota, Virginia, and in the unicameral legislature of Nebraska. Fourteen states use the push-button machines for their larger houses only.[7]

---

[5] In 1952 the West Virginia supreme court indicated its disfavor of the practice of stopping the clock when it said "It cannot in law stop the actual passage of time or lawfully continue or prolong a regular session of the legislature." In Nevada, where the clock is stopped to circumvent the 60-day session limitation, the threat has been made recently to challenge the constitutionality of all enactments occurring after the actual end of the session.

[6] California has operated under the split session since 1911; West Virginia and New Mexico discontinued it after short periods; in Massachusetts it is constitutionally authorized but never used. Alabama, Georgia, New Jersey, and Wisconsin also utilize the recess device during regular sessions. Constitutional amendments in Arkansas and Florida were awaiting action by the electorate in 1953. See T. S. Barclay, "The Split Session of the California Legislature," *California Law Review,* 20 (November, 1931), 43-59.

[7] States using the machines in their lower houses are Alabama, Arkansas, California, Florida, Illinois, Iowa, Maryland, Michigan, Mississippi, New Jersey, Tennessee, Texas, West Virginia, Wisconsin. Wisconsin originated the practice in 1917. Beginning with the 1955 session Arkansas and California plan to use the machines in their senates, and Ohio in the house.

Effects of Sessional Limitations

Limiting sessions intensifies all evils associated with legislative halls. Taking advantage of the short time for deliberation, a strong minority may thwart the interest of the majority through delaying tactics. Bills piled up at the end of a session are rushed through without adequate consideration. This tendency to defer action on bills until the closing days does not create a situation suitable for debate and deliberation. The restrictions on length of sessions are the real reasons for bad laws—not extended periods of discussion. Certainly it would be impossible to say that legislation or the quality of legislators has been improved by limiting the sessions.

The argument that lengthy and frequent sessions are an excessive expense was exploded by a survey conducted by the American Legislators' Association some years ago. For the period studied, 1927-1932, legislative costs were less than one per cent of the total state expenditures. It was observed in this study that annual sessions were not necessarily more expensive than biennial sessions.[8] Based upon figures compiled by the Bureau of the Census on the costs of state government, the percentage allotted to legislative costs in 1948, was much smaller than for the period of 1927-1932. Some economies would result from more efficient handling of administrative matters by legislative bodies, but no real economies can be effected by reduction of legislative sessions—certainly not in terms of total state costs. As the Committee on Legislative Processes and Procedures of The Council of State Governments has wisely observed: "The important consideration is that the legislature be enabled to meet as often and as long as, in the judgment of its leaders, its responsibilities require." No state constitution protects the interests of all the people when the question of length and frequency of legislative sessions is a forbidden topic for legislative determination. The purpose of lengthening sessions is not to deny to the governors the right to call special sessions, for they are frequently more aware of the necessity than a majority of the legislature. However, to freeze into a state constitution a restriction upon the length and frequency of legislative sessions is a

---

[8] See W. Brooke Graves, *American State Government* (3rd ed., Heath, 1946), p. 256; (4th ed., 1953), pp. 230-36.

reactionary and negative approach to a problem that requires the most positive and constructive analysis and remedy.

LEGISLATIVE OFFICERS AND EMPLOYEES

Legislative Officers

The principal officers chosen by a legislative house are the presiding officer, the clerk or secretary, the sergeant-at-arms, the doorkeeper, the postmaster, and the chaplain. Other persons on the legislative pay roll, excluding members, are known as employees and vary in number and method of appointment from state to state. The employees include the expert assistants and office staffs of the officers, committees, and other agencies, and individual members of the particular house or legislature as a whole. The officers are chosen by the house to which they are attached, usually for political reasons. Employees are appointed by the officers, committees, or individual members, and their selection likewise is usually on a political basis rather than one of merit.

The presiding officer of the lower house is uniformly known as the speaker; in three fourths of the states the voters elect a lieutenant governor who has the function of presiding over the senate, although all senates elect presidents or presidents pro tempore. Speakers in all lower houses and presiding officers in all but fifteen of the senates appoint the members of standing committees. Presiding officers, other than lieutenant governors, are invariably identified with the major party or faction in control of the house to which they are attached and frequently use their powers to further the cause of their party or faction. Although they are usually powerful politically, their importance as leaders varies considerably, depending upon the type of political organizations obtaining within the chamber over which they preside.[9] The other elective officers perform for the most part routine functions, which need not be described here. Their duties are of such character that political considerations should not enter into their election.

---

[9] Consult Chapter 12.

Legislative Employees

Legislative employees are dealt with in various respects in other parts of this report. The *Interim Report of the New York State Joint Legislative Committee on Legislative Methods, Practices, Procedures and Expenditures*[10] deals extensively with the problems of legislative staff. Various other studies and recommendations have been made, but few legislatures have progressed very far in providing efficient staffs for their officers, committees, and individual members. Most legislatures have not approached the problem from the standpoint of adequacy of staff or its selection on the basis of merit. Useless employees are carried on the legislative payroll whose places could be taken by others to whom necessary duties not now performed could be assigned. Politics rather than need and merit have governed the number and recruitment of legislative employees. The possibilities of applying the merit system to legislative appointments, as in Wisconsin, seem quite promising. The whole problem of what constitutes an efficient and useful legislative staff needs thorough investigation in most states. The lack of such a staff is a very serious handicap to the effectiveness of most legislatures.[11]

THE COMMITTEE SYSTEM

General Characteristics

The most important work of the state legislatures, like that of Congress, is conducted by standing and special committees. The tendency everywhere is for the debates on the floors of both houses of the state legislature to decline in importance, and for the real consideration of proposed legislation to be given by the committees. The large number of measures that are considered at each session, as well as their complexity and the wide range of subjects covered, make it necessary for the legislature to delegate most of the work of preparing, considering, and revising legislative proposals to its committees, retaining for itself only the final approval or disapproval of their

---

[10] Legislative Document 1945, No. 35. For further treatment of the matter of legislative research and clerical staff, see Chapter 9.

[11] See discussion of this problem in Chapters 8 and 9.

recommendations. The inability of the legislature itself to give adequate consideration to the great mass of proposed legislation, moreover, has made it generally necessary to accept committee recommendations without change. The successful functioning of a state legislature thus depends in large measure on the organization and operations of its committees.

It is generally recognized that the existing committee system of most state legislatures is poorly constituted to handle the large volume of important legislation. In practically all states there are too many standing committees in each house, resulting in some cases in needless duplication, confusion, waste of legislative talents, and the absence of clear-cut responsibility of each committee for legislation in its assigned field. The large number of standing committees has resulted from the accidental nature of their growth. Committees once created have been continued largely because of the desire of members for committee chairmanships and the added prestige of membership on several committees. The great bulk of work in most states is done by a few of the most important committees. The major committees are assigned more legislative business than they can adequately consider, whereas minor committees languish with little to do. As a result, many members of the legislature assigned to only minor committees are denied effective participation in the most important work of legislation. Because of the log jam in a few committees either legislative sessions are unduly prolonged or bills suffer from little or no consideration. Under this system the opening of the legislative session witnesses a mad scramble of members for good committee assignments, which are often made on the basis of trades and political deals rather than careful consideration of the qualifications of members.

The increasing volume of state legislation makes it imperative that the committee system be reorganized. If, because of an ineffectual committee setup, the length of the legislative sessions is prolonged, the situation can be corrected only through the establishment of a more efficient and better organized committee system. Several states have recently reorganized their committee systems, drastically reducing the number of committees and assigning to each committee an important and well-defined field of legislation.[12]   This reduction has made it possible for each member of the legislature to be assigned to at least one active, working committee.   The existence of committees with such well-defined areas of legislation somewhat limits the power of the presiding officer to refer bills on the basis of personal influence or favoritism rather than the subject matter contained in the bill.

The committee system of state legislatures needs to be reorganized to provide greater responsibility of the individual committees to the legislative body that they serve.   It is not in accord with public policy for the standing committees to become "little legislatures," each a law unto itself with irresponsible power.   Some of the most severe criticism of our state legislatures today is due to the irresponsible actions of a few committees.

A Sound Committee System

The essential features of a sound committee system are generally agreed upon by authorities on state legislatures.   They include the following:

1. A substantial reduction of the number of standing committees, and the assignment to each committee of a broad area or related areas of legislation.

2. The utilization of joint committees by the two houses of the legislature where practicable in order that committee work may be effectively coordinated, the consideration of pending legislation expedited, and the wasted effort and expense of duplicate hearings on the same legislation avoided.   The use of joint committees requires that each house establish substantially identical committees.

3. The reduction of the number of committee assignments of members of the legislature so that each member can give the necessary attention to the work of the committee to which he is assigned.   The ideal, it would appear, has been achieved by the United States House of Representatives, which limits each member to one committee

---

[12] For example, in 1952 Kentucky reduced the number of house committees from 71 to 44.   North Carolina reduced its senate committees since 1951 from 52 to 28.

assignment, although the smaller size of most state senates might necessitate each senator serving on a minimum of two committees.

4. The appointment of committee chairmen who can provide able leadership, and the assignment of members to committees with due regard to their special qualifications. Attention should be given also to making each committee representative of the public interest and of the political complexion of the legislative house to which it is attached.

5. The establishment of rules that provide for advance notice of hearings and adequate committee records and require prompt consideration of measures referred to committees, thus avoiding the last minute rush. Of especial importance is the establishment of an effective and workable discharge rule through which the legislative body may prevent the arbitrary pigeonholing of bills by a committee.

6. The utilization of a permanent legislative council or a limited number of interim committees to investigate the most important subjects of legislation and to propose suitable legislation in advance of sessions.[13]

7. Adequate and competent committee staffs to assemble data needed by each committee, to aid in the preparation of bills, reports, and the scheduling of hearings, and otherwise to assist the committees in their work.[14]

These features of a sound committee system are discussed below.

The Number of Committees. A survey conducted by The Council of State Governments in 1953 indicates that the lower houses of the state legislatures have on the average 32 standing committees, whereas the state senates have an average of 25 committees. Georgia has 63 house committees; Missouri has 60, Arkansas 56, Tennessee 55, Florida 54, and South Dakota 51. Fourteen states have 40 or more committees in the lower house, and fourteen have 30 or more in the senate. At the other extreme, Wisconsin has only 10 senate committees (bills are referred to only 9), and South Carolina has only 8 house committees.

Among the states that have drastically reduced the number of the standing committees in one or both houses since 1949 may be men-

[13] See Chapter 8.
[14] See Chapter 9.

tioned Arkansas, Colorado, Kentucky, Maryland, Nevada, North Carolina, Oregon, South Carolina, and South Dakota. Further reductions are needed in most states. In 1946 Congress reduced the number of standing committees in the House of Representatives from 48 to 19, and in the Senate from 33 to 15.

Studies made in several states of the reference of legislative bills to the standing committees of the legislature uniformly show that a few of the most important committees receive the great bulk of the bills, whereas other committees have few bills referred to them, and a few committees are assigned none at all. In the New York Senate, for example, in the 1945 session two committees (judiciary and finance) received 26.6 per cent of all bills referred; the nine highest committees received a total of 1,587 bills—70 per cent of all bills referred to committees, an average of 176 bills per committee. The ten committees with the smallest number of bills referred to them had a combined total of only 116, or an average of only 11.6 per committee. In the New York Assembly at the same session five committees, out of the total of thirty-six, received more than half of all bills referred, or an average of 315 each, whereas six other committees received a combined total of only 16 bills.[15] Studies of the reference of bills to standing committees in other states present a similar picture. The great bulk of legislative measures is referred to a few committees, which, because of the sheer volume of legislative business, are not able to give them adequate consideration, while some committees have little or nothing to do.

The number of standing committees in most state legislatures should continue to be drastically reduced after a careful analysis has been made of the work load of present committees. Each committee should be assigned a definite field or related area of legislation of sufficient importance that every committee will have a reasonable amount of legislative business. By keeping the number of committees small the common practice of having several committees with similar or duplicating assignments will be avoided.

Through the use of a small number of committees and a corres-

---

[15] That this situation in New York has shown no recent improvement may be checked by comparing these figures with those of the 1935 session, in Belle Zeller, *Pressure Politics in New York* (Prentice-Hall, 1937), pp. 296-97.

ponding reduction of the committee assignments of individual members it will be possible for each committee to schedule regular meetings and proceed promptly with its work, without running into conflicts with other committees. Also, each committee can readily be provided with adequate rooms for meetings and hearings, and with a capable staff, and the legislature itself will be better able to hold each committee responsible for its work.

If the Congress of the United States is able to operate with only 15 major standing committees in the Senate and 19 in the House of Representatives, it would appear that the state legislatures could get along with this number or even fewer. It would be feasible for state legislatures to limit the number of standing committees to around 12. The following list of committees is merely suggestive and is based on an analysis of the typical legislative load:

Judiciary	Transportation and highways
Revenue and taxation	Health and welfare
Appropriations and finance	Education
Governmental efficiency	Local Government
Agriculture	Conservation
Labor and industry	Elections

It is impossible to suggest a committee arrangement that would be feasible for all state legislative houses. Moreover, some committees, particularly the judiciary committee, have such a large volume of legislative measures that their work would be expedited by providing a larger number of members than for others, permitting the use of subcommittees.

The Use of Joint Committees. The greatest use of joint committees has been made by the states of Massachusetts, Maine, and Connecticut, in which the joint committee system has been utilized for years with eminently satisfactory results. It is notable that a total of twenty-three states use one or more joint committees, though outside of New England their use is exceptional rather than the rule. Joint legislative committees have the following advantages:

1. They avoid the necessity for dual consideration of bills, which is both time-consuming and expensive.

2. They provide the means for better coordination of the work of the two houses, avoiding much of the usual friction and misunderstanding.

3. They facilitate the expeditious consideration of legislation and afford some of the advantages of a unicameral legislature while retaining a bicameral system.

4. They provide, as a rule, for more thorough consideration of legislation and the better utilization of qualified staff than is possible with separate committees.

5. They reduce the use of companion bills, as well as the need for conference committees.

The Reduction of Committee Assignments.   One of the results of an excessive number of committees is that each member of the legislature is assigned to several committees, and committee chairmen find it difficult to secure a quorum because of the conflicts with meetings of other committees.   It is not unusual in many legislatures for members to belong to from six to nine separate committees, and thus to be unable to give adequate attention to the work of any committee without neglecting that of others.   The average number of committees on which members serve varies widely.   In the house the number ranges from one in Maine and New Hampshire to twelve in North Carolina, and in the senate from two in Indiana, Maine, and Rhode Island to fourteen in Tennessee.   The mean of these averages is 4.37 in the house and 6.09 in the senate.   In contrast, the rule in Congress now is that no Representative may, with certain exceptions, serve on more than a single committee, and no Senator on more than two.   If similar limitations were adopted by the state legislatures, it would be possible for each committee to hold regular and frequent meetings and to keep abreast of its calendar, thus making possible shorter legislative sessions and avoidance of the last minute rush.

The Selection of Chairmen and Members of Committees.   As a general rule the assignment of members to committees of the lower house is made by the speaker.   In fifteen state senates, however, the rule is for committee assignments to be made by a committee on committees.   In two-party states the actual selection in both houses is sometimes made by the leaders of the two major political parties and approved in a party caucus.

The making of committee assignments requires consideration of the qualifications, interest, and experience of members and their stand on public issues, as well as a balancing of sectional, economic, and other interests. The task would be greatly simplified by reducing the number of committees and the number of committee assignments of individual members. If political parties are to have any meaning in state legislatures, it would seem essential that the legislative party leaders be given a controlling voice in making the committee assignments. It should be borne in mind that the primary purpose of the committee assignments is to produce effective, working committees.

The selection of committee chairmen is of the utmost importance, for upon the chairmen will necessarily fall the leadership that will determine in large part the effectiveness of the committee. The rule of seniority, if strictly followed, will often elevate members who are not equipped to exercise that leadership to the post of chairman. Although legislative experience is an important consideration in selecting committee chairmen, the length of service alone is a poor guide and in effect greatly weakens the leadership in the legislature.

The Rules Governing the Work of Committees. It is important that each legislative body adopt a set of rules that will assure prompt and orderly consideration of the bills assigned to the committees and avoid the abuses that unfortunately have at times marred their work. The rules should require a regular schedule of committee meetings. Hearings on specific bills should be publicly scheduled and announced a week ahead of time so that interested citizens will be able to appear and testify. Frequently committees keep extremely meager records. This situation can be corrected by a specific set of rules requiring each committee to keep records, including among other items the vote of its members on all measures. As the deliberations of committees are often conducted in executive or closed sessions, it is desirable that the decisions of the committee and the votes theron be made a matter of public record. This is the practice in a number of states at present.

In eighteen states committees are required to report out all bills referred to them and in some within a specified time. This rule prevents committees from killing proposed measures by holding them in the committee and takes away what virtually amounts to a veto power by the committee, or sometimes by the chairman. However, in Massachusetts, where such a rule has been in use for many years, it has operated to prolong the legislative session. It would appear preferable not to require committees to report out all bills, but to provide instead a workable discharge rule. Experience indicates that the requirement of a constitutional majority vote for discharge of a committee is somewhat excessive. The new constitution of Missouri, it may be noted, provides that a vote of one third of the members elected to either house may recall a bill from a committee and place it on the calendar.

RECOMMENDATIONS

With reference to legislative organization the following summary of recommendations may be presented:

1. The substitution of annual regular sessions of state legislatures for the prevailing biennial regular sessions would be desirable for the more populous states. Legislation is now a continuous process and cannot be confined to infrequent intervals between long periods of inactivity. The frequency of special sessions in later years and the need for financial planning on an annual basis demonstrate the necessity for a return to the original American principle of annual sessions. If need be, the regular sessions in even-numbered years could be limited to financial and emergency matters. Nevertheless, the call for special sessions should be authorized by the governor or by petition of a majority of the legislators, and these special sessions should be permitted to transact any public business whether mentioned in the call or not.

2. The elimination of time and pay limitations on the length of regular and special sessions is equally necessary. The legislative process has become complex and time-consuming as well as continuous. Such limitations are conducive to hasty and ill-considered legislation and have not proved to be the safeguards against excessive and bad legislation that the authors of such limitations originally

anticipated. The subterfuges sometimes resorted to by legislatures in circumventing these limitations are demoralizing and disgraceful and should be rendered unnecessary. Mechanical systems of recording legislative votes and roll calls have demonstrated their time-saving effectiveness in states that have already installed them.

3. The reorganization of legislative staffs with a view to providing an adequate and efficient research and secretarial service for the use of officers, committees, and individual members of the legislature is greatly needed in most states. The substitution of a merit system in the place of political considerations in the appointment of legislative employees is the best means of securing a more proficient legislative staff.

4. Streamlining the committee system is a long overdue reform in most state legislatures. This involves first a substantial reduction in the number of standing committees and the assignment to each committee of a broad area or related areas of legislation. If the committee system of each house is to remain distinct, duplicate or companion committees should be established in each in order to facilitate joint meetings and hearings. The time-saving character of a joint committee system for a bicameral legislature is emphasized and is recommended for more widespread adoption.

5. The reduction of the number of committee assignments of members and the more careful selection of committee chairmen and members with due recognition of seniority, experience, and political and regional factors are recommended as means of improving the quality of committee work. The provision of adequate and competent committee staffs is a necessary complement to the improvement of committee personnel.

6. The improvement of committee operations requires the adoption of regular, nonconflicting, and duly publicized schedules for committee meetings and hearings, the keeping of adequate committee records, and the establishment of workable discharge rules that would enable a substantial minority of the house to secure floor consideration of a bill held by a committee beyond a reasonable length of time.

7

Rules of Procedure

MUCH MORE INTEREST attaches to the policy decisions made by a legislative body than to the procedural steps involved in arriving at these decisions. This situation is neither surprising nor undesirable, since what is accomplished will in the ordinary case be more significant than the details of the hurdles surmounted or tripped upon. Yet the procedures followed may have a really heavy impact upon the results reached and upon the probabilities of acquiescence in those results. The passage or defeat of a bill with the aid of a tactic not authorized by the customary interpretations of the rules of procedure governing the body violates traditions of fair play in lawmaking even if it does not actually give rise to litigation in the courts. And even if all accept the results to which the maneuver contributed, such action weakens the future value of prescribed procedures as a foundation for orderly deliberation and action in the representative tradition.

PARLIAMENTARY SOURCES OF RULES

At least five distinct sources of parliamentary guidance and restriction can be identified as applicable to a legislative body in its organization and procedure: constitutional provisions, occasional statutes dealing with procedure, general parliamentary law and precedents, perhaps *Robert's Rules* or another's manual of procedure adopted by reference, and the standing rules written by the chambers for their own use. Constitutional provisions, unless held to be merely directory rather than mandatory, have, of course, a special force that cannot be avoided except through the subterfuge of journal entries that conform to the constitution rather than giving a literal report. Statutory provisions (commonly necessary at least for occurrences in the interval between *sine die* adjournment and the convening of a new legislature) are not likely to curb passing whims for change, if only because it is difficult for one legislature to bind its successors in matters of internal procedure when each legislature has the constitutional authority to adopt its own rules. General parliamentary law or precedents and unofficial manuals have corresponding limitations.

IMPLEMENTATION OF RULES

Although much of the business of any legislature is conducted in near defiance of the standing rules by an informal unanimous-consent process, the rulebooks are not rendered any more ineffective than are most other rules of conduct. Relatively rigid compliance with basic rules (as well as with constitutional restraints) may be secured whenever a few members are willing to risk unpopularity with their colleagues by insisting upon adherence to procedural safeguards. A notable instance of such an action, which, if only for the time being, stopped introduction and passage of skeleton bills, has been reported from California. There the lieutenant governor as president of the senate announced he would not advance skeleton bills, and if overruled in such decisions by the chamber would either refuse to certify the bills as passed or would append thereto the skeleton bill as introduced—thus inviting litigation.[1] Other states can report similar instances, though perhaps the protestants were motivated in their insistence on compliance with the set standards by obstructionist goals rather than by a desire that dubious practices be avoided.

[1] Clement C. Young, *The Legislature of California: Its Membership, Procedure and Work* (San Francisco: Commonwealth Club of California, 1943), p. 224.

Even with strict adherence to prescribed procedures, the rules governing deliberation cannot be credited with all the saving graces nor be held responsible for all the shortcomings of the legislative body. Nevertheless, it is equally obvious that the rules should be so drawn as to be conducive to orderly and effective deliberation, neither so sketchy as to provide inadequate guideposts nor so cumbersome as to require suspension of the rules on a wholesale basis whenever something must be accomplished.

In a report to The Council of State Governments it was stated that "the customs, traditions, and practices of the states vary too widely to make practical the drafting of a general set of recommendations respecting legislative rules."[2]   An optimum set of rules can best be drawn by each legislature for itself in the light of local conditions— and even then can be maintained as a code of maximum utility only if re-examined either on a continuing basis or at frequent intervals. Legislative councils, reference bureaus, and similar legislative service agencies sometimes are charged with the responsibility of studying existing rules to determine needs for revision; where they are not, their staffs are frequently able to assist those legislative leaders who do evidence an interest in the problem.

STANDARDS FOR LEGISLATIVE RULES

For the state legislatures as a group—and for individual legislators by way of stimulant to action—it should be possible to block out standards for an adequate set of rules and to give other guidance on problems that are particularly troublesome. Had the Legislative Reference Service of the Library of Congress been allowed to bring to fruition its projected publication of the texts of the rulebooks, or were someone able to publish even the index-digest of these manuals, shortcomings and solutions could be more easily identified. As it is, each analyst or group of analysts must first collect the often elusive volumes, do his own reading and tabulating, and from the resultant mass either derive significant comparisons or seek to distill

---

[2] *Our State Legislatures,* Report of the Committee on Legislative Processes and Procedures (rev. ed., Chicago: The Council of State Governments, 1948), p. 18.

some standards. This chapter attempts to provide the basis for a few such standards.

Physical Format

It should be accepted as routine that the adopted rules are published in a format permitting ready reference by both the legislator with years of experience and by his newly elected colleague, and that current editions exist. The inherent power of a legislative chamber to formulate rules that suit its convenience is presumably also a power to remain "elastic" by failing to adopt written rules, but that is an abnormal happening, and no state legislature attempts such a course on a continuing basis.

The common practice is for a legislature to have three sets of standing rules: one for each chamber plus a third covering matters concerning joint action by the two houses, with occasional additional sets of rules governing combined sessions of the two chambers (as when hearing an address by the governor) or controlling the senate when it sits to consider appointments by the chief executive. Nebraska's unicameral legislature has but a single set of rules. South Dakota alone of the bicameral states has developed the practice of placing most procedural matters in a single code that serves both houses. For a few states joint rules are not found in the published rulebooks, but it appears that this, at least in all but isolated cases, is an omission in compilation and not a gap in practice.

Uniformity is also to be found to the extent that a rectangular booklet is the common edition used by members, though sizes, format, and other features vary widely. Some of the pamphlets, indeed, seem so inconvenient to use that one is tempted to invoke a ban on paper under a given weight, as well as on vest-pocket editions generally.

Indexing or the absence thereof is, however, more deserving of attention. In about one third of the states the editions of the rules that must be commonly used by legislators contain nothing resembling an index or detailed table of contents for even one house.[3] More-

---

[3] These states are: Alabama, Arizona, Connecticut, Delaware, Maine, Maryland, Michigan, Mississippi, Nebraska, New Hampshire, North Carolina, Rhode Island, Utah, West Virginia, and Wyoming.

over, in many states where an index is provided, it is sketchy and of little value for rapid reference. On the other hand, the Wisconsin pocket manual is a notable example of systematic indexing. Here the rules of both houses, the joint rules, and appropriate constitutional and statutory provisions are indexed together, with code letters being used to distinguish each authority.

Some of the chambers include in their rulebooks special or unusual aids throwing added light on procedure. The addenda in the Arkansas rules contain a condensation of the rules, including a listing of the stages of bill action and a table of motions with the procedure in relation to them. In Louisiana, Maryland, and New York, either in the rules or as an appendix, there is a table or listing of the motions in the house, showing their scope and effect. In the volume containing the rules of the North Carolina house there is a listing of procedural data, including the vote required for various actions and motions; the Washington house has a similar tabulation.

The rules of several legislative chambers have a listing of the precedents of that house either as a part of the rules or as an appendix; a few other states give the precedents as separate publications. Miscellaneous data published along with the rules often include listings of personnel and occasionally guides to bill drafting.

Features such as those described above constitute a minimum for an adequate rulebook as concerns format and types of information. Seasonable publication in legible type on a page of convenient size and adequate indexing are routine needs. Tabular summarization of basic procedural data on motions and some recording of major precedents are necessary if the relative newcomer to the assembly is not to be under a continuing disadvantage when dealing with his seniors in parliamentary experience.

Organization and General Content

Most of the rules seem at first glance to contain a rather full exposition of the different points of legislative procedure, but the truly fragmentary nature of many becomes apparent when comparisons are made with other states or when one seeks to discover the practice on a point that does not arise frequently. Two simple tests for omissions in the rules offer themselves: Does the text say what happens when a committee reports a bill out adversely or without any recommendation? Do the rules tell clearly at what stages amendments may be offered to bills? These, however, are but rules of thumb, and an attempt at an over-all analysis has so far proved to be sufficiently difficult that no classification of the states as having reasonably complete, moderately complete, or fragmentary rules is at hand, though some have rules that contain liberal amounts of language concerning formalities in relation to modest amounts of substance.

Even when the published rules seem ample, much of the procedure that governs the chamber is to be found only in unwritten understandings or in volumes incorporated into the written rules by way of reference as a supplement. Imagine the chagrin of a seasoned member who has spent a week-end preparing dilatory amendments to be offered at second reading when a colleague is recognized ahead of him for a surprise motion to advance the bill to final passage without amendment. Imagine, moreover, the accentuated chagrin of the vanquished a biennium or so later when he desires to offer such a guillotine motion himself only to find that the clerk of the body was not enough of a parliamentarian to have recorded the details of the affair for *stare decisis* application and had merely reported that the bill was advanced without amendments being offered.

In some states the rules contain too much detail. These rules usually deal with matters relative to the routine management of the chamber, much of which could be excised and replaced with a brief designation of the presiding officer or a committee as the administrative superior of employees. Other provisions that serve little purpose deal with inconsequential formalities. Here an extreme case is the serious declaration in the rules of the Texas house that: "Only children of House Members under the age of twelve years shall be eligible for election to the honorary office of mascot. . . ."[4]

The order of presentation of the several rules also requires consideration. Some of the rules are so arranged that no attempt at

---

[4] Rule 2, sec. 2, of the *Texas Legislative Manual, Fifty-first Legislature* (1949), p. 132. The parliamentarian adds a note pointing out that "sweethearts" are also chosen.

a logical presentation with regard to the flow of procedure is apparent. Others not only follow a coherent plan but make for additional utility through well-considered use of divisional headings.

The rules of procedure should contain language adequate to outline at least the main steps in procedure and to present them in an order that would permit utilization by the ordinary member despite handicaps imposed by the faults of such extraneous aids as an index. At the same time, inconsequential language serving no useful purpose should be marked for deletion.

Cautions against Excessive Rule Making

There is an actual danger in rules that prescribe in detail procedures upon which there is no desire for compliance, even by a vigorous minority. For example, a rule imposing a deadline on introduction of bills may too easily mean that whereas all or most bills are introduced before the specified date, many are in skeleton form to be completed or completely rewritten at a later date. Not only would the rule lack utility in such a case, but the introduction of skeleton bills would adversely affect the preparation of a meaningful digest or synopsis of proposals before the legislature, and so make a positive contribution to confusion.

Occasionally objection is heard even to the adoption of an intrinsically desirable rule that is likely to be accepted as routine, on the score that its adoption would merely create another opportunity for a legalistic challenge to statutes in instances of noncompliance with prescribed procedures. As is generally known, noncompliance—though a fact—is in the ordinary case of no consequence if the official journals contain entries that conceal such faults, since the courts will not normally search behind the official record or allow it to be contradicted. Moreover, an offending statute is sometimes upheld on the score that the rule is merely directory and not mandatory, or that the rule has been suspended by an implicit unanimous-consent understanding. If these escapes are not deemed adequate, it is possible to draw a specific proviso to the effect that protest against noncompliance not made in the chamber before the bill has been advanced to passage stage shall be deemed waived. This type of

TABLE 6

Major Limitations on Debate in State Legislatures

State	Number of Times Member May Speak without Leave[a]		Length of Time Member May Speak without Leave[b]		Is Previous Question Authorized?[c]		Other Cloture Rules[d]	
	Senate	House	Senate	House	Senate	House	Senate	House
Alabama	2	2	1 hr.	10 min.		Yes	Rule 34	
Arizona		2	1 hr.	1 hr.	Yes	Yes	Rule[e]	Rule 9 (9)
Arkansas	1	1		1 hr.	Yes	Yes		Rule 15
California	2	1		5 min.	Yes	Yes		
Colorado	2	1	2 hrs.	10 min.	Yes	Yes	Rule 10 (3)	
Connecticut	2	2				Yes		
Delaware	2	2				Yes		
Florida	2	2	30 min.	30 min.		Yes		
Georgia	2	2	30 min.	1 hr.	Yes	Yes		
Idaho	2	2		1 hr.	Yes	Yes		
Illinois	2	1	15 min.	30 min.	Yes	Yes	Rule 51 (2)	
Indiana	1	2	30 min.		Yes	Yes		
Iowa		1			Yes	Yes		
Kansas	2	1			Yes	Yes		
Kentucky		2	1 hr.	30 min.	Yes	Yes		Rule 12
Louisiana	2	2		30 min.	Yes	Yes	Rule 9	

112

State								
Maine	3	2				Yes		
Maryland		2				Yes	Rule 47	Rule 85
Massachusetts	2	1				Yes		
Michigan	2	2			Yes	Yes		
Minnesota	2				Yes	Yes		
Mississippi	1	2	5-20 min.	5-10 min.	Yes	Yes	Rule[f]	
Missouri	2	1		15 min.	Yes	Yes		
Montana	2[g]			30 min.	Yes[g]			
Nebraska	2				Yes	Yes		
Nevada	2	2			Yes	Yes		
New Hampshire	3	2				Yes		
New Jersey	2	2		5-15 min.		Yes		
New Mexico	2				Yes	Yes	Rule 65	Rule 78
New York	2	2		15 min.	Yes	Yes	Rule 14 (3, 4)	Rule 19
North Carolina	2	2	30 min.	10-30 min.	Yes	Yes		
North Dakota	2	2	5-10 min.	5-10 min.	Yes	Yes		
Ohio	2	2		20 min.	Yes	Yes		
Oklahoma	2	2	5-10 min.	5 min.	Yes	Yes		Rules 36, 37
Oregon	2	2			Yes	Yes		
Pennsylvania	2	2			Yes	Yes	Rule 9	
Rhode Island	2	2	2 hrs.		Yes	Yes	Rule 23	Rule 21
South Carolina	2	2	10 min.	10 min.	Yes	Yes	Rule 14	
South Dakota	2	2	10-20 min.	10-15 min.	Yes	Yes		
Tennessee	2			10 min.	Yes	Yes		
Texas	2				Prohibited	Yes		
Utah	2	2			Prohibited	Yes		Rule 29
Vermont	2	2				Yes		
Virginia	2	2			Yes	Yes		
Washington	2	2		10 min.	Yes	Yes		

113

T A B L E 6—continued

Major Limitations on Debate in State Legislatures

State	Number of Times Member May Speak without Leave[a]		Length of Time Member May Speak without Leave[b]		Is Previous Question Authorized?[c]		Other Cloture Rules[d]	
	Senate	House	Senate	House	Senate	House	Senate	House
West Virginia	2	2			Yes	Yes		
Wisconsin	2	2			Yes	Yes		
Wyoming	2	2	5 min.		Yes	Yes		Rule 38

[a] These are the general provisions as to the number of times a member may speak on a given issue. Exceptions and qualifications to these general provisions are omitted.

[b] These are the general provisions as to the duration of permissible debate by an individual member. Special limits sometimes exist for particular classes of members or types of business.

[c] An entry here reflects the issue of whether the written rules allow, prohibit, or fail to mention the motion for the previous question as a form of cloture.

[d] The reference in these columns is to cloture rules that may be regarded as distinct from the motion for the previous question either by way of supplement thereto or substitute therefor.

[e] Sec. 2 of unnumbered rule on the previous question.

[f] In listing the precedence of motions, there is (preceding Rule 64) a reference to a motion to close debate at a specific time.

[g] Unicameral legislature.

"saving clause" will allow experimentation with modernized rules while avoiding any basis for increased judicial scrutiny of legislative procedure.

Table 6 may be used to illustrate the considerable detail in which some points are covered by rules of procedure and to show that, at least in matters of debate limitation, the states are not backward. Substantially all of the ninety-five state legislative chambers have provisions limiting the number of times a member may speak on a given point—usually twice—with appropriate and inappropriate exceptions. A common exception is one that allows a mover of the motion under discussion to close debate even though he has already fully exercised his right to debate as a member of the chamber. About half the chambers also have standing time limits that, when enforced, limit the duration of any speech to perhaps a matter of minutes. Added to this are the provisions—in all but a baker's dozen of the chambers—authorizing the use of the motion for the previous question (in many cases by a simple majority vote) as a means of closing debate. Finally, many chambers have specially devised cloture rules.

The fact that several pages of footnotes would be necessary to supply the detailed qualifications and exceptions to these provisions limiting debate is conclusive evidence that what is acceptable to and practicable in one legislative chamber may not be suitable for even the second house of the same state. Furthermore, only on carefully selected topics is there a real possibility of drafting specific suggestions for rule improvement that will be widely accepted—and generally adhered to when adopted. These rules are most likely to relate to the printing of bills or amendments and to easing the load of business in the last day or two of a session.

Possibilities for Legislative Improvements through Rule Changes

A more-than-obvious basis exists for concluding that the striking features of the legislative process do not lend themselves to suggestions for reform through relatively standard rule changes. The following reasons may be assigned for this conclusion: (1) some aspects of the legislative process are sufficiently basic to require regulation through constitutional mandate; (2) others are not susceptible to uniform proposals that can reasonably appeal to, or be enforced by, very many of the ninety-five state legislative chambers; and (3) still other aspects are even now well in hand.   Requirements as to voting on final passage are in the first category; provisions for eliminating end-of-the-session jams are in the second; debate limitation, treated above, seems to be in the third.

Turning to a positive approach, a number of areas can be identified where significant possibilities for improvement through rule changes do appear.   These areas may be described generally as aspects of the legislative process involving sound procedures in the conduct of the administrative phases of legislative work.   Nine such topics, with indications extracted from existing rules of the form that tentative recommendations may well take, should serve to advance this thesis into the discussion stage for testing of utility and probabilities of acceptance in practice.

1. Informal introduction of bills, that is, merely placing them in the hopper, rather than time-consuming introduction from the floor, plus checking of bills for proper form by legislative draftsmen:

Bills introduced by members shall be deposited at any time in the bill box.   Bills so deposited shall be given to the presiding officer before or at the opening of the session.   Bills may by unanimous consent be introduced from the floor.   *(New York Senate, 1950 Rule 23, sec. 6.)*

Each bill intended for presentation by any member shall be first presented to the legislative draftsmen whose duty it shall be, within three days after receiving a bill, to examine and revise the same as to form and expression, so far as it may require.   *(Vermont Senate and House, 1951 Rule 41.)*

The purpose here is, of course, to minimize time spent on formalities and to provide reasonable assurance that a bill being considered in committee or on the floor has been properly drafted.

2. Printing of all bills upon introduction, and subsequent amendments in a form that as nearly as possible would show intended changes in existing law:

All bills when introduced shall be ordered printed.   In the case of a bill which amends a statute the author of the bill shall indicate the particular changes in the following manner: (a) all new matter shall be underscored; (b) all matter which is to be omitted or superseded shall be shown crossed with a line. Bills shall be printed with new matter in italics and omitted or superseded matter enclosed in brackets and underlined.

When requested by five (5) or more members, amendments shall be printed and properly filed in the binders before such amendments may be voted upon. Amendments to bills that propose to change an existing law shall be in writing and shall indicate the changes proposed in the existing law as is required for the introduction of bills. *(Illinois Senate, 1951 Rules 5 and 16.)*

Without provisions of this general type citizens cannot be adequately acquainted with proposals that are before the legislature; the membership of the general assembly itself may be uncertain of the content of proposed legislation; and a bill that is passed may be so defective in form as to be obviously invalid as law.

3. Proper scheduling of committee hearings and adequate notice of meetings:

The committee on committees (or other appropriate agency) shall arrange and publish a schedule of regular standing committee meetings in such manner as to avoid, as far as possible, conflicts in the assignments of members to such committees, and shall cause a copy of such schedule to be posted in some conspicuous place in the capitol near the legislative chamber. *(Nebraska Legislature, 1950 Rule 5, sec. 4.)*

No uniform notice provision for individual meetings is likely to be found practicable, since the states vary from the absence of any requirement to the customary publication of notice days, weeks, or even months in advance of the meeting date. However, unless provision is made for a reasonable amount of advance notice of committee hearings the legislature is denying itself an opportunity to obtain the views of all interested persons and groups.

4. Adequate committee records:

The chairman or acting chairman of each committee shall cause to be kept a record in which there shall be entered: (a) the time and place of each hearing and each meeting of such committee; (b) the attendance of committee members at each meeting; (c) the name and address of each person appearing before the committee, with the names and addresses of the person, persons, firm, or corporation in whose behalf such appearance is made; and (d) the vote of each member on all motions, bills, resolutions, and amendments acted upon.

Such record shall be ready and approved by the chairman before the expiration of.................days after each committee meeting or at the next regular meeting of the committee. *(Illinois House, 1951 Rule 18.)*

To this should be appended an appropriate provision for preservation of the record at the end of the session. Some would want to add a requirement for a summarization of the reasons for the committee action. The latter is common in Congress, and such reasoned committee reports may well tend to make committtee action more acceptable to the membership of the chamber as a whole. Basic committee records in adequate form also serve to permit more careful weighing of committee action and—depending on their scope— provide a source for later study of the background of proposals.

5. Installation of procedures that could routinely minimize opportunities for irregularities in the mechanical handling and reporting of bills:

The chief clerk shall retain the original copy of every bill, resolution, or memorial for the use of the house and its committees, releasing these from safekeeping only upon proper order of the house and taking a receipt therefor. All committee reports shall be signed by the chairman, or, in his absence, by the vice chairman, be made on forms furnished by the clerk, and be delivered to his office. (Substantially as embodied in *Proposed Rules for the Florida House of Representatives,* 1949 House Rule 7, sec. 13, and Proposed Rule 8, sec. 19.)

The need for such "good housekeeping" practices is probably evident to any who have witnessed their breakdown when a highly controversial measure is under consideration and have seen the legislative body as a result lose some of its confidence in the integrity of its officials.

6. At least a minimum impetus to time-saving joint action by the two chambers of the typical bicameral body:

Whenever any standing committee of either house shall desire to arrange for a public hearing upon any subject of legislation pending before such committee, it shall be the duty of the chairman of such committee to consult with the chairman of the corresponding committee of the other house and endeavor to arrange a hearing by the joint committees of the two houses. *(Washington,* 1951 Joint Rule 27.)

Such a provision may neither contribute to nor tend to weaken the arguments for a change to the unicameral system, but if utilized it should not only conserve the time of legislators and those who appear before them but also improve working relations between the two houses.

7. Daily publication during the last days of the session of a calendar that is a meaningful guide to the business actually to be transacted rather than a listing of all the matters that might be taken up, and that is determined by the recognized leaders as a group rather than by arbitrary decision of the presiding officer or by an aggressive minority:

The committee on rules, during the last................days of each session (or after a prescribed date) shall arrange and fix the calendar of business for each day, and such calendar of business shall be a standing and continuing special order during said period; and no matter shall be taken up or acted on otherwise than in the order and manner fixed by such calendar, except by a............................vote of those present. *(Georgia Senate,* 1951 Rule 44.)

This rule should be in addition to one calling for the publication of a daily calendar of some type throughout the session a minimum number of hours or days in advance of each daily meeting.

8. Creation of some specific discouragement to tactics that contribute to the overly common rush of business in the last days of the session:

No bills transmitted by either house to the other after the forty-seventh day of the session, and no amendments so transmitted after the fifty-seventh day of the session, shall be considered, with the exception of bills reported by a joint conference committee. Bills from said committees may be transmitted at any time up to and including the sixtieth day. *(Montana,* 1951 Joint Rule 22.)

The dates here provided would, of course, need to be altered to suit the particular state involved. The same goal of discouraging the end-of-the-session peak may in some states effectively be sought by imposing a less rigid hurdle, for instance, re-reference of bills to some policy committee if reported out of the regular committee after two thirds of the session has passed. For those who prefer to go even further and impose a series of specific discouragements to procrastination in acting upon bills attention should be called to the deadline-in-series type of provision that Michigan has been using, whereby bills introduced after a set date are not printed, and committee reports in the house of origin must be made within a specified number of days after the session convenes.[5]

9. Placing responsibility for suggesting needed revisions in the standing rules upon some agency likely to act at least at intervals:

The committee on rules is charged with the general responsibility for the administrative functioning of the chamber. The committee shall also have the duty of making studies and recommendations designed to promote, improve, and expedite the business and procedure of the house and of the committees thereof, and of proposing any amendments to the rules deemed necessary to accomplish such purposes. *(California Senate,* 1941 Rule 13.)

Some would, of course, give this function to the legislative council where such a body exists; other locations of the authority are also feasible.

These approaches represent, obviously, merely one set of conclusions, based on views arrived at on a national basis, on what might be considered by legislative bodies in individual states when seeking to improve their functioning through better internal rules of procedure. The items listed are substantially in the words of the cited rule books, but are not exact quotations. The slight departures involved should not militate too severely against consideration of these rules in halls where academic paraphernalia are submerged by very practical considerations. And it is believed that the practices prescribed by these excerpts, if experimented with by other state

---

[5] See Illinois Legislative Council, *Scheduling Legislative Workloads,* Publication 108, May, 1952, p. 30.

legislatures, may point the way to increasingly successful steps in effective legislative functioning.

Need for Fuller Methods

The rules of the state legislatures are either completely silent or generally inadequate on the subject of keeping records of chamber and committee proceedings in such a manner as to show the substance of debate. It is therefore not surprising to find that in practice the legislatures suffer not only from varied and inadequate records of committee proceedings, but, most palpably, from a lack of records of the deliberations in the full chambers.[6] The journal, the basic official record of legislative action, reports only parliamentary actions and for the most part omits debate. Only seven states—Connecticut, Maine, New York, North Dakota, Pennsylvania, Tennessee, and West Virginia—keep a stenographic or sound-recorded report of debates. But not even all of these states record or publish the debates. They are merely preserved for future reference. "The absence of a record of debates, however, means lack of a full opportunity for public knowledge of legislative proceedings, and, particularly, the lack of a ready source for later determination of the factors motivating bill enactment and of the 'legislative intent' where statutory language is not clear."[7] In the absence of a counterpart of the *Congressional Record* the best and often the only explanatory reports of state legislative proceedings are the incomplete accounts found in the newspapers. Assignment of space in state legislative chambers for newspaper correspondents has now become routine, with a number even providing press rooms in the state capitol. The merits of radio broadcasting and televising of committee hearings and sessions of the legislature have recently been subjected to serious and extensive debate. In 1953 legislative sessions had been broadcast in nineteen states and telecast in twelve, while fifteen states had taken the first step in the

---

[6] See Phillips Bradley, "Legislative Recording in the United States," *American Political Science Review,* 29 (February, 1935), 74-83. Only Pennsylvania has a full, verbatim report of debates, which may be published somewhat late if the sessions are long. Maine records a condensed version.

[7] Illinois Legislative Council, *Legislative Broadcasting and Recording,* Publication 106, February, 1952, p. i.

direction of full broadcast by using one or more kinds of recording equipment. The problem of adequate facilities for originating broadcasts in legislative halls will have to be met, if and when the practice is more extensively and regularly used.[8]

There is no doubt that legislators are sensitive to the heavy expense involved in the costly reporting and publication of debates. However, tape-recording and other sound-recording techniques have minimized the argument of cost, and the more adequate reporting and publication of legislative debates may be anticipated.

RECOMMENDATIONS

1. Rules should be so drawn as to be conducive to orderly and effective deliberation. Often they are either too sketchy to be helpful or too cumbersome to allow action without wholesale suspension.

2. Each legislative body should maintain an optimum set of rules subject to re-examination by the legislative council or other appropriate agency on a continuing basis or at frequent intervals. Adequate standards would require the publication of the current rules in a format permitting ready reference by the experienced and inexperienced legislator alike, and in a single code with joint rules, where possible, which would serve both houses of a bicameral legislature. Uniform manuals on thin yet durable paper and with a systematic index should be minimum requirements for all states.

3. In general, rules of procedure should contain the main, rather than the detailed, procedure. Rule changes to insure sound procedures in the conduct of administrative phases of legislative work are recommended. These changes should deal especially with informal and early introduction of bills to provide opportunity for check by legislative draftsmen, with the printing of bills in such typographical form as would clearly indicate the nature of the proposed changes,

---

[8] In most of the states there are occasional broadcasts or telecasts when the legislature convenes or adjourns, or when the governor is inaugurated or addresses the legislature. Oklahoma, however, televised the state legislative sessions twice a week in 1951 and 1953, and Illinois broadcast its legislative sessions once a week in 1953 on a trial basis. See *State Government,* 24 (October, 1951), 249-50, 260. See also William L. Day, "Legislative Broadcasting and Recording," *State Government,* 25 (October, 1952), 225-26, 238.

with proper scheduling of separate and joint committee hearings, with keeping of adequate committee records, with installation of enforceable procedures in mechanical features of bill handling, with daily publication of calendars, especially during closing days of sessions, and with other devices to discourage the overly common rush of business during the last days of session.

4. Adequate records for the legislature should include not only the journal of proceedings, but also a full record of debate and other legislative transactions, and should be available to the public in published form or recordings.

8

Legislative Services:

COUNCILS AND INTERIM COMMITTEES

UNDER MODERN CONDITIONS legislative business has become increasingly voluminous, technical, and continuous. Practically all the problems of the modern community at one time or another are tossed into the lap of the state legislature for solution. The total annual volume of proposals is staggering, not only in terms of quantity, but also in the complexity of the issues and alternatives involved. The state legislature and its committees are expected to pass upon policies not infrequently of novel and sweeping character, to determine the desirability of creating new administrative agencies, and to deliberate upon the policies of existing administrative organization, power, and finance.

NEED FOR LEGISLATIVE AIDS

Legislation—an Expert Business

As a result of changing conditions, therefore, the making of laws needs more and more to be done by "experienced and exercised minds" and "by minds trained to the task through long and laborious study." This need has required the creation of "agencies of knowledge" that can provide the "element of intelligence" in the construction of laws and in watching and controlling the conduct of state business.

The "expert" in government has not been popular in America, especially with legislators. To what extent this attitude reflects the traditional jealousy of the executive branch, from which most experts have emanated, it is hard to determine. Lawmakers have, however, commonly adhered to the Jacksonian concept that government should be conducted by the political amateur who simply gives expression to the will of the sovereign people without regard to such factual knowledge as may be available through systematic studies in administration, politics, economics, or sociology. But the fact remains that the problems of government can be solved today only by synthesizing the contributions of the expert and the legislator.

Legislatures also need assistance in bridging the long gap between sessions. The process of legislation has become continuous; thus "research and discussion in advance of a legislative session are fundamentally as much a party of the legislative process as the actual session of the legislature itself." Moreover, in order to screen the facts and to judge of the validity of requests for legislation emanating from governors, administrative agencies, pressure groups, and local constituents the legislatures need fact-finding agencies and expert assistance of their own creation that will be free from the bias of special pleaders from the outside, whether they be public or private.

Principal Aids

Most important among the legislative agencies or aids are: legislative councils; interim committees; legislative reference, bill drafting, statutory revision, and codification services; and adequate technical and secretarial staffs and facilities for committees and individual legislators. Although much progress has been made in recent years in providing these services, it has been quite uneven from state to state. Many states are lacking in some and a few in all or nearly all of these necessary adjuncts of the legislative process. It cannot be emphasized too strongly that only with such expert service can a state legislature adequately or intelligently fulfill its proper functions under present-day conditions.

Legislative councils and interim committees are without doubt the most significant devices for improving the work of state legislatures.

Since 1933 councils or their equivalents have been established in thirty-three states and Alaska. Although interim committees are of longer standing, councils have become increasingly important in recent years. The mounting volume of legislative work and the necessity for intersessional legislative activity in preparation for the meeting of the legislature have pushed both councils and interim committees to the forefront as legislative adjuncts.[1] Exclusive attention will, therefore, be given to these agencies in the present chapter; other legislative aids will be considered in the succeeding chapter.

LEGISLATIVE COUNCILS—HISTORY AND GENERAL FUNCTIONS

The Movement for Legislative Councils

The first legislative council was established in Kansas in 1933—an historical leadership that has come to mean primacy among the councils both in research and in program preparation. Michigan also established a legislative council in 1933, but owing to abuse of the privileges by council members, party changes, and the failure to provide a technical staff for research, it fell into disrepute and was abolished in 1939. Virginia created an advisory legislative council in 1935. The powers of the latter are considerably weaker than those of the Kansas council because it has no authority to initiate proposals for legislation. It does produce, however, a small number of excel-

---

[1] In 1933 a model legislative reference bureau act—now outdated—was drafted by a committee on which the then American Legislators' Association was represented. No extensive up-to-date treatment of legislative councils has been published. However, there is in progress a comprehensive study of all legislative services by the Legislative Service Conference. (See its revised preliminary report [Chicago: The Council of State Governments, September, 1953].) For a recent bibliography consult Frederic H. Guild, "Legislative Councils," *Law Library Journal,* 42, no. 2 (May, 1949), 60-75. See also Lawrence W. O'Rourke, *Legislative Assistance* (Los Angeles: University of California Bureau of Government Research, June, 1951); Frederic H. Guild, "Legislative Councils: Objectives and Accomplishments," *State Government,* 22 (September, 1949), 217-19, 226; Harold W. Davey, "The Legislative Council Movement in the United States, 1933-1953," *American Political Science Review,* 47 (September, 1953), 785-97; *The Book of the States, 1950-51* (Chicago: The Council of State Governments), pp. 125-28; *1952-53,* pp. 122-23; and Christian L. Larsen and Miles F. Ryan, Jr., *Aids for State Legislators* (Bureau of Public Administration, University of South Carolina, 1947).

lent reports each biennium. In keeping with its "advisory" character, it investigates only those subjects assigned to it for study by the general assembly or by the governor. The statute in 1936 establishing a legislative council for Kentucky was repealed in 1948, when a legislative research commission with the powers of a council was created in its place.

The legislative year of 1937 saw the establishment of legislative councils in Connecticut, Illinois, Nebraska, and Pennsylvania. These are all considered "strong" councils. The Pennsylvania legislative council, known as the Joint State Government Commission, was continued from session to session until 1943, when it was made permanent. The Illinois council was originally given a life of only four years. It has since been made permanent, and to assure its future it has refrained from putting forth specific legislative programs. Both the Illinois and Nebraska councils are authorized to prepare legislative programs, but in practice neither does so.

The next legislative year, 1939, witnessed the setting up of the Maryland and Oklahoma legislative councils. The latter, however, was not activated until 1947. A council was also established in Rhode Island in 1939 but became inoperative after minority members refused to serve. In 1940 Maine established its Legislative Research Committee. Ten years after the establishment of the first council Missouri became the eleventh state to adopt this legislative device by providing for a committee on legislative research. This so-called committee has all the powers of a council including that of the right to make legislative recommendations (which it does not exercise). In 1945 the new constitution of Missouri provided directly for a council, thus making it the only council with constitutional status.

Councils were established in 1945 in Alabama, Indiana (Legislative Advisory Commission), Nevada (Legislative Counsel Bureau), and North Dakota (Legislative Research Committee). The movement took another forward step in 1947, when five new councils were established, and the Oklahoma council, as noted above, was made active. The Arkansas Legislative Council, created in 1947, was not given a state appropriation until 1949. Also in 1947 the Minnesota Legislative Research Committee, the Wisconsin Joint Legislative Council, and the legislative councils of Utah and Washington were established. Wyoming at the same time dignified its Legislative Interim Committee by giving it power to prepare information concerning long-range legislative programs without specific suggestions.[2] This action brought the total number of councils to twenty-one.

In 1949 legislative councils were established in Florida, South Carolina, and Texas, and Ohio created the Ohio Program Commission, which exercises many of the functions of a legislative council. In 1951 New Hampshire, New Mexico, and South Dakota also established legislative councils, followed by Louisiana in 1952, and Arizona, Colorado, Montana, and Tennessee in 1953.

The legislative council movement is obviously growing. Its spread has been comparable to the swift adoption of the executive budget in many states in the few years before and after World War I. During the period 1933-1953 thirty-three councils have been established, eighteen of them in the legislative years 1945, 1947, 1949, and 1951, one in 1952, and four in 1953.

Legislative Council—A General Interim Committee

The legislative council as found in most states is essentially a super interim committee with an area of action as wide as that of the legislature itself. It has not displaced the interim committees, although it has minimized the need for their creation. Where such committees have existed alongside a council, the council has usually either cooperated with them or steered clear of their assignments. On the whole, legislative councils have proved to be more objective in their approach and more successful in getting legislatures to adopt their recommendations. An interim committee is frequently confined to a single problem, and its assignment is usually temporary, whereas the scope of council work is general and the body is permanent. A council, therefore, can give an over-all consideration to legislative problems.

The membership of the councils varies from 3 in South Carolina

---

[2] In 1953 the legislature revised the act under which the Wyoming Legislative Interim Committee operates. The committee was instructed to report with recommendations at each session of the legislature, and $60,000 was appropriated for the biennium.

and 4 in Nevada to 27 in Kansas. In addition, three states—Oklahoma, Nebraska and South Dakota—follow the more unusual practice of including the full membership of the legislature in the council. The mean number of members for the whole group of councils is fifteen. Since councils in most cases consist exclusively of legislators, the most common means of selection is by the presiding officers of the houses.[3] Consideration is usually given to political affiliation, and minority party representation is assured. When not made by the presiding officers, the selection is confined in some manner to the legislature itself.

The *annual* budgets for 1947-1948, which included funds for research service, varied from $8,000 in Wyoming and $10,000 in Nevada to $100,000 in Pennsylvania and $110,000 in Missouri. The mean was $30,000 in 1947-1948, and in more recent years the appropriations have been more generous. For example, for the *biennium* 1951-1953 the sums varied from the low of $5,000 for the new council in New Hampshire to the high for Pennsylvania of $300,000. For its newly-established council the legislature of Louisiana appropriated $60,000 a year for 1953-1954, and the new Arizona council began its operation in July, 1953, with a biennial appropriation of $100,000. The councils recognized as being very effective have what appear to be the most sizable appropriations.

Most councils hold to quarterly meeting dates, but they may meet more often when business is pressing. In Maryland the council meets twice a month and sometimes holds two-day sessions. It should be noted that many councils operate through small subject-matter subcommittees to which legislative projects are assigned. These subcommittees usually consist of council members, although other legislators are added in some states, and in Pennsylvania non-legislators as well serve in advisory capacities. The addition of other legislators allows wider legislative participation in the work of the council and relieves council members of excessive subcommittee assignments. In a few states the subcommittees seem to perform the

---

[3] Among the recent states to establish a legislative council is New Hampshire. The council is composed of fifteen members, three of whom are nonlegislative members appointed by the governor.

bulk of the council's work.   For example, the 1953 biennial report of the Wisconsin legislative council disclosed that over 100 persons served on its eleven committees and numerous subcommittees, which held 123 meetings totaling 160 days.   It is interesting to note that the committee meetings are open to the public, and it is customary for representatives of the press to be present.

Some legislative councils have received very broad statutory assignments of duties; some have been restricted by statute; and others have limited their tasks by their own action.   All councils have conducted objective research and fact-finding in aid of legislation and have been provided with some sort of a research agency subject to their direction.   Some councils are confined or have confined themselves to this research function and have submitted only factual reports on subjects of major legislative interest.   Most councils, however, prepare and present positive recommendations for legislative action in the form of general proposals, drafted bills, or both.   The Illinois Legislative Council presents only recommendations, the Maryland council drafts bills, and the Kansas council does both.   Some councils restrict themselves to a few major subjects; others submit a comprehensive legislative program.   The newer councils are cautious about making recommendations.   The Minnesota Legislative Research Committee is forbidden by law to make recommendations or draft bills.   The policy there and in Kentucky is to let the facts speak for themselves, and the legislators are free to draw such conclusions as expediency permits.   Such a policy, it is felt, precludes the development of jealousy on the basis that the council is too powerful and opinionated.

The Pennsylvania Joint State Government Commission, on the other hand, discovered that when it made no recommendations its reports gathered dust, and the commission was threatened with extinction.   Now recommendations are made and bills prepared to accompany the reports.   In Pennsylvania legislative approval is given to over 80 per cent of the recommendations, and in Kansas during recent sessions legislative approval has been given to about 72 per cent of the council's recommendations.   Since the establishment of the council in 1933, the Kansas legislature has overruled the council on only one occasion, when the council recommended that no legislation was required. In Nevada the recommendations of the council constitute the bulk of the legislation considered by the legislature. In fact the Nevada director of the council, known as the legislative counsel, holds a uniquely powerful position, in that he is required by law to present directly to the legislature recommendations of his own that have not been adopted by the council. The experienced councils and their staffs make forthright recommendations to the legislature. In doing so they are realistic. They realize that simply to present the facts is something of a recommendation. It is the feeling of the councils that make specific recommendations that to do less is to cut down on their utility.

A few states have granted the power of subpoena to their legislative councils. For example, Kentucky, Maryland, and Oklahoma have this power but do not use it. Kansas has used the power of subpoena only once. Also, in 1951 one of the committees of the Wisconsin legislative council did exercise its power of subpoena. It is believed that ordinarily legislative councils can function effectively without the subpoena; however, it has been found valuable in the case of a subordinate employee who hesitates to volunteer adverse testimony against his superior administrator.

Another matter that legislative councils have had to decide is the extent to which proposals should be received from outside the membership of the councils. Certainly any member of the legislature should be permitted to present proposals for study, but to what extent should executive officials, administrative agencies, private organizations, and citizens be allowed to place matters before the council? The Minnesota Legislative Research Committee, as the council is called, requires that administrative proposals of legislation be screened through the committee, and the North Dakota council has been very successful in screening administrative proposals. The Oklahoma legislative council reports that in 1952 over 200 citizen organizations appeared before it and that 90 per cent of the council's proposals have come from these private organizations and citizens.

Practices in other states with legislative councils show considerable variation in this respect.[4]   In any event, the legislative council must select the proposals it deems most worthy of consideration.

LEGISLATIVE COUNCILS—OPERATION

Research Staff

The greatest contribution that the legislative council movement has made to the functioning of state legislatures has been the provision of a research staff.   The success of a council is definitely dependent upon an adequate staff.   The matter of clerical, technical, and professional assistance requires considerable thought and deliberation. Here the setup from state to state varies a great deal.   Some states creating legislative councils have had or have provided for well-organized legislative aids in the form of fully manned and adequately equipped legislative reference and bill-drafting agencies and other available facilities for fact-finding, research, and technical assistance in the legislative process.   These agencies have been coordinated with the legislative council's research division by some sort of cooperative arrangement.   In order to coordinate these facilities and to provide immediate assistance most legislative councils employ a director of research, who usually serves as the executive secretary of the council.

The director and his staff are subject to the council and its executive committee and are available to render expert assistance to the council and its subcommittees and to the officers, committees, and members of the legislature as far as possible.   The council should determine the major projects to be undertaken; the director should assign such projects to members of his staff or to whatever agencies of the state might be best prepared to undertake them.   He should be responsible for all work undertaken and for the preparation of all reports, recommendations, and bills required by the council and its officers and subcommittees.   Some state laws creating legislative

---

[4] In 1947, when Arkansas established its council, it encouraged citizen participation to the extent of actually providing membership in the council for representatives of bar associations and farm and other citizen groups.   This provision was repealed in 1949 "because it did not work well."

councils have attempted to lay down qualifications for a director. It seems obvious that he should be a man with graduate training, preferably in government, other social sciences, or public administration, and should have knowledge of the law. He should be competent to direct research in the legislative field and should be able to deal amicably with legislators, public officials, and the general public. Above all, he should be thoroughly objective on public problems and issues and should not be selected for political reasons. Much of the success of a legislative council depends upon the proper selection of such a director.

The director should have under him several competent full-time research and office assistants. This staff need not be large. In the words of the *Final Report of the New York State Joint Legislative Committee on Legislative Methods, Practices, Procedures and Expenditures:* ". . . the scope of legislative activity is so broad that to retain a staff of specialists equipped to deal with such a variety of subjects would be so costly as to be prohibitive."[5] A legislative research staff is not needed to gather exhaustive primary data. Its function is "rather to collate and synthesize data already culled by administrative agencies and private organizations of various kinds . . . the overall research requirements of the legislature can be satisfied by the employment of three or four experts of broad training and inside experience in public administration, economics, government and taxation and finance, assisted by a small clerical and research staff." Like the director, the staff should be free of politics, subject to merit selection, and assured of reasonable tenure. Discussions with council staff members disclose that there is an awareness of the partisan axe hanging over them. Partisanship is a matter of greater concern, of course, in states like Missouri, where there are frequent shifts in party domination.

Fact-finding should not be left exclusively to the director and staff. Council members themselves should participate in research. As practical politicians they have much to contribute in tempering the proposals of the staff to what the legislature and the public will stand for. Furthermore, council members learn more about a sub-

---

[5] Legislative Document 1946, No. 31, p. 152.

ject in the process of working through the problem to recommendations than is possible by reading a research report prepared by others. One experienced council director believes the legislator must participate in building the report if he is to retain much of it. He points out that the average legislator is not a reader; he learns by ear and is not visual minded. This director also deduces that the quality of debate on bills has greatly improved owing to research reports. Not only are the reports read and referred to in the preparation for and progress of debates, but the legislators by participating in research become thoroughly versed in the issues. The research function itself is shared by members searching their minds for answers to questions that are certain to arise in floor discussion.

Although the staff is attached to the council and in most states devotes a major share of its efforts to projects proposed or at least approved by the council, it serves the legislative membership as a whole in bringing together "short order" research reports upon request. Some of the legislative councils are inoperative during legislative sessions. The council staff then becomes available to do research work for the standing committees. In Kansas a steering committee of the council informs each standing committee at the beginning of the session what council reports are ready for each, thus effectively bridging the gap between the council, staff, and standing committees.

The tendency of legislative councils to staff themselves to give assistance to the legislators on appropriations is also a matter of special interest. The proper relationship of the legislature's own finance agent and the executive budget machinery has yet to be worked out. The need for such assistance in the legislature stems from weaknesses inherent in our system of separation of powers. It is accentuated by the frequent turnover in the office of budget director owing to short tenure in the gubernatorial post, the failure of budget departments to staff themselves adequately, partisan differences between the executive and legislative branches, and the lack of post-audit machinery to carry out the legislative function of audit. The legislature's desire for help under the prevailing circumstances is understandable, but if the legislature endeavors to usurp administrative functions by means of such research staff, this particular development will do more harm than good. The staff of a legislative council can be of high value in the performance of this budgetary function.[6]

Appraisal

Almost without exception, the legislative councils that have been established for some years have proved to be invaluable aids to the state legislatures and have contributed greatly toward improving the character of legislative work. As fact-finding and recommending agencies of the legislatures, working in the interims between sessions, they have served to make the legislative process continuous and have provided lawmaking bodies with substantial programs with which to start their sessions. Legislatures in the past, meeting infrequently and for limited sessions, have worked largely in the dark. A legislative council with a competent research staff is a purely legislative agency that furnishes the lawmakers with unbiased information, gives careful presession analysis to important pending legislative problems, and restores to the legislature something of the independent role in policy framing that was no doubt the original intent of our constitutional system.

Legislative councils have also proved to be of great assistance to legislators in informing the public on imminent problems and issues. Walter Bagehot pointed out many years ago that the educational function was one of the most important that a legislative body had to perform. It is well known that debates are seldom of a quality to warrant lengthy press reports. The committee system in American legislatures has had much to do with submerging the educational function. The council, a new variety of legislative committee, may enable the legislature to perform its educational work in a more satisfactory manner. By periodic research reports to legislators between sessions the council provides a means by which they can take matters to their constituents at regular intervals for grass-roots reaction. Keeping legislative problems continuously before the public may make possible a crystallization of public sentiment before the session. If this informational function is performed judiciously, it may create

---

[6] See fuller discussion of this problem in Chapter 11.

public confidence and aid in restoring the legislature to public esteem. Whereas advance material is useful to old-time legislators in understanding new problems and in apprising their home folks of what is going on, it is of inestimable aid in giving background to the new, inexperienced legislator.

It may be noted that since legislative council members are drawn from both houses, the existence of a council helps to build up a common understanding by means of comprehensive research reports submitted to members of both houses well in advance of the session. Thus many possible differences between the houses of a bicameral legislature can be obviated and the need for conference committees reduced. Legislative councils have helped to provide real leadership for legislatures. Lack of capable leadership from within themselves has been a weakness in legislatures, most of which now are of a size to require direction from some outside source to make any progress. The council provides a leadership drawn from within and accountable to both houses of the legislature. Such leadership is more acceptable than that coming from the governor's office or from the administrative departments. Rightly or wrongly, legislators suspect this leadership from without as being molded by partisan and personal motives and ambitions. Although the council should not nullify the leadership traditionally offered and, indeed, needed from the executive branch, the council provides a mechanism for legislators to weigh the executive proposals. The council and its staff in performing this sifting and appraisal function should help to provide smoother legislative-executive relationships. Conflict often has arisen out of the failure of one branch of the state government to understand the problems and objectives of the other.

Finally, with a well-substantiated research report redrafts of bills and multifarious amendments can be cut down. Senator Joseph R. Burns of the Maryland Legislative Council declared recently that the legislative council had greatly shortened the session. This council introduces at the outset of a session thirty to seventy-five bills. Before a session opens public hearings have been held and the entire membership of the legislature has received copies of these bills.

INTERIM COMMITTEES

Recent Importance

Although the legislative council is considered to be an outstanding innovation so far as legislatures are concerned, the interim committees, which are closely akin to it, and for which it is a partial substitute, date from the earliest days of state legislatures. As has been noted, the interim committee may be distinguished from the legislative council in two respects: First, it is a temporary agency specifically created to gather information about a particular subject or problem for proposed legislation. Second, the interim committee, until recently at least, gave little thought to the problem of research staff.

Interim committees were common in the early 1900's, widely used in the 1920's, were operating in twenty-nine different states by the mid-thirties, and in thirty-five states in 1951. Between-session investigations by interim committees and commissions and legislative councils reached a high point in 1949, when the states reported 323 special study groups with a total appropriation of $7,700,000, as compared with 302 studies in 1951 with total appropriations of $6,350,000.[7]

The close relationship between interim committees and legislative councils is indicated by the fact that a number of these committees were making studies under the direction of the legislative councils in states where they existed, but in states where there were no councils the interim committees were compelled to work alone without the coordinating influnces of the councils. It should be noted that interim committees are more common in states that do not have legislative councils. Michigan, Massachusetts, New York, and California are examples. In 1947 there were 18 interim committees in Michigan, 21 in New York, 34 in Massachusetts, and 51 in California; by 1951 there were 41 in Michigan, 28 in New York, 37 in Massachusetts,

---

[7] See "Legislative Research in the States," *State Government,* 25 (October, 1952), 233-36. The *Legislative Research Checklist* of The Council of State Governments (March 13, 1953) reported the total of $8,096,029 appropriated for the 1951-1952 biennium.

and 59 in California. Many of these interim committees and commissions have been continued by each succeeding legislature over a period of many years. In 1951 the total appropriation in these four states alone was nearly two million dollars.

Comparison with Legislative Councils

The interim committees, no matter what their number, cannot operate in all respects as satisfactorily as a council. There is no assurance that an interim committee will be set up to study every vital subject requiring legislative attention. The choice of subjects to be dealt with in the interim between sessions is prompted by the interests of individual members. The interim committee does not insure a planned or comprehensive approach to subjects needing legislative attention.

A second weakness of the interim committee is that each one starts *de novo*. Much time is wasted in getting organized and setting up a pattern of action, which often differs with each committee. So much time is absorbed in this process that there is little opportunity for study and formulation of recommendations.

A third difficulty encountered in the interim committee is the lack of experienced staff. Capable people cannot readily be brought together on short notice to serve for a limited period of time. Without expert assistance the committees are quite helpless. It is difficult for a group by itself to organize a study, go about assembling materials, separate the wheat from the chaff, and quickly acquire enough background to prevent the committee from becoming lost in details.

Lastly, without the help of a staff it is difficult to produce a final report as evidence of having worked through the problem and cleared the way for legislative action. Moreover, each interim committee tends to pursue its work without relationship to other committees and the general program of the legislature. The reports of interim committee are likely to pour into the legislature during the opening days of the session; yet legislators find much more time to consider reports when they are submitted well ahead of the opening of a session. If these reports are not digested by the general membership, their impact on the decision-making process is indirect and greatly reduced. The usefulness of a report is also improved by adequate publication, distribution, and custody. Most interim committee reports are not attractively processed or well distributed. File copies of reports are not always kept, and the work done may be wasted or subsequently repeated by another committee.[8]

The interim committee, in spite of certain weaknesses, has some advantages when compared to the legislative council that are not to be overlooked. Interim committees offer opportunity for wider participation between sessions by more members of the legislature than most legislative councils. When there are a number of interim committees at work, a considerable percentage of all the members may be involved in program planning. The feeling of jealousy that sometimes has developed toward members of legislative councils is not so apt to develop where interim committees are also used. Second, the individual members of interim committees are usually much interested in the subject matter to be studied, as they are commonly appointed because of their particular interest. Although it may be true that more than 50 per cent of interim committee assignments have been of little value, some very notable contributions have been made in recent years by interim committees in a number of states.[9]

The advantages of the interim committee system need not be lost in the adoption of a legislative council. The legislative council and the interim committee system can be combined to eliminate the difficulties inherent in each without losing the advantages of either.

The legislative council is an indispensable legislative aid for all state legislatures for several reasons: First of all, it provides a research staff on a continuing basis. Second, it is needed to make sure that all aspects of the state government are considered and programmed. Program and research upon it cannot be left to the interest or the political acumen of individual members of the legislature to create an interim committee. The council is in a position, too, to decide

---

[8] The New Hampshire legislature at its 1953 session made several amendments to the 1951 act establishing the legislative council, among these the interpretative statement that "it is the declared intention of this act to eliminate the establishing of interim commissions in the future."

[9] See Rae Files Still, *The Gilmer-Aiken Bills* (Austin, Texas: Steck Co., 1950).

what problems will be given research attention and in what order of priority as far as staff time is needed. The council can also effectively publish and distribute research reports. However, interim committees should still be used by legislatures with councils. Interim committees may work completely independently, may be interlocked in membership with the legislative council, or may secure close collaboration from the staff of the legislative council.

COMMISSIONS ON INTERSTATE COOPERATION

Commissions on interstate cooperation now exist in all 48 states. Created by statute and directly affiliated with The Council of State Governments, they are composed entirely or for the most part of members of the legislature and operate chiefly during the interim. These commissions study problems of interest to the various states in the fields of interstate and federal-state relations in particular and develop recommendations, which usually take the form of reciprocal and uniform legislation, interstate compacts, enabling legislation to mesh state operations with those of the federal government in cooperative programs, and administrative agreements.[10] The commissions call on the staff of The Council of State Governments for assistance in connection with various problems. An increasing number of them —about ten at the present time—employ their own staffs, which vary from one to ten persons.[11]

---

[10] See *The Book of the States, 1952-53,* for recent examples of the diversified character of interstate cooperation. See especially discussion on interstate compacts, pp. 20-39, and uniform state laws, pp. 135-39.

[11] For conclusions and recommendations applying to this chapter, see the end of Chapter 9.

9

Legislative Services:

STAFF FACILITIES

THE LEGISLATURES have created a wide variety of facilities other than legislative councils and interim committees that operate during both the interim and the session. The most widespread are the legislative reference services, now functioning in all but four of the states, but with activities that vary considerably from state to state. Specialized agencies have been created in many states to draft bills and in several states to revise the statutes continuously or at frequent intervals. The office of legislative counsel has been created as a full-time agency in several states, notably in California and Massachusetts, to provide bill-drafting assistance and to counsel members of the legislature concerning the form, substance, and effect of the law.[1] In addition, many special agencies have been created to give assistance to legislators on state fiscal matters. Continuing or semipermanent research agencies have been created in several states to provide independent analysis of fiscal and administrative operations for the benefit of the legislature. The New York Temporary State Commission on Coordination of State Activities, equipped with a full-time staff, has been re-created from session to session to provide a means for continuing review of the departments and agencies of the state. Similar

---

[1] The office of legislative counsel has been created in several other states including Idaho and Nevada. The Idaho agency has not been activated, and the Nevada agency functions as a legislative *council*. In Oregon the office of legislative counsel became effective in January, 1954.

agencies in California, Iowa, and South Carolina have been continued for at least two sessions each. They resemble in some respects the state government reorganization agencies that more than thirty of the states have created.[2]   Finally, note should be taken of the efforts of legislatures to afford adequate technical and secretarial staffs to assist committees and individual members and to provide office space and facilities for members.

LEGISLATIVE REFERENCE SERVICES

Functions of Reference Services

Legislative reference services are among the oldest aids state legislatures have provided for themselves.   New York and particularly Wisconsin, near the opening of the present century, were the pioneers in creating such services.   A number of other states followed suit before 1916, and since the establishment of the Interstate Reference Bureau by the American Legislators' Association in 1930 notable extensions and improvements in state reference facilities have been made.   In some states the establishment of legislative councils has led to the creation or improvement of reference work.   Increasing need for such assistance, however, has been generally responsible for its expansion.

In the words of Larsen and Ryan:

The general purpose of legislative reference services has been to collect all available information relating to any subject on which the legislature might take action; to collect and compare legislation of all the states and pertinent material on the practical operation of that legislation; to collect such works of reference as may be of general use to the lawmakers; and to undertake, when requested by the legislators, such research studies as facilities may permit.[3]

The range of legislative reference activity, however, varies greatly from state to state, depending upon the functions assumed, the size and character of the staff assigned to the work, the facilities avail-

---

[2] See Chapter 10.
[3] Christian L. Larsen and Miles F. Ryan, Jr.., *Aids for State Legislators* (Bureau of Public Administration, University of South Carolina, 1947), pp. 29-30.

able, and the appropriations allowed. Although legislative research is the primary and most universal function of these agencies, bill drafting, statutory revision, the publication of analyses, summaries, and reports dealing with legislative and other subjects of interest to legislators, and providing a general information service for citizens are among the services rendered by a number of them.

Extent of Reference Services

At the present time forty-four states have official legislative reference services.[4] The four remaining states provide no reference facilities whatsoever.[5] In several states reference services are independent agencies;[6] in others legislative reference work is assigned to one or more of the following agencies: the state libraries,[7] the legislative councils,[8] or some state department.[9] The spread of activities of the legislative reference agencies ranges from active engagement in bill drafting, statutory revision, preparation of bill and law summaries, and assistance to legislators and to standing and interim committees in states like Illinois, Indiana, Michigan, and Vermont, to state libraries restricted to legislative reference services in states like California and Montana.

Although many employees of legislative reference bureaus are not engaged exclusively in reference work, it may be stated fairly accurately that the interim personnel ranges from one part-time to eight full-time persons. The more effective reference services employ extra help during legislative sessions. A very few states provide for a merit system of selection; however, in many selection is made in a variety of ways not controlled by merit system regulations. Complete infor-

---

[4] Consult *The Book of the States, 1952-53* (Chicago: The Council of State Governments), pp. 114-24.

[5] Idaho, Nevada, Utah, West Virginia.

[6] Among these states are Delaware, Illinois, Maryland, Michigan, Ohio, Pennsylvania, Tennessee, Virginia.

[7] Thirty-three states.

[8] Arkansas, Florida, Indiana, Kansas, Kentucky, Minnesota, Missouri, Nebraska, North Dakota. In Utah the statute permits, but appropriation is inadequate.

[9] Colorado—attorney general; North Carolina—department of state; Wisconsin—free library commission.

mation is not available as to appropriations and expenditures, but apparently the range from state to state is from $75 to more than $75,000 annually.[10]

BILL DRAFTING

Laws are the main product of any state legislature, and their quality is the chief measure of the service rendered by the lawmaking body. The legislature is properly responsible for the form as well as the substance of laws. Few pieces of literary composition are subjected to more searching analysis and criticism than are statutes. Certainly a bill must be drafted in such language that it can be readily understood and that it cannot be misunderstood.

Requirements of Bill Drafting

Bill drafting requires an accurate and technical knowledge of law and judicial interpretation, a knowledge of the methods of accomplishing the revision and amendment of statutes and the introduction of new measures, an appreciation of the importance of precision in the use of terms and phrases, and great skill in the use of the English language. The principles of the common law involved, as well as the statutory and constitutional provisions on the subject, must be understood in order to secure effective legislation.

The professional bill drafter must do five important things:

1. He must master the subject matter; that is, he must know the statutes and court decisions on the subject. He must not propose a measure that will create conflicts or undesirable results.

2. He must consider whether the desired proposal may be adequately dealt with by amendment to existing law or whether it requires a new law. If an amendment is to be used it must avoid contradictions and ambiguities. If a new act is written he must decide whether to consolidate all existing law or merely include certain phases of the subject.

3. He must carefully examine administrative precedents and meth-

---

[10] Larsen and Ryan, *op. cit.,* p. 31.

ods of enforcement as disclosed by the statutes of other states and as reported by successful administrators.

4. He must consider who will be affected by the measure. He must determine whether any principle of law will be affected, beyond the statute to be amended.

5. He must carefully consider constitutional requirements, such as whether the proposed act includes only one subject.

6. He must also consider whether all appropriate details have been inserted into a bill that affects administrative organization and procedure.[11]

In addition to its technical nature bill drafting in most states is conducted as a highly confidential matter between the legislator and the bill-drafting agency. However, in Texas, where the office of the attorney general is in charge of all bill drafting, a public file is kept of every bill drafted. This unusual practice is partly conditioned by the fact that the governor follows the practice of seeking the opinion of the attorney general on the constitutionality of bills before him for signature.[12] Bill drafting must be carried out in a wholly impartial, nonpartisan atmosphere. The members of an official bill-drafting agency who divulged the subject matter of proposed measures or sought to promote legislation would quickly lose public confidence. Those engaged in this work rapidly acquire (if they do not have it at the start) a professional code of ethics that regards as cardinal sins the promotion of legislation or outside discussion of pending bills. This code forms a practical safeguard against any abuse of their position as expert advisors in the technique of bill drafting.[13]

Bill-Drafting Facilities

In the past bills were frequently drafted by a private attorney em-

[11] D. L. Kennedy, *Drafting Bills for the Minnesota Legislature* (St. Paul: West Publishing Co., 1946), pp. 4-5; Chester Lloyd Jones, *Statute Lawmaking* (Boston Book Co., 1912); Ernst Freund, *Standards of American Legislation* (University of Chicago Press, 1917).

[12] At one time there were 173 such requests in the attorney general's office, with a 40-day period for gubernatorial action.

[13] Howard F. Ohm, *A Law Making Laboratory* (Wisconsin, 1944), pp. 9-10.

TABLE 7

Location of Official Bill-Drafting Services for State Legislatures

State	Attorney General	Legislative Reference Bureau or Library	Legislative Council	Statutory and Code Revisor	Legislative Counsel	Special	None
Alabama		X					
Arizona			Xª				
Arkansas	X		X				
California					X		
Colorado	X						
Connecticut				X			
Delaware		X					
Florida	Xᵇ	X					
Georgia	X						
Idaho	X						
Illinois		X					
Indiana	X	Xᵇ					
Iowa		X					
Kansas				X			
Kentucky				X			
Louisiana			Xª				
Maine			X				
Maryland		Xᵇ	X				
Massachusetts					X		
Michigan		X					
Minnesota				X			
Mississippi	X						
Missouri			X				
Montana	X						
Nebraska				X			
Nevada				Xª			
New Hampshire	X						
New Jersey				X			

ployed by the legislator or by a private agent serving as legislative representative for a pressure group. Such practices did not make for accurate or responsible drafting of measures. Although a high degree of informality still exists among the states in their bill-drafting procedures, most states now have authorized at least one agency to perform this service. In addition, in some states, as a matter of

TABLE 7—continued

Location of Official Bill-Drafting Services for State Legislatures

State	Attorney General	Legislative Reference Bureau or Library	Legis- lative Council	Statu- tory and Code Revisor	Legisla- tive Counsel	Spe- cial	None
New Mexico		X[a]					
New York						X	
North Carolina	X						
North Dakota			X				
Ohio		X					
Oklahoma	X[c]	X[c]					
Oregon					X[a]		
Pennsylvania		X					
Rhode Island		X[b]		X			
South Carolina			X				
South Dakota	X						
Tennessee			X[a]				
Texas	X						
Utah	X						
Vermont		X					
Virginia		X					
Washington				X[a]			
West Virginia							X
Wisconsin		X[b]	X				
Wyoming	X						

[a] By legislative enactment in 1951, 1952, or 1953.

[b] Drafts major portion of bills.

[c] About equally divided.

custom or courtesy rather than by statutory direction, a second agency may draft bills for legislators. The office of the attorney general in several states serves as this second agency, or as the only agency.[14]

---

[14] See table on pages 146-47. For example, in Indiana the attorney general drafted about one third of the bills of a recent session of the legislature as a matter of custom, while the Indiana Legislative Bureau by statutory require- ment drafted the rest of the bills. In Texas, the attorney general as a matter of custom is the only official agency to draft bills—in a recent session the number was almost half of the bills introduced in the session.

West Virginia is the only state that has no official permanent bill-drafting agency.[15]

In over thirty states the office of the attorney general participates in bill drafting, but only in the eleven following states did this office draft at least half of the bills: Colorado, Florida, Georgia, Mississippi, Nevada, New Hampshire, North Carolina, Oregon, South Dakota, Tennessee, Washington.[16]   Changes were made in 1954 in Nevada, Oregon, Tennessee, and Washington (see Table 7).   Various agencies under the jurisdiction of the legislature also play a large part in the bill-drafting functions of their states.   Among these are the legislative reference bureaus, the legislative councils, statutory and code revision agencies, legislative counsels, and the specially constituted Bill Drafting Commission in the State of New York.   For example, the reference bureaus of libraries draft a major portion of the bills in the eleven states of Alabama, Illinois, Indiana, Iowa, Maryland, Michigan, Ohio, Pennsylvania, Rhode Island, Virginia, and Wisconsin.   Among the states whose reference bureaus engage in drafting bills on a smaller scale are Arizona, Florida, and Tennessee.[17]   The Vermont Board of

[15] In 1951 the house of delegates of West Virginia provided a small appropriation for the employment of an attorney for this purpose.   In the senate the clerk follows the custom of providing such assistance upon request.

[16] In Nevada, North Carolina, and Washington the office of the attorney general drafted 80 per cent or more of the bills.

[17] The legislative reference bureaus in Illinois, Michigan, Ohio, and Wisconsin draft well over 90 per cent of the proposed bills.

The Pennsylvania Legislative Reference Bureau drafts a large number of bills each session, in addition to a similar service on a smaller scale rendered by the office of the attorney general.

Maryland provides for bill-drafting services for its legislators by the Department of Legislative Reference as well as the attorney general.   This department drafts about 80 to 85 per cent of the proposed bills introduced.

In 1949 the general assembly of Tennessee created a legislative reference bureau consisting of an assistant attorney general and two members of the State Planning Commission.   They were empowered to draft bills.   The newly created (1953) legislative council has bill-drafting functions.

In 1949 Oklahoma created a legislative reference division in the State Library that was assigned bill-drafting functions and drafts about 40 per cent of the bills.   Heretofore the attorney general drafted the bulk of the proposed statutes.

In Iowa the largest proportion of bills is drafted by special attorneys employed by the legislature and assigned to the Iowa State Library, although the attorney general also drafts a small percentage.

In Arizona the newly created (1953) legislative council is charged with bill drafting.

Legislative Draftsmen, consisting of two attorneys, drafts most of the bills introduced in the legislature, and all bills must be approved as to form and uniformity by this board before introduction. The librarian of the legislative reference bureau is an ex officio member of the board, and during the session of the legislature the board is housed in the office of the bureau.

Four states turn over a major portion of bill drafting to their legislative councils: Maine, Missouri, North Dakota, and South Carolina. By statute in 1951 the legislature of New Mexico directed its newly established legislative council to furnish the assistance of expert draftsmen to its legislators. Subsequently the new legislative councils in Arizona, Louisiana, and Tennessee were directed to perform similar functions. Legislative councils that draft a small percentage of bills, usually their own recommended bills, are found in Arkansas, Maryland, Nevada, and Wisconsin.

Bill drafting is a function of the statutory and code revision agency or the revisor of the statutes in eight states: Connecticut, Kansas, Kentucky, Minnesota, Nebraska, New Jersey, Oregon, and Rhode Island. California and Massachusetts follow the more unusual practice of providing bill-drafting services through the offices of the legislative counsel.[18]

Special attention should be called to the State of New York, where the legislature established a Bill Drafting Commission whose sole task is the drafting of bills. The commission is composed of two com-

---

[18] In January, 1954, the Oregon office of the legislative counsel began drafting bills. In Connecticut about 75 per cent of the 2,900 bills introduced in a recent session came from the office of the legislative commissioner, who is appointed by the legislature for a four-year term.

The revisor of the statutes in Kansas is responsible for 90 to 99 per cent of all bills introduced.

Minnesota assigns bill drafting to a revisor of statutes, as well as a small number to the attorney general's office. In 1949, however, no appropriations were made for bill-drafting services, so only 25 per cent of the bills came from the revisor's office.

In Kentucky the revisor of statutes drafts about 85 per cent of the bills, whereas in Nebraska this same office drafts about 98 per cent of the bills.

The director of statutory research and drafting in Virginia employed five full-time workers for sixty days to draft a considerable number of bills that were presented to the legislature.

Massachusetts empowers the counsel of the senate and counsel of the house of representatives to draft bills for introduction to the general court.

missioners and a deputy commissioner, all of whom must be attorneys with at least five years of experience. A substantial staff assists the commission shortly before and during the legislative session.

STATUTORY AND LAW REVISION

Revision of the law, the statutes, and the code may take different forms and represent widely varying activities. An explanation of terminology may help dispel some of the misunderstanding and confusion that have developed in the area. As sometimes used, though erroneously, "revision" may mean mere "compilation" of the statutes, as undertaken frequently by private publishers, that is, bringing together of pre-existing statutes with latest amendments under an arrangement designed to facilitate use of them. This process may simplify reference to the statutes, but it cannot remedy confusion of expression and inconsistency, nor can it make any change in the effect of statutes that it includes or omits. "Revision" in the sense of "codification," in contrast, is the process of collecting and arranging the laws into a complete system of positive law, scientifically arranged and affirmatively approved by the legislature itself. A code, then, is more than evidentiary of the law; it becomes the law itself.

Revision of the statutes or of the code cannot be accomplished except by enactment—or re-enactment—of the finished product. It involves change in expression, and its purpose may be either to accomplish substantive change in the statute law or to improve its form. "Substantive revision" is the process by which the meaning and effect of pre-existing statutes are changed to accommodate them to changing conditions; "formal revision" of statutes, on the other hand, is concerned with the form and expression of the statutes, and revision in this sense is for the purpose of producing certainty and conciseness in expression and logic in arrangement.

Substantive Revision

All modifications of the substance and effect of the law are revisions of the law, and most of the work of the legislative session is concerned with making changes of this nature. For the most part, such changes have to do with the substance of the so-called public law—areas concerning relationships with government—and the various vocal, organized groups in the state or the agencies of government ordinarily may be counted on to generate interest in such changes. One particular aspect of substantive revision, however, is the process of making changes in the great body of private law, which affects persons in their dealings with each other—an area in which organized groups or adversaries ordinarily cannot be counted on to express views or call for change. This is one of the areas in which a few of the states have sought in recent years to create agencies that might give continuous examination to the common law, statutes, and judicial decisions for the purpose of discovering defects and anachronisms and recommending needed reforms.

New York and Louisiana are leaders among the states that have set up agencies primarily designed to effect substantive revision of the law, particularly of private law. In New York the Law Revision Commission is concerned with that function. That commission, created in 1934 and located at Cornell University, has a commendable record. The commission consists of the judiciary and code committees of both houses of the legislature as ex officio members and five additional members appointed by the governor, of whom four must be attorneys. Its functions are:

(1) to receive suggestions from judges, public officers, bar associations, the American Law Institute, the National Conference of Commissioners of Uniform State Laws and the public regarding defects and anachronisms in the law of the State; (2) to observe and identify such inconsistencies, ambiguities, and obsolescent sections of the law; (3) to study the problems raised by all data indicating apparent defects in the law and to formulate a correct and complete statement of the existing law; (4) to consider whether statutory changes are desirable and to formulate changes approved by the Commission; (5) to report its proceedings to the legislature and in addition to submit recommendations proposing specific statutory changes, accompanied by bills embodying such changes.[19]

Another example is the system that has been established in Louisi-

---

[19] *Final Report of the New York State Joint Legislative Committee on Legislative Methods, Practices, Procedures and Expenditures,* Legislative Document 1946, No. 31, p. 161. In 1953 the California legislature created a Law Revision Commission modeled after that of New York (California Statutes 1953, ch. 1445).

ana. In 1938 the Louisiana State Law Institute was organized, which is located at Louisiana State University. The legislature declared that the purpose of this institute was "to promote and encourage the clarification and simplification of the law of Louisiana and its better adaptation to present social needs; to secure the better administration of justice and to carry on scholarly legal research and scientific legal work."[20]   The institute is explicitly required to consider needed improvements in the law and to make recommendations concerning them; to study the civil law with a view to discovering defects and inequities and recommending needed reforms proposed by learned societies and associations; to recommend from time to time such changes in the law as are deemed necessary to modify or eliminate antiquated and inequitable rules of law; and to bring the law of Louisiana, both civil and criminal, into harmony with modern conditions.   The personnel of the institute is made up of ex officio members and others, all of whom are attorneys or judges except for the chairmen of the judiciary committees of the two houses who, in turn, may very well be lawyers.   The Louisiana institute has made a creditable record in the short period in which it has operated.   It has completed and submitted a criminal code, presented a revision of the general statutes, and completed an extensive project of background studies and analyses looking toward revision of the state constitution.[21]

Substantive revision responsibilities have also been conferred upon the New Jersey Law Revision and Bill Drafting Commission established in 1944, and the North Carolina General Statutes Commission. In North Carolina the revisor of the statutes, whose office was created in 1947, is ex officio secretary to the General Statutes Commission.

Formal Revision

In recent years a large and increasing number of states have estab-

---

[20] *Law Revision Agencies,* Illinois Legislative Council Research Memorandum, File 845, January, 1949, p. 13.

[21] *Ibid.,* p. 14.   The Louisiana legislature has provided an appropriation of $50,000 for each fiscal year, 1952-1954.

lished permanent agencies to provide formal revision of the law, that is, to consolidate overlapping provinces; correct inaccurate, prolix, or redundant expressions; eliminate obscurities and conflicts; and collect and enact the whole into a logical, compact arrangement without change in effect. The enacting, of course, is accomplished by the legislature, passing upon the completed revision.

Wisconsin led the way in this field with the establishment in 1909 of the office of revisor. By 1952 half of the states had authorized permanent revision facilities; some are engaged in making initial bulk revisions of their statutes. Others, having completed their bulk revisions, now are engaged in continuous revision—fitting new enactments into the code, spotting inconsistencies and bringing them to legislative attention, counseling with legislative bill sponsors and legislative committees to eliminate or alter unconstitutional and inconsistent matter from pending legislation, and performing similar tasks designed to maintain a consistent and logical pattern in the statutes.

The following brief survey indicates the revision facilities and programs that many of the states have inaugurated:

The California legislative counsel reported that his duties include the codification of the statutory law and the continuous formal revision of the statutory law to better express the legislative intent, making recommendations thereon to the legislature at the beginning of each general session.

The legislative commission's office in Hartford, Connecticut, maintains a continuous revision of the General Statutes. The Connecticut *Cumulative Supplement* is in itself a revision of all laws passed since the last revision of the General Statutes.

A number of legislative councils, for example that of Illinois, created in 1937, have been authorized to examine the effects of constitutional provisions and previously enacted statutes and recommended amendments thereto.

Kansas adopted complete revision in 1923, then issued a revised compilation, the General Statutes of 1935, and a subsequent compilation, the General Statutes of 1949. These compilations and biennial cumulative supplements are prepared and regularly issued by the Kansas revisor of the statutes.

The office of revisor of statutes in Wisconsin was created by law in 1909. The revisor, appointed by the justices of the supreme court and the attorney general, works principally on the continuous revision of the statutes. This revision includes the clarification of the language and the arrangement of the statutes, the elimination of obsolete and unconstitutional provisions, and the reconciliation of conflicting provisions. The revision work is presented to the judiciary committee of the senate in "revision bills," which carry full explanation of any proposed changes in the law. The revisor edits and annotates the Wisconsin Statutes, which are issued biennially. These statutes include the permanent general laws of the state then in force.

In Maine the director of legislative research maintains a system of continuous statutory revision. At each legislative session a so-called omnibus bill is prepared to correct errors and inconsistencies in the law, and complete revisions of chapters of the revised statutes are also introduced. The counsel of the senate and the counsel for the house of representatives in the Massachusetts General Court act as agents for the continuous consolidation of statutes.

The revisor of statutes in Minnesota is required by law to provide for biennial publication of the statutes. The text is kept constantly up to date, and when copy for an edition of the statutes is sent to the printer a new dummy is created for the next edition, any required changes being made. Mississippi established a system of continuous revision of laws in 1944, but organization plans have not yet been completed, so nothing has been accomplished. The 1950 session clarified the revision function, which is lodged in the attorney general's office. The New Jersey Law Revision and Bill Drafting Commission is empowered to provide formal continuous revision of state statutes, as well as the substantive revision already noted.

Law revision in Washington is done at each session of the legislature by the repeal or amendment of existing statutes and the enactment of new laws. Work on a bulk revision of the law in Washington was commenced in 1945 and completed in 1951, when the legislature enacted the code. In the same session of 1951 continuous revision was provided for when the legislature established the permanent statute law committee.

Other states that provide continuous revision include: Florida (through the statutory revision and bill-drafting departments in the attorney general's office), Iowa (through the code editor), Kentucky (through the Statute Revision Commission), Maryland, Missouri (through the Legislative Research Committee), Nebraska (through the statute revisor), North Carolina (through the Division of Legislative Drafting and Codification of Statutes in the attorney general's office), Ohio (through the Bureau of Code Revision), Oregon (through the Statute Revision Council), Pennsylvania (through the Joint State Government Commission), Rhode Island, and South Carolina (through the code commissioner).[22]

Permanent Statutory Publication

All of the states now utilize some method of permanent statutory publication. These range all the way from the publication of the statutes in bulk at long intervals (ten to twenty or even more years apart in some instances) to methods that effectively keep the permanent laws of the states currently available—through pocket parts, supplemental volumes, looseleaf or loosepart replacements, or through frequent publication, perhaps at biennial intervals, of the statutes. Although most of the states at one time followed the practice of publishing their permanent statutes at long intervals with no intervening supplements, only six states—Delaware, Maine, New Hampshire, Pennsylvania, Rhode Island, and Vermont—still rely upon this method. At the opposite extreme are several states—Wisconsin, Illinois, Florida, Iowa, Kentucky, and Minnesota—that publish the entire body of statutory law every two to four years. The latter method, although initiated by Wisconsin in 1911, took hold only within the past decade.

Various factors such as cost, ease of reference, and mass or bulk of statutes have led the several states to utilize different publication policies. The overwhelming majority of the states have found, however, that publication only in bulk and only at long intervals is unsat-

---

[22] See Robert K. Cullen, "The Advantages of a System of Continuous Statutory Revision," *Missouri Law Review,* 10 (April, 1945), 113-27.

isfactory, and that the other methods indicated above are more satisfactory.

SESSIONAL STAFF AND OTHER FACILITIES

Reference was made earlier to the need for an adequate and well-selected staff, but further emphasis is required at this point because a good research and clerical staff is an indispensable aid to the legislature.[23]   About one fourth of the states provide special research or technical assistance to serve the committees during the session.   In Connecticut, Iowa, Michigan, North Dakota, and West Virginia standing committees generally may obtain outside technical assistance as needed.   Florida, Massachusetts, Mississippi, New York, Pennsylvania, and Texas limit such assistance to the finance and appropriations committees, and in Arizona and Montana the judiciary committees have access to outside assistance.   In three quarters of the states, however, it appears that the permanent agencies, including those under legislative and executive control, provide such research and technical assistance as is available.   The permanent legislative service agencies are available to assist committees, of course, even though special committee staffs may be provided.

Since much of the legislature's work is done in committee, most states provide clerical and secretarial assistance for their standing committees.   According to the most recent information on this subject, such assistance as needed is furnished all committees in 29 states; it is available to the major committees only in 7 states, to one or two of the most important committees in 8 states, and to no committees in only 2 states.

The provision of secretarial and stenographic assistance to the individual members of the legislature is, on the whole, less adequate. Fewer than twenty of the states assume the responsibility for providing the individual legislators with needed assistance in adequate quantity. In five states—Florida, Iowa, Missouri, Oregon, and Texas—almost all legislators have individually assigned stenographic or secretarial aid.   Each Pennsylvania legislator receives $2,400 a biennium for

[23] See Chapters 6, 10, and 11 especially.

TABLE 8

State Legislative Office Space

A. Thirty-six states do *not* provide individual office space for members of either house:

1. Alabama	13. Kentucky	25. New Mexico
2. Arizona	14. Louisiana	26. North Carolina
3. Arkansas	15. Maine	27. North Dakota
4. Colorado	16. Massachusetts	28. Ohio
5. Connecticut	17. Michigan	29. Oregon
6. Delaware	18. Minnesota	30. Rhode Island
7. Georgia	19. Mississippi	31. South Carolina
8. Idaho	20. Montana	32. South Dakota
9. Illinois	21. Nebraska[a]	33. Tennessee
10. Indiana	22. Nevada	34. Utah
11. Iowa	23. New Hampshire	35. Virginia
12. Kansas	24. New Jersey	36. Wyoming

B. Three states provide individual office space for senate members:

1. Maryland	2. Missouri	3. Texas

C. Eight states provide office space to be shared by varying numbers of senators:

1. Florida	4. Pennsylvania	7. West Virginia
2. New York[b]	5. Vermont	8. Wisconsin
3. Oklahoma[b]	6. Washington	

D. Five states provide office space to be shared by varying numbers of representatives, assemblymen, or delegates:

1. Maryland[c]	3. Oklahoma[c]	5. West Virginia
2. Missouri	4. Washington	

[a] Nebraska, of course, is unicameral.

[b] New York has individual office space for about 50 per cent of the senators; Oklahoma has two senators per office.

[c] In Maryland separate office space is provided for each county delegation and for Baltimore city delegation; in Oklahoma about two thirds of house members share offices.

TABLE 8—*continued*

State Legislative Office Space

E. Twenty-four states provide individual office space for president of senate:

1. Alabama	9. Maryland	17. Ohio
2. Arkansas	10. Massachusetts	18. Oklahoma
3. Colorado	11. Minnesota	19. Oregon
4. Connecticut	12. Mississippi	20. Tennessee
5. Kansas	13. Missouri	21. Texas
6. Kentucky	14. New Jersey	22. Virginia
7. Louisiana	15. New York	23. Washington
8. Illinois	16. North Dakota	24. Wisconsin

F. Fifteen states provide individual office space for the president pro tempore of the senate:

1. Delaware	6. Minnesota	11. Oklahoma
2. Indiana	7. Mississippi	12. Pennsylvania
3. Kansas	8. Missouri	13. Tennessee
4. Illinois	9. New York	14. Texas
5. Maryland	10. Ohio	15. Washington

G. Twenty-six states provide individual office space for the speaker of the house or assembly:

1. Alabama	10. Louisiana	19. Oregon
2. Arkansas	11. Massachusetts	20. Pennsylvania
3. Colorado	12. Minnesota	21. Rhode Island
4. Connecticut	13. Mississippi	22. Tennessee
5. Delaware	14. Missouri	23. Texas
6. Florida	15. New Jersey	24. Virginia
7. Illinois	16. North Dakota	25. Washington
8. Kansas	17. Ohio	26. Wisconsin
9. Kentucky	18. Oklahoma	

clerical assistance. In about a dozen other states the pool of available assistance is sufficiently large to serve all or most legislators. These states include Illinois, Kansas, Maryland, Minnesota, Nebraska, New Jersey, New York, Oklahoma, Washington, West Virginia, and Wisconsin. In most of the other states secretarial assistance is inadequate or nonexistent insofar as most of the legislators are concerned.[24] Partly this is a question of cost, partly it is a space problem. The latter bears particularly hard on the legislators, as it affects office space. Space in the state capitols is at a premium at all times, but at no time as much as it is during the session, when continuing agencies of the states frequently have to vacate their space and set up shop in the corridors in order to provide the legislative leaders with officers.

No state provides all its legislators with individual offices. Maryland, Missouri, and Texas have individual offices for their senators; eight other states provide shared offices for the senate membership; and the representatives in five states have offices that they share. But thirty-six states provide no individual office space at all for either house or senate members, with the exception of the leaders and a few committee chairmen.[25]

CONCLUSIONS AND RECOMMENDATIONS

From the material presented in Chapters 8 and 9, which deal with the legislative aids and services required as adjuncts of the legislative process in all the states,[26] a number of important factors become quite clear. In the first place, the legislative services provided in all the states are incomplete and inadequate. Although legislative councils exist in more than two thirds of the states, there is still heavy

---

[24] For a full consideration of the following problems: "factors influencing legislative employment"; "personal service expenditures"; "job classification for legislative employees"; and "personnel requirements of the legislature" as they pertain to the New York legislature, see *Interim Report of the New York State Joint Legislative Committee on Legislative Methods, Practices, Procedures and Expenditures,* Legislative Document 1945, No. 35, pp. 30-64.

[25] Herbert L. Wiltsee, "Staffing for Legislatures," at panel on American Legislatures, annual meeting of American Political Science Association, New York, December, 1949.

[26] Attention should again be called to the work of the Legislative Service Conference, which was organized in 1948. Its purpose is to provide more effective service to the legislatures and to help in improving legislative processes and procedures. The conference has already made some contribution in helping to expand, improve, and coordinate legislative services in the states. See discussion in Chapter 1, p. 12, and *The Book of the States, 1950-51* (Chicago: The Council of State Governments), p. 18, and *1952-53,* pp. 16-17.

reliance upon interim or ad hoc committees for information gathering, research, and planning work, in spite of the many serious defects of this procedure.

It is clear that the existing services are poorly organized, and that in no case do they collectively provide a complete service for the legislature.   Not only are there miscellaneous agencies, created independently over a period of many years, that cannot offer members and committees a complete and comprehensive service, but some of the agencies that do exist are not even under legislative control. Security of tenure for the staff engaged in these legislative activities, and efforts to build a professional status for them, with proper public appreciation and respect, has been achieved in few states.

Recommendations in the area of legislative facilities may be summarized as follows:

1. There is urgent need for a single legislative service, organized and equipped, adequately financed, and functioning exclusively under legislative control, to provide a complete and integrated service for the members and committees of the state legislatures.   Such a service should be organized under a professionally qualified director of legislative service, selected by a legislative council of possibly ten or twelve members.   Under the supervision of the council on matters of policy and under the administrative supervision of the director might be five divisions or bureaus, each headed by a professional, qualified person, as follows:

> Reference and Information
> Research and Planning
> Bill Drafting
> Law Revision and Codification
> Budgetary and Fiscal Analysis

The above recommendation represents the ideal goal of organization. It is recognized that practical considerations peculiar to the individual states may make its acceptance impossible in the near future, for it is not intended that an existing service be sacrificed to accomplish this organizational set-up.   However, it is hoped that all states will move in this direction, and that states now having meager facilities might well benefit from the immediate application of this recommendation.

2. Legislative councils should be established in all states and further improved in some of the states where they are already in operation. Without doubt they fill the greatest single need of the state legislatures by coordinating their interim investigatory and research activities, by securing and preparing in advance of legislative sessions needed information and recommendations with respect to matters likely to come up for consideration, and by affording an internal legislative agency of leadership in developing a program of legislation for each session.

3. Interim committees, which have been increasing in number and importance in recent years, fulfill a real legislative need in those states that as yet have no permanent agency for legislative research, such as a legislative council. In view of the continuous character of the legislative process, research facilities in some form are needed to carry on the interim activities of the legislature; where interim committees are used in conjunction with a legislative council, their work may be coordinated with, or may supplement that of the council. The objective should be to strengthen the council to such an extent as to make unnecessary under ordinary circumstances the use of interim committees.

4. Legislative reference services need to be established in the few remaining states that do not provide them, to be expanded in many states so as to constitute more effective aids to committees and individual legislators, and to be coordinated with the research staffs of legislative councils where such are established.

5. There is need in many states for the creation of specialized bill-drafting factilities adequately staffed to provide efficient service to committees and members of the legislature in this highly technical phase of lawmaking. Proper bill drafting is imperative if the state legislative product is to be improved. Other state agencies should not be depended upon to fulfill this service on a part-time and inadequate basis.

6. In order that the laws governing the people be clear, consistent, and easily found:

(a) Each state should establish permanent facilities and programs for carrying on continuous formal revision of the statutes. When necessary, a bulk revision should be undertaken, and upon its completion and adoption continuous revision should be commenced as a permanent program. Provision should be made in all cases for the legislature to act upon all revisions completed in order that the product may be enacted as law.

(b) States should explore the problem of substantive revision of private law. In the more populous and economically diversified states—particularly where an integrated organizational setup of legislative facilities does not exist—an official agency might be established to review court decisions, statutes, and other sources and to recommend needed simplifications and improvements in the rules that govern private relationships.

(c) All states should adopt policies for permanent statute publication to facilitate and expedite reference to the permanent law. A variety of methods is available for the states to consider, but consideration of cost should be counterbalanced by the great desirability of assuring that basic statutory sources shall be easy to refer to and as current as possible.

7. Most legislatures need to increase the clerical staffs provided for committees and members and to provide adequate office space for the staff and for individual members of the legislature.

10

Legislative-Executive Relations:
THE ROLE OF THE EXECUTIVE

THE PREPARATION and initiation of legislation is no longer the exclusive prerogative of the legislature itself, though final decision rests with that body. The last two generations have witnessed a remarkable increase in the role of the chief executive and the administrative agencies in the state legislative process. Early in the twentieth century the governor emerged as the state-wide representative and spokesman of the people, the majority political or party leader, and the chief legislator. The state administration, as it has subsequently expanded, has become a principal source of legislative proposals. In addition, the increasingly technical character of a constantly growing volume of social and economic legislation has necessitated extensive delegations of quasi-legislative rule-making powers to administrative authorities. Finally, since the decade of the twenties considerable progress has been made by some states in the consolidation and integration of state administrative organization under the governor; thus his administrative control, and in consequence his importance as a political and legislative leader, has been greatly augmented.

It is well recognized that the state legislature has not kept pace with these developments and has not revised its organization and procedures to enable it to cope adequately with the greatly increased volume of legislation. Out of this situation, aggravated as it has been by the overwhelming problems of depression, war, and postwar adjustment, has arisen much of the recent interest in legislative reform. Realistic students of government have recognized that the formulation of public policy is essentially an indivisible process that should be shared by both the legislature and the administration.

NEED FOR A WORKING PARTNERSHIP

The fundamental problem is, therefore, not only that of rendering the legislature more effective in taking its part, but of bridging the gap created by the separation-of-powers system and of producing greater harmony between the legislative and executive departments. Legislative reform is not exclusively a matter of improving the powers, structure, personnel, organization, and procedure of the legislature; it must also be concerned with bettering the relationship between these two major governmental agencies that participate in fundamental policy decisions.

Despite general acceptance of the goal, considerable disagreement exists as to the purpose and means of establishing a better working liaison. Some would realize it largely through formal changes; others would alter practical political relationships. Some have proposed the abandonment of the principle of separation of powers and the adoption of the parliamentary system, with a view to giving ultimate and final power to the representative body. Whatever the merits of this proposal, the difficulties of securing the adoption of the parliamentary system and of adapting it to American conditions would seem to be insuperable. One approach toward obtaining better relationships is to strengthen the legislative role of the governor; another is to concentrate on improving the legislature so as better to equip it to carry on the long-standing tug-of-war with the executive. Indeed, it would seem that many who are preoccupied with streamlining the lawmaking assembly have only this aim in view, which, if realized, could only serve to intensify the interminable struggle between the legislature and the executive. The best solution would seem to be to avoid the supremacy of either branch, but to devise the conditions of a working partnership that would assure greater harmony without destroying the essential independence of either. In the words of one writer:

It is of the utmost importance for the future of popular government in the United States that the legislature and the executive work out some sort of division of labor by which each, in accordance with its peculiar capacity, and under leadership that spans both branches, will work with the other for the promotion of the general welfare.[1]

THE LEGISLATIVE ROLE OF THE GOVERNOR

The legislative role of the governor stems from three sources, namely, his constitutional and legal status as chief executive; his constitutional powers, which make him a participant in the legislative process; and his extra-constitutional role as a popular or party leader. All three are more or less inseparable and interrelated and must be taken into account in formulating any proposals for making the chief executive a more effective legislative leader and for developing a better working relationship between him and the legislature.

Head of State Administration

The first essential is that the governor be made the responsible head of the state administration with real authority to speak for it to the legislature and the public. Regardless of all other considerations, it is almost inevitable that where the governor has become in fact the chief executive officer of the state, he has been much better prepared to assume an intelligent and effective initiative in lawmaking. What this involves has been fairly well determined. In the first place, he should be the only elective executive officer, and his term should be four years in all states with re-eligibility for at least a second consecutive term. Only twenty-nine states now provide gubernatorial elections at four-year intervals.[2] The four-year term allows him ample time to develop well-considered policies, and the opportunity for immediate re-election strengthens his political leadership.

---

[1] George W. Spicer, "Gubernatorial Leadership in Virginia," *Public Administration Review*, I, No. 5 (Autumn, 1941), 457.

[2] In addition, fourteen states do not permit the gubernatorial incumbent to succeed himself; at least three governors have been re-elected after waiting the necessary term out of office. Nine states provide a shorter term for the governor than for their state senators. See Samuel R. Solomon, "U. S. Governors, 1940-1950," *National Municipal Review*, 41 (April, 1952), 195.

The governor should also be made the master of his own executive household. This action involves the shortening of the state ballot and the reduction of the administrative agencies of the state to a logical and manageable number, properly integrated and coordinated, with their heads appointed and removed by the chief executive. The governor should also have full power to determine their over-all policies and to direct their activities, and the agency heads should serve collectively as his cabinet.[3]

In his capacities as chief executive and legislative leader the governor should have complete control over the preparation of the budget, the date for the presentation of which should be set late enough to allow a new governor time to prepare his own budget proposals. Moreover, the many nonfiscal legislative projects, which in all states originate in the administrative departments and agencies and which frequently reach the legislature through channels independent of the governor, should be cleared through his office in order to unify the legislative policies of the executive. One of the greatest evils, destructive of the governor's legislative and administrative responsibilities, is the common practice of independent departmental and institutional lobbying. Only by eliminating or controlling such legislative activities can the executive head fulfill his role as legislative leader. If such concentration of the power to initiate administrative proposals could be effected, it would go far to eradicate unholy alliances between administrative agencies and private pressure groups.

The governor should be relieved of routine and detailed work by the creation of a state administrative officer or agency to whom he could delegate many of his administrative tasks. Several states have recently established a department of administration that integrates these "housekeeping" activities directly under the immediate supervision and control of the governor.[4] The governor must also have

---

[3] If the commission type of organization is retained for certain quasi-judicial functions, the commissions should be subject to the same policy clearance and staff supervision as is applied to single-headed departments.

[4] By 1951 these states included Kansas, Minnesota, Michigan, Oregon, and Rhode Island. See Homer E. Scace, "The Governor Needs Staff," *National Municipal Review*, 40 (October, 1951), 462-67, *The Organization of the Executive Office of the Governor* (New York: Institute of Public Administration, November, 1950), and "Kansas Administration Department Created," *National Municipal Review*, 42 (June, 1953), 283.

available adequate facilities for legislative research and bill drafting. He should have "enough professional staff assistance to keep him fully informed, relieve him of detail and enable him to concentrate on important questions of policy,"[5] whether such questions be classified as administrative or legislative or both.

Establishing More Effective Relationships between the Governor and the Legislature

In all state constitutions the governor is granted certain powers or functions with regard to legislation. In every state he is authorized and directed to make recommendations of needed legislation; in all but one state (North Carolina) he is given a veto power, and in thirty-eight states he is granted an item veto on appropriation bills. "Constitutionally, the governor's veto power today is at its zenith and the trend is toward strengthening it."[6]

In practically every state the governor submits an executive budget to the legislature and has the power to call the legislature into special session, ordinarily with the added authority of defining the agenda of legislation that may be considered at such a session. In addition to these powers, his influence over legislation may be considerably enhanced by his authority as the chief executive of the state, particularly his appointing power. As chief executive he may also focus public attention on problems requiring legislation and arouse public opinion in favor of his legislative program. Lastly, he is in many states the recognized leader of his political party, and through the wise and able exercise of political leadership may be able to secure the adop-

---

[5] "Retooling State Government," *National Municipal Review*, 37 (June, 1948), 292.

[6] Frank W. Prescott, "The Executive Veto in American States," *Western Political Quarterly*, 3 (March, 1950), 111. However, Alabama governors (1903-1943) vetoed a total of 108 complete bills, 70 per cent of which were overriden by the legislature. Between 1931 and 1943 Alabama governors pocket vetoed 19 per cent of the bills passed.—Hallie Farmer, *The Legislative Process in Alabama* (University of Alabama, 1949), pp. 181, 184.

In New York State four governors during the period 1927-1952 vetoed 7,877 complete bills, or 26.1 per cent of the bills sent them. During this period the number of bills vetoed by a New York Republican governor with the legislature controlled by the same party was not only not lower, but was in fact higher than that of Democratic governors working with a legislature controlled in one or both houses by Republicans.

tion or at least the serious consideration of his legislative program.[7]

While the governor exercises these powers and functions with respect to legislation, the state legislature possesses equal and corresponding powers with regard to administration. All state departments and agencies, except those created by the state constitution, are established by act of the legislature, and their organization, powers, functions, and broad policies are defined and prescribed by statute. Their programs are brought constantly under the review of the legislature in connection with amendments to their basic legislation, and also when they come before the legislature for funds with which to carry on their work. From time to time the legislature conducts special investigations of departments and agencies, or of particular problems with which they deal. One of the most important duties of the head of an administrative department is to maintain good relations with the legislature. If the purpose, program, and policies of the department are well understood and supported by the legislature, its operation is greatly facilitated; if the department head does not enjoy the confidence of the legislature, his path is usually a thorny one.

The problem at hand is, how may the relationships between the legislature and the executive be made closer, more harmonious, and more cooperative and be marked by a greater degree of mutual respect and confidence, which is essential to the effective functioning of both branches? The following specific suggestions are made to accomplish this purpose:

1. All administrative proposals or requests for legislation should be cleared through the office of the governor and receive his approval. This practice is accepted in the federal government, where it has been formalized through the clearance procedure in the Bureau of the Budget. Many states now provide similar if less formal clearance through the office of the governor with respect to both fiscal and policy matters. Such clearance enables the governor's office to coordinate and reconcile conflicting legislative requests and to see to

---

[7] See "Governors' Messages" annually in the March issue of recent years in *State Government* (Chicago: The Council of State Governments), and Harvey Walker, *The Legislative Process* (Ronald Press, 1948), pp. 374-77.

it that legislative proposals initiated by executive departments are brought to the attention of other departments that may be affected before they are submitted to the legislature. It avoids interdepartmental squabbles before the committees of the legislature and saves the time of the legislature.

2. The governor's office should be adequately staffed to study legislative proposals, to prepare drafts of bills to be submitted to the legislature, to carry on the necessary clearance work, and otherwise to assist the governor in his legislative duties. In this connection, the staff of the governor should work in close cooperation with the legislative reference and bill-drafting service of the legislature and with the legislative counsel on pending legislation.

3. Bills submitted by administrative departments with the approval of the governor should be clearly identified so that they may be recognized as such, and should be given special treatment and review.

Administration measures and bills originating in administrative agencies have a special significance in the legislative process. While constituting a small portion of all bills introduced in some states, they certainly represent a substantial portion of the laws enacted during any one session.[8] For the most part these bills are the heart of the governor's program and are apt to be controversial in nature. More likely than not, such bills, in sharp contrast to the usual legislative offerings, will have been carefully worked on in the months preceding the legislative session.

In view of the importance of administration measures, such bills should probably be segregated by the legislative leaders for special review and analysis. There would appear to be a need for more than normal understanding between the governor and the legislative leaders. Prior to the legislative session, therefore, administration bills should be considered at conferences held by the governor and the proposed legislative policy committee of the governor's party, which would in effect constitute a presession program review. Chairmen of legislative councils, interim legislative committees, and com-

---

[8] See E. M. Scott and Belle Zeller, "State Agencies and Lawmaking," *Public Administration Review,* 2 (Summer, 1942), 205-20; Harvey Walker, "Well Springs of Our Laws," *National Municipal Review,* 28 (October, 1939), 689-93.

missions should attend such conferences if the subject matter is pertinent to the work of their groups.

At the time of introduction in the legislature administration measures should be clearly identified as such. Because of their importance they should be introduced before other legislation, as is done in Massachusetts and New York.

4. Department heads should give priority to their function of advising the legislature concerning questions affecting their departments and making available the information and technical resources of the department to the legislature. To accomplish this purpose they should appoint departmental officers to act as liaison officers or departmental legislative representatives. The heads of smaller administrative departments will perform this function themselves.

During legislative sessions a valuable function is performed by departmental legislative representatives who make available to legislators pertinent data regarding measures originating in their departments. They are in a position to draw upon specialized sources of knowledge to assist legislators in appraising bills affecting their agencies. Despite this key role the status of departmental representatives is uncertain. Some agencies make little attempt to keep legislators informed on a systematic basis. Too often the activities of departmental representatives are greeted with suspicion by some legislators who resent "lobbying" and "pressuring."

The potentialities for good in the work of departmental representatives have been overlooked. Given a dignified and acceptable role, departmental legislative representatives would help to further understanding between the legislature and the executive departments. Legislative insight into administrative operations would be facilitated if a departmental spokesman were continuously available. The agencies in turn would find a keener appreciation of their problems among legislators.

5. Closer legislative-executive relations should be achieved through the participation of both legislators and representatives of the governor on interim study committees and commissions. Customarily legislative investigating committees are restricted solely to legislators, whereas commissions appointed by the governor are usually composed

of administrators and individuals from private life, and this rigid pattern should be relaxed to permit the appointment of administrators to legislative committees and of legislators to executive commissions. Short of actual representation of both sides, closer legislative-executive cooperation should be maintained on interim committees and commissions and the legislative councils where they exist.

6. The establishment of close and cooperative relationships between the governor and the leaders of the legislature requires continuous personal conference and consultation, for there is no substitute for personal contacts to develop the mutual respect and confidence that are essential. The organization of the legislature itself so as to provide for effective internal leadership is the *sine qua non* to such relationship. The governor cannot establish effective working relationships with a group of over one hundred individuals; he must have a group of recognized legislative leaders with whom he can consult about pending legislation. The proposal has often been made that conferences between the governor and the legislative leadership be formalized through the establishment of a legislative policy committee to meet regularly with the governor during the legislative session. In opposition, however, has been the view that any fixed, formal arrangement is apt to impede rather than to facilitate such conferences for several reasons: the group whom the governor consults should vary somewhat, depending upon the legislative subjects for discussion;[9] any formal arrangement is likely to lead to jealousies and to break down when animosities of particular individuals are incurred; members of the legislature are apt to rebel against a small, unvarying group that attempts to exercise leadership. Therefore a more flexible arrangement is advocated to take full advantage of the abilities, interest, and enthusiasm represented in the legislative body.

---

[9] The Sunday night conferences held by Governor Dewey of New York with legislative leaders and others during the legislative session might well serve as a model.

Legislative-Executive Relations:
OVERSIGHT OF THE EXECUTIVE

THE MOST IMPORTANT FUNCTION of state legislatures today is to exercise broad control over the state executive departments. The legislature enacts laws establishing state departments and agencies and authorizing them to carry on prescribed activities and programs. These laws define the broad policies and prescribe the limits of the work of executive agencies, and the legislature then appropriates the funds to carry out the programs. The legislative role does not stop here, however, for the executive branch is constantly calling upon the legislature to revise and amend and extend existing legislation; in fact, a substantial portion of its time today is devoted to considering legislation that originates directly or indirectly with the executive departments.

CHARACTER OF LEGISLATIVE SUPERVISION

Although administering the laws that it passes is not the function of the legislature—this is the responsibility of the governor, and department heads, and other executive officers—the legislature nevertheless needs adequate information concerning the work of the executive departments in order to pass upon legislative policies, to determine the amount of funds to be appropriated, and to be able to take action to correct or improve administration when necessary. In short, the legislature cannot perform its legislative functions unless it exercises effective legislative oversight of administration. But should it go further and attempt to exercise detailed supervision over executive departments, it will undertake a task for which it is not suited and inevitably will encroach on the executive function.

Effective legislative supervision of the executive will remain less than a reality unless (1) the legislature provides itself with the necessary organizational machinery and (2) its supervisory techniques are geared to its role as a deliberative body that meets infrequently. Responsibility for legislative action, diffused among numerous committee chairmen, must give way to a well-defined legislative leadership with the authority to administer the affairs of each house, to coordinate the work of assorted legislative groups, and to receive and act on communications from the executive branch. Practically, this means under bicameral legislatures that the powers of the speaker of the lower house, the temporary president of the senate, and the chairmen of fiscal committees should be extended and reinforced.

While legislative leadership should be strengthened, the legislative body itself should not sacrifice its major role as a "general court" to a preoccupation with self-defeating detail. Chiefly, its function is to act on broad questions of public policy and administrative programs and to serve as a forum where its own committee reports, differing opinions, and public pressures may be considered.

In its attempt to keep up with the executive branch, the legislature may be tempted to establish a permanent legislative staff who would (1) constantly audit, even preaudit, administrative decisions and (2) independently develop the same data prepared by administrative agencies. This course of action would lead to legislative involvement in the differences of opinion among competing bureaucrats and to legislative participation in administration at the expense of its own independence as a critic. It is preferable for the legislature to limit itself to a relatively small staff of high competence, equipped to make special investigations as needed, but not large enough to duplicate the functions of the executive departments in supplying the legislature with information about the various programs of the state. There is some danger that the case for "independent" legislative information can be overstated.

At the same time that the legislature organizes itself for effective oversight it must be aware of the need to organize the executive branch for effective administration. It cannot properly hold the executive to account if the executive's own house is not in order. Numerous, overlapping, and uncoordinated agencies of government invite administrative confusion and make the job of legislative supervision difficult if not impossible. Where there is a clearly focused center of responsibility in the executive branch and in the legislative branch, the ground is laid for supervision as well as partnership and cooperation.[1]

STRENGTHENING LEGISLATIVE SUPERVISION

There are several areas that should be explored for possible means of strengthening legislative supervision over the executive:

The Role of Legislative Fiscal Committees

Legislative review of the budget is the chief instrument for oversight of the executive branch. Whereas at one time the initiative in budget-making lay with the legislature, which was not equipped to exercise it, today in most states the governor submits the budget to the legislature for review and approval, Arkansas being the only state with an exclusively legislative budget. Budget-making and control continue through the year, and a permanent staff is needed to follow the budget process. In only a few states, however, is the legislature organized and adequately staffed to give the budget effective consideration. In New York State, the senate finance committee and the assembly ways and means committee depend on year-round staffs for this purpose. In Kansas and Nebraska the legislature depends on

---

[1] This certainly is one of the aims of the "little Hoover commissions," which by 1952 had been established in thirty-three states and two territories. See *The Book of the States, 1952-53* (Chicago: The Council of State Governments, 1952), pp. 147-53, and Ferrel Heady, "States Try Reorganization," *National Municipal Review,* 41 (July, 1952), 334-38.

legislative fiscal officers. The Massachusetts house ways and means committee and the legislative fiscal committees in Pennsylvania employ full-time staffs for analysis of the budget. In California, Michigan, and West Virginia the legislature has established an officer known as a legislative auditor, whose function is to analyze and review the executive budget and to make recommendations to the appropriations committees;[2] in some respects, this officer and his staff constitute a legislative budget agency, duplicating the work of the budget office under the governor. Is this arrangement for such large states as California and Michigan preferable to providing a small, competent, year-round staff for the appropriations committees? In middle-sized and smaller states the appropriations committees often use the staff of the budget office.

Undoubtedly, legislative review of the budget would be facilitated by the creation of joint legislative fiscal committees in most states. Important economies would be effected, and the efforts of both houses would be better coordinated. However, in those states where there is likelihood of the control of each house by a different party, the use of joint committees might not be practical. The budget is essentially a political document, reflecting the policies and programs of the party in control of the state administration. Consideration of the budget by a joint committee equally divided between the two parties would inevitably lead to a stalemate. The prescription for joint standing fiscal committees can therefore not be applied in all instances. Obviously, a unicameral legislature avoids this difficulty.

Fiscal committees in most state legislatures are not organized to obtain an integrated picture of state finance. Senate appropriations committees and ways and means committees of the lower house typically are concerned with proposed expenditures. The taxation com-

---

[2] In California the legislative auditor, independent of the budget office, is required to make specific recommendations of approval or disapproval to the legislature on every item of appropriation. In 1950 the legislative auditor analyzed the cost factors of 1,000 appropriation bills, or 20 per cent of the total, which were based on estimates submitted by the budget office. The report of the legislative auditor appears concurrently with the governor's budget report. In West Virginia the post of legislative auditor was established by the legislature in 1953. A new office of legislative auditor in Arkansas, established in 1953, is charged with auditing all agencies of the state government.

mittees in both houses pass upon revenue measures. Budget review requires that proposed expenditures be closely related to anticipated tax yields, a task that can be performed effectively only by a single committee (joint meetings of appropriations and taxation committees would undoubtedly prove to be too unwieldy).

Review of Budget Preparation. Cost-conscious fiscal committees should seek to avoid duplication of effort in reviewing budget estimates. In employing a permanent staff they should therefore not attempt to duplicate the functions of the state budget agency. Close and effective relations should be established between the appropriations committees of the legislature (and their staffs) and the budget officer of the governor (and his staff), to avoid duplication and at the same time make available to the appropriations committees the information they need to evaluate departmental requests. The practice in New York, where annual legislative sessions are held, is significant in this regard. The chairmen of the appropriations committees of the legislature and their staffs participate in the executive hearings on the departmental requests in the preparatory stage, and are consulted by the governor before he sends his budget to the legislature. The appropriations committees of the legislature do not conduct hearings at which the department heads appear to justify their requests, and the governor's budget is usually adopted without change. This practice, which differs widely from that of other states, indicates one way in which effective legislative-executive relations in the preparation and adoption of the budget can be accomplished. Since the legislative leaders are consulted about the budget before it is submitted and participate in the preparatory stages, they do not feel called upon to conduct lengthy detailed sessions with each department, as is customary in most states. There is, however, some feeling that the New York practice results in less public reporting and therefore less public understanding of the appropriations than in most other states.

Committee Review of the Budget. Budgets today consist of hundreds of pages. For committee review to be effective, therefore, staff members of the fiscal committees should summarize all pertinent information and the results of committee hearings. Data developed by the operating agencies and the budget office should be drawn on heavily, summarized, and interpreted.

Numerous questions on the extent, timing, and validity of expenditures must be resolved at committee sessions; however, they are not the sole tests that should be applied to proposed appropriations. The fiscal committee is but one of a number of standing committees and, in order to coordinate legislative action, should consider the views of other committees. All appropriation bills imply certain policies, which should be cleared with the appropriate subject-matter committees. Such a course may delay action on the budget, but mature deliberation should not be sacrified to speed. Fiscal committees should also ascertain whether appropriations are intended for activities previously authorized by statute, and disapprove appropriations where functions have not been authorized, thus safeguarding the legislature's primacy in framing policy and preventing policy making by indirection.

Segregated Funds. The widespread use of segregated funds constitutes one of the most serious obstacles to effective budgeting in the states. To the extent that this device is permitted in any given state it bedevils both the legislature and the administrative fiscal officers alike, curtailing the exercise of proper controls of each branch of government over the finances of the state. In some jurisdictions legislative and executive control over state funds is largely a fiction and a mockery, the special funds being numbered by the dozens, scores, or even hundreds, and removing from normal fiscal controls as much as 75 or 80 per cent of the revenues of the state. Fiscal management under such circumstances is not only difficult, it is impossible.

Special funds are variously referred to as segregated, designated, or earmarked funds; they consist of revenues pledged by law to specified purposes. Their history during the last half century has been an interesting one. The philosophy on which they have been established is easy to understand. One writer has summarized the situation in these words:

A particular group of taxpayers, being required to pay licenses or fees, feels that the revenues derived therefrom belong to them as a group. If they are motorists paying gasoline taxes, motor license fees, and operators' license fees, they feel that this money should go into the highway fund and be used for road construction and maintenance, and they resist *en masse* any attempt at diversion, regardless of the worthiness of the purpose. If they are hunters or fishermen, they feel that the funds derived from their license fees should be used for the acquisition and stocking of additional game preserves and streams and not for the regular operating expenses of government. . . .

These groups do not confine their efforts to a single state or to any single campaign. They are well financed, well organized, and persistent. They work both in Washington and in the state capitals. The highway organizations secured an antidiversion clause in the Hayden-Cartwright Act of 1934 and promptly set to work to obtain antidiversion amendments to the constitutions of the several states. And they had made progress— if such it may be called. In the 1945 sessions the subject was considered in eighteen states and, in five, amendments received legislative approval. By 1948 twenty states had adopted such amendments. Similarly, tax funds are earmarked for educational or welfare purposes in a growing number of states.[3]

In Alabama, for instance, according to official reports, there were 7 funds in 1900; 54 in 1936; and 100 in 1942, which expended 91 per cent of the total net disbursements made by the state. In Kansas it is reported that "by a curious patchwork process extending over a period of more than sixty years, Kansas has built up a large number of these funds, in which at the present time more than four fifths of all state receipts are set aside for specific purposes. Such funds are more than bookkeeping accounts; they represent actual physical segregation of cash resources." A few years ago there were 32 such funds in California and 65 in Louisiana. In Illinois there were 4 general revenue reserve funds, 42 special funds, and 16 separate funds that may be regarded as trust funds for various types of federal grants. Large numbers exist also in Missouri, New York, and Ohio. A few years ago New Jersey had more than 40, controlling approximately three fourths of the state's revenues. But it would be difficult to surpass the records of Colorado, in which it is reported that there

---

[3] W. Brooke Graves, *Public Administration in a Democratic Society* (Heath, 1950), p. 384.

were 231 special funds, or of South Dakota, where the number has varied between 454 and 530 since 1930.

This vicious system reacts to the serious detriment of governments and people in a number of different ways. It prevents any over-all planning of the fiscal program of the governmental unit as a whole; the money is there, but the hands of management are tied. Moreover, the legislature, whose responsibility it is not only to lay and collect taxes but to spend the receipts in the best interests of all the people, abdicates its authority and responsibility every time it submits to the demands of a persistent pressure group representing some part of the public. In addition, the operation of the system makes needlessly difficult the payment of the state's bills when due; often there is money in the treasury, but if it is earmarked for some other purpose, it cannot be used. Finally, the system may lead to still another unfortunate condition—the expenditure of a major portion of the government's total receipts by an agency supported by earmarked revenues. In some states more than half of the money of the state is spent without the kind of budgeting that is common for the general fund. Such a situation may be a major contributing factor in explaining deficits and financial difficulties for the state as a whole.

The thinking of Congress with respect to legislative control of the budget can best be explained in the measure that passed the United States Senate in 1952.[4] A Joint Committee on the Budget is authorized to be composed of 14 members: (a) 7 from the Senate Appropriations Committee, 4 of the majority party and 3 of the minority party; (b) 7 from the House Appropriations Committee, 4 of the majority party and 3 of the minority party. The joint committee is authorized to:

1. Employ a staff director, appointed by and responsible to the majority party.

2. Employ an associate director, appointed by and responsible to the minority party.

3. Employ professional, technical, clerical, and other employees without regard to civil-service laws.

---

[4] Senate Bill 913 passed the United States Senate, April 8, 1952; pending in the House committee when the 82d Congress adjourned.

4. Inform itself on all matters relating to the annual budget of Government agencies, consider the President's messages on the State of the Union, and the Economic Report; consider all information relating to estimated revenues essential programs, and changing economic conditions.

5. Report its findings to the Appropriations Committees of the House and Senate relating to budget estimates and revisions in appropriations required to hold expenditures to a minimum.

6. Recommend to the appropriate standing committee of both the House and Senate such changes in existing laws as may effect greater efficiency and economy in government.

7. Hold hearings within or without the District of Columbia; require by subpoena or otherwise attendance of witnesses; administer oaths, and take testimony.

8. Assist the staffs of both the Senate and House Appropriations Committees during the periods when appropriation bills are pending.

9. Examine the fiscal books and reports of Government agencies upon the written authority of the chairman or vice chairman.

Review of the Execution of the Budget.   Too often legislative involvement in the budget process ends with the approval of the appropriation bills.   This situation is particularly true of those legislatures that meet biennially or that lack well-staffed fiscal committees operating on a continuous basis.   As significant as the adoption of the budget is the supervision of its execution.   To what extent are the objectives in the budget approved by the legislature being attained?   Unless the legislature is in a position to answer this question there can be no genuine oversight of the executive.

There is a need, therefore, for the routine forwarding of information on allocation of funds and on expenditures from the budget office and other agencies to the fiscal committees.   Where lump sums have been appropriated, the fiscal committees should receive copies of itemized allocations and allotments from those funds.   All transfers and interchanges of funds should likewise be reported in this fashion. In at least thirty-five states legislatures have made appropriations for a central emergency or contingent fund that can be tapped when unanticipated needs arise.   If this fund is not to become a "blank check," legislative leaders should be consulted before allocations are made. In New York State no expenditures can be made from the governmental emergency fund unless legislative leaders certify that they will recommend the replenishment of the fund at the next legislative session. This pattern of action is recommended, for it provides legislative review of expenditures in those instances where no specific appropriations have been made.

Continuous information should also be made available on expenditures. In a number of states a centralized reporting system has been developed by the state accounting office. This system permits the periodic reporting of expenditures, unpaid obligations, and unencumbered balance of appropriations. Usually this information is made available to the governor and to the state budget office and is invaluable for the purpose of determining the over-all pattern of expenditures in relation to available appropriations and to the revenue trend. Data of this nature should also be made available to the fiscal committees, as is done to a limited extent in New York and California, inasmuch as an understanding of the expenditure pattern is essential for review of the budget for the ensuing fiscal year.

Data on expenditures alone will not indicate to the legislature whether the highest grade of service is being delivered at the lowest possible cost. Information of this nature can be obtained in two ways: (1) providing for a systematic and organized review of departmental reports of accomplishments, and (2) spot-checking and reviewing administrative operations in the field. These functions would also be appropriate responsibilities of the fiscal committees because of the close relationship between expenditures and departmental management. Not that the fiscal committees should retain a large staff of administrative analysts to intervene continuously in administrative operations—continuous review of this nature should be the responsibility of the department and the budget office; rather, a number of specialists should be available to committees to explore carefully selected areas of administration where there is some evidence of inefficiency. As far as can be determined, this practice is followed only by the California Joint Legislative Budget Committee, which employs six administrative analysts.

In sixteen states permanent legislative councils or research committees are specifically authorized to investigate administrative agencies to effect economy.[5] Reorganization commissions and "little Hoover commissions" are currently in vogue. Valuable as these agencies are, they do not provide for a permanent and systematic analysis and follow-up of administrative operating problems.

Legislative Postaudit of Fiscal Transactions

A postaudit of fiscal transactions involves a thorough examination, in both the state accounting office and the operating agencies, of all accounts relating to receipts and expenditures. Through such an examination it is hoped to answer these questions: To what extent have the appropriation acts and other statutes been complied with? Is there any evidence of fraud and dishonesty? Clearly, as the appropriating body, the legislature is entitled to receive these facts routinely and systematically, but in most states the legislature has no clear-cut responsibilities with respect to postauditing. Thus it is formally shut out from this vital area where close supervision of the executive might be exercised.

Among the states there is wide diversity in the allocation of responsibility for the postaudit. In twenty-three states accounts are postaudited by the same agency that preaudits or approves claims before payment, an arrangement that, in effect, puts an agency in the position of evaluating its own work. Most officials responsible for postauditing are either elected or appointed by the governor. This practice is questionable in these respects:

1. An official elected by the people can make an independent audit, but the people are not organized to act on the results of the audit or to put his recommendations in effect. In addition, an elected auditor is independent of the legislature and is not responsible for furnishing information to it.[6]

---

[5] California, Connecticut, Illinois, Indiana, Kansas, Maine, Missouri, Nebraska, Nevada, Ohio, Oklahoma, Pennsylvania, Utah, Washington, Wisconsin. The newly created (1953) legislative councils of Montana and Tennessee may be added. The Minnesota statute creating the Legislative Research Committee has been interpreted as broad enough to permit, for example, a 1950 study of state inspectional activities with a view to the achievement of consolidation and economy.

[6] For a good discussion of the point, see Victor Jones, *Legislature and the Budget* (University of California Press, 1941).

2. A postauditor appointed by the executive is not independent of the executive. He should be completely free to review the fiscal transactions of all administrative agencies.

Preferable by far is the situation in *seven* states where the auditor (postauditor) is appointed by the legislature.[7] In these states the legislature is in a better position to evaluate independently the fiscal decisions of the state accounting office, an operating agency. It is an appropriate legislative function to know whether the laws are being faithfully administered and whether claims are approved wisely or unwisely.

Constitutional barriers in most states may make it difficult to strip the governor of his power to appoint a postauditor or to make the position a nonelective post with the appointive power vested in the legislature. Although of major importance, these considerations should not deter the legislature from obtaining an independent postaudit for its own purposes. The legislature has ample powers to appoint its own employees and to investigate, and under these powers, it is free to audit administrative accounts. It is not suggested, however, that every fiscal operation be audited in those states where postauditing is done by elected officials or officials appointed by the governor; it would be sufficient for legislative purposes to spot-check fiscal transactions. Postauditing by a legislative agency would be vitiated unless the legislature is organized to receive and to act on the reports of its auditors.

Need for Strong Legislative Leadership

The central place of fiscal committees with respect to supervision of the executive has been stressed. Equally important is the focusing of responsibility for legislative affairs in the temporary president of the senate and in the speaker of the house, as has been done in New York State. The authority to appoint committee chairmen and legis-

---

[7] Connecticut, Georgia, Maine, Nevada, New Jersey, Texas, Virginia. In South Carolina, the state auditor is selected by the budget committee, which consists of the governor and the chairmen of the house ways and means committee and the senate finance committee. In Arizona the governor and the presiding officers of the legislature select the postauditor. Oklahoma provides for a legislative audit committee within the legislative council.

lative personnel should be clearly vested in these leaders, thus ending the existing fragmentation of responsibility.

The objective of concentrating responsibility in the hands of a few leaders would also be furthered by having these leaders serve not only during the session but also during the recess.   Of course, they should be well compensated for such service—under no circumstances should the salaries of legislative leaders be less than that of department heads.   Continuous service with adequate compensation would serve to point up the prestige and responsibilities of the office.

Especially in states where there is no legislative council, offices of legislative leaders should be adequately staffed throughout the year.[8] Not only clerical assistance but also high-grade research assistance should be available to legislative leaders if they are to fulfill their functions.   It should be possible for them to have all legislative proposals and all memoranda for and against legislation summarized. Access to all available data would tend to equalize their position with respect to the executive and competing pressure groups whose views are usually well if not impartially documented.

Facilities for obtaining full information should be freely extended to the minority leadership as well.   A well-fortified minority will tend to improve bill drafting and legislative debate and can become a genuine "loyal opposition."   Moreover, from the standpoint of practical politics there will be fewer reprisals and less of a wholesale firing of legislative employees in the event of a change in party control if the minority is given its share of clerical and research assistance.

An important test of legislative leadership is the extent to which the leaders can coordinate the views of the legislature and present to the executive an integrated legislative viewpoint.   In the absence of clearly defined legislative thinking regarding administrative policies and programs there can only be unheeded sniping at the executive from the legislative sidelines.   Mechanisms in addition to the traditional caucuses must therefore be developed to crystallize legislative thinking and to formulate legislative policy.

---

[8] See discussion of legislative councils in Chapter 8 and recommendation for integration of all legislative research under a director of legislative services selected by the legislative council (page 160).

To an increasing extent the legislature depends on legislative councils and interim committees and commissions for fact-finding, and these agencies are influential in developing legislative thinking on the major issues of the day. As a major step in coordinating legislative viewpoints, majority and minority leaders should be appointed as ex officio members of all interim groups. This action has been taken with considerable success in the interim committees of New York State, where party leadership is clearly defined. In 23 of the 33 state legislatures that have established legislative councils and research committees legislative leaders serve as ex officio members of such bodies.

In many state legislatures, especially those lacking legislative councils, the influential rules committee or steering committee determines the fate of much legislation. Because these committees are usually composed of ranking members of the legislature they can easily be converted into effective instruments of legislative policy making. It is recommended, therefore, that the rules (or steering) committee be composed solely of legislative leaders and chairmen and ranking minority members of the major standing committees and that it become, in effect, the legislative policy committee. The majority-party members of the committee would constitute the policy committee for that party, with the minority group performing a comparable function for the minority party.

Examining Legislation from the Standpoint of Administrative Feasibility

The legislature cannot properly hold the executive to account if a statute is so written as to impede effective administration. It is desirable, therefore, that the test of administrative feasibility be applied to all legislation in the same manner that bills are reviewed to determine whether they comply with technical bill-drafting requirements. Among the tests of administrative feasibility should be the following:

1. The administrator should be given the maximum amount of flexibility in administering the law. Administrative details should not be frozen in the law.

2. Organizational structure within major departments or agencies should not be prescribed in the law. The department head should have freedom in this respect.

3. Responsibility for administrative functions should be given to the department head. His authority should be commensurate with the responsibilities.

4. Responsibility for one function should not be divided among a number of agencies.

5. The law should carry a clear-cut expression of legislative policy for guidance of the administrator.

State legislative committees should follow the practice of the committees of Congress, which usually refer proposed legislation to the departments affected for their comments and advice. This practice often avoids mistakes and gives the committee the benefit of the advice of the departments concerned.

Developing Management Controls within the Executive Departments

Through its fiscal and policy-making powers the legislature should seek to develop an administrative framework that will promote effective administration, for it cannot expect an administrator to do a job without adequate tools. The legislature should be particularly alert to provide for such organizational units as will improve management practices, such as methods and procedures offices, effective business offices, and adequate research offices. Units of this type would continuously furnish data on the effectiveness of agency programs and operations to the administrator and at the same time would enable the legislature to obtain more information on administrative operations than might otherwise be accessible and to obtain data from these key points on routine matters.

CONCLUSIONS AND RECOMMENDATIONS

With reference to legislative-executive relations the following conclusions and recommendations may be made:

1. Within the framework of the system of checks and balances a better working partnership between the executive and legislature

should be encouraged. This working liaison should recognize the state executive as a leader in policy formulation and formal lawmaking. On the one hand, this legislative role requires that the legislature make it possible for the governor to be master of his own executive household through a well-integrated administrative setup; complete control over the preparation of the budget; and an adequate professional and clerical staff for general supervision of staff agencies, for legislative research, and for bill drafting.

The ever-increasing importance of administration-sponsored bills should also be recognized, for effective coordination requires formal or informal but responsible clearance through the governor's office before early legislative introduction. While there is no substitute for personal contacts and continuous consultation, there is need for regularized machinery such as frequent periodic conferences of the governor and other key administrators with recognized legislative leaders. In addition, good legislative-executive relations require very close cooperation, if not actual representation, of legislative and administrative officials on interim committees, commissions, and legislative councils.

2. Any enumeration of proper legislative functions must include legislative oversight of the administration. If such supervision is to be effective, there must be recognition of the need for well-defined legislative leadership for legislatures that meet infrequently and whose machinery is commonly diffused among numerous committee chairmen. Since much legislative supervision is conducted through the budget, caution must be exercised in not duplicating the functions of the executive budget agency. A small but well-trained staff attached particularly to a consolidated appropriation and taxation committee in a unicameral legislature or joint legislative appropriations and joint tax committees working in close cooperation with one another and with the executive budget staff could channel sufficient information to the legislature for valid decisions on administrative policies.

If the state should go so far as to adopt the completely integrated organization of all legislative services under a director of legislative service appointed by the legislative council, as suggested in connection with the chapters on legislative facilities, then consideration should be given to assigning legislative budgetary supervision to the division of budgetary and fiscal analysis of the council.

The widespread use of segregated and earmarked funds should be recognized as a serious obstacle to the exercise of proper control over the finances of the state by the legislature and administration alike. These special funds should be re-examined with the view of freeing as many as possible in the interest of effective budgeting.

It is strongly urged that there be thorough postauditing of all fiscal transactions by an independent auditor appointed by the legislature. This method is now followed by only seven states. The legislative auditor should have access to all administrative accounts for the purpose of making postaudits without intervention in current administrative fiscal operations. This recommendation implies the abolition of the popularly elected state auditor where he exists and a separation of the function of an administrative controller subordinate to the executive from that of the legislative auditor.

Preauditing by the legislature should be eliminated or kept to a minimum. The general power of legislative investigations may be used for a detailed examination of administrative and financial operations as the need arises.

Party Organization and Control

MANY OF THE DESCRIPTIONS and analyses of American state legislatures have been confined to the formal structural and organizational features of these bodies and have not taken adequately into account the forces of practical politics that determine their activities. Political control or guidance emanating from the legislative leaders, the governor, or the cooperation of both assumes a different form in almost every state and depends in a large measure upon the practical political conditions existing either permanently or at a given time within each state. "In our forty-eight state legislatures," writes Willoughby, "may be found every shade of belief as to the importance of leadership and organization. . . ."[1]

Political leadership is usually thought of in terms of party leadership, but it has been generally assumed that partisanship counts for less in most state legislatures than it does in Congress. Luce states that "everywhere except in New York there is much less partisanship than is commonly supposed," and that "leadership is rarely now and in our time rarely has been a matter of party control."[2] One explanation for this has been that the two major national parties are divided mainly on national issues that do not figure greatly in the

---

[1] W. F. Willoughby, *Principles of Legislative Organization and Administration* (Washington: The Brookings Institution, 1934), pp. 522-23.

[2] Robert Luce, *Legislative Procedure* (Houghton Mifflin, 1922), pp. 472-73.

TABLE 9

Party Cohesion, Pressure Politics, Local and National Issues in State Legislatures

State	Party Cohesion Strong	Party Cohesion Moderate	Party Cohesion Weak	Pressure Politics Strong	Pressure Politics Moderate	Pressure Politics Weak	Local Issues Strong	Local Issues Moderate	Local Issues Weak	National Issues Strong	National Issues Moderate	National Issues Weak
Alabama			X	X			X					X
Arizona			X	X				X				X
Arkansas			X	X			X					X
California			X	X				X				X
Colorado	X					X			X			X
Connecticut	X					X			X		X	
Delaware	X				X						X	
Florida			X	X			X				X	
Georgia			X	X			X					X
Idaho	X							X				X
Illinois		X			X			X				X
Indiana	X					X		X				X
Iowa	X			X					X		X	
Kansas	X				X				X			X
Kentucky			X	X			X				X	
Louisiana			X	X			X					X
Maine			X	X								X
Maryland	X				X		X				X	
Massachusetts	X				X		X					X
Michigan	X			X				X			X	
Minnesota			N[a]	X			X					X
Mississippi	X		X	X			X					X

State												
Missouri	X											
Montana		X		X			X	X				X
Nebraska		X		X			X	X				X
Nevada			N[a]		X	X						X
New Hampshire	X				X							X
New Jersey			X	X								X
New Mexico	X							X				
New York	X			X	X				X			X
North Carolina			F[b]	X				X				X
North Dakota						X		X				X
Ohio	X			X	X				X			X
Oklahoma			X	X			X	X				X
Oregon	X		X	X			X	X			X	
Pennsylvania	X			X							X	X
Rhode Island	X				X	X						
South Carolina			X	X			X	X				X
South Dakota				X								
Tennessee		X	X	X			X	X				X
Texas		X	X	X			X	X				X
Utah	X				X				X		X	X
Vermont	X				X				X		X	X
Virginia			F[b]	X	X				X		X	X
Washington	X			X	X		X					
West Virginia	X			X		X		X				X
Wisconsin		X	X	X			X	X				X
Wyoming		X	X			X		X				X
TOTALS	17	11	20	24	14	7	20	12	15	0	15	33

Source: Questionnaires sent to each state.   [a] Nonpartisan.   [b] Strong factions.

politics of the states. More significant is the fact that the type of
two-party system operating in national politics is found in not many
more than a third of the states. In the remainder one of the major
parties holds a predominant position of control in the state government. However, factionalism here may have much the same effect
as the two-party system. In fact, many gradations from the vigorous
two-party system of New York to the chaotic factionalism within the
one party of Florida may be found in the forty-eight states; in no
two states are the party systems alike. It would seem, therefore, that
in the majority of the states factions, blocs, pressure groups, personal
followings, local interests, and logrolling combinations play a much
greater part in supplying legislative leadership than does partisanship.

In order to secure a comprehensive and accurate picture of the
political situation in all the state legislatures for the biennium 1949-
1951 a questionnaire was sent to two or more competent persons
in each state, including political scientists specializing in legislation,
political parties, or state government, directors of governmental or
administrative research agencies or bureaus, legislative officers, and
politicians. At least one reply was received from each of the forty-
eight states—in most cases two or three. The committee is indebted
to all for their courtesy and care in preparing their answers.

In digesting and summarizing the results of the questionnaire two
approaches have been made: (1) A general summary has been undertaken without regard to any classification of states according to
varying types of party systems. (2) In a succeeding section such a
classification has been presented with a view to pointing up more
clearly the marked differences between states with two-party systems,
states with large majority and small minority parties, one-party states,
and, finally, the two states with nonpartisan legislatures.

PARTY ORGANIZATION—THE STATES IN GENERAL

Party Cohesion and Organization

With respect to the degree of parity spirit or cohesion within the
legislatures of all the states 17 states replied that it was strong, 11

TABLE 10

Substitutes for Party Divisions

Pattern	Number of States	
Pressure politics	24	
Local issues	20	
Factionalism	17	
Rural vs. urban	10	
Sectionalism	6	
Combinations on particular issues	5	
Conservative vs. liberal	5	
Administration vs. anti-administration	4	
Personalities	4	
Nationality groups	1	(N. H.)
Religious groups	1	(Mass.)

that it was only occasionally or moderately strong, and 20 that it was weak or nonexistent.[3] Table 10 summarizes the answers from the thirty-one states in the last two categories[4] and lists the patterns of majority versus minority alignments that are more important than major party divisions or that entirely take their place.[5] It is noteworthy that in the replies from 45 states it was indicated that pressure politics played a more important part than party politics in 24 states, at least an equal part in 14, and a less important part in only 7. Out of 47 states 20 reported that local issues overshadowed statewide issues, 12 assigned local issues an important place, and 15 indicated that they were of less significance. Thirty-three states asserted that national issues had no effect in determining legislative votes, and 15 states assigned them only a very limited or occasional importance.[6]

In the matter of the degree of effectiveness of internal majority party organization in controlling the formal organization and procedure of the legislatures, the replies indicated that majority party

---

[3] See Table 9.

[4] For the most part one-party states and states in which the minority party is numerically weak in the legislatures.

[5] Some of these patterns are overlapping and compete for control in given legislatures.

[6] See Table 9.

control was strong in 28 senates and 29 houses, moderately effective in 6 senates and 5 houses, and weak or nonexistent in 11 senates and 10 houses. Administrative leadership was stated to be dominant in controlling the internal organization of both houses of the legislature in five states.[7] Minority parties were reported to be well organized within one or both houses of the legislatures of 18 states, moderately so in 10, and weak or nonexistent in 18. Majority and minority party organization as such is entirely absent in Minnesota and Nebraska, where elections to the legislatures are nonpartisan. Well-defined and continuous factional leadership and organization within the majority party exist in twenty-four states. Factionalism within the all-important majority party in the legislatures of North Dakota and Virginia was indicated as sufficiently strong to constitute the practical equivalent of a two-party system. A dual factional division in the "nonpartisan" Minnesota legislature produces the same effect.[8]

Agencies of Party Organization—The Caucus

The replies with respect to the existence or nonexistence of familiar agencies of internal majority party organization are summarized in Table 11, which shows that majority party caucuses are nonexistent in 15 senates and 14 houses.[9] In only thirteen states do majority caucuses meet frequently and exert or attempt to exert any significant control over their members or the program of the legislature. Facts with respect to the latter states are presented in Table 12. In the remaining states in which majority party caucuses function[10] they meet usually once a session, largely for organizational purposes.

---

[7] Alabama, Georgia, Louisiana, New Mexico, Tennessee. In these states the governor exercises a dictatorial or strong hand in the selection and/or control of the internal formal, party, or factional leaders or agencies, which in turn dominate the legislative houses.

[8] See pages 211-12.

[9] California is the only genuinely two-party state where majority caucuses are of no importance. Majority party caucuses are nonexistent in most of the one-party states.

[10] The joint caucus is the exclusive form for both parties in Wisconsin, and meetings are held more or less frequently, but no party discipline is attempted. The joint caucus is used in Virginia for nominating judges. Joint caucuses elsewhere are rare.

TABLE 11

Party Agencies in Legislatures

Agency		Senate	House
1. Majority caucus	Existent[a]	25	24
	Existent but of little or no significance	8	9
	Nonexistent	15	14
2. Majority party leadership of presiding officers	Strong	14	35
	Moderate	5	1
	Weak	27	9
3. Steering or policy committees	Existent	11	11
	Occasional	5	4
	Nonexistent	23	24
4. Rules or sifting committees as majority party agencies	Existent	13	14
	Occasional	7	7
	Nonexistent	20	19
5. Floor leaders	Existent	31	30
	Occasional	6	6
	Nonexistent	7	8
6. Committee on committees	Existent	9	0
	Nonexistent	39	47
7. Position of standing committees	Dominant	27	29
	Sometimes dominant	12	10
	Subordinate	4	4
8. Other forms	Governors[b]	12 states	
	Party committees, officials, or leaders outside the legislature	5 states	

[a] The joint majority caucus is the only form in Wisconsin.
[b] The power of the governor over the internal workings of the legislature—exceptionally strong.

In a few states, where meetings occur somewhat oftener to consider party policy as to legislative measures, attempts to bind members either are not made, or when made are futile.

Minority party caucuses were reported by 25 states, but are of some importance only in 15, where the minority party strength in the legislatures is considerable. In the remaining 10 states, in which the majority party holds a much larger proportion of seats, minority

TABLE 12

States with Strong Majority Party Caucuses

State	Meetings during Session		Binding Character of Decisions		
	Senate	House	Character of Measures	Release of Members	
Colorado	Weekly	Weekly	Few	(Not stated)	
Connecticut	Frequent	On call	"State-wide"	Reserves right	
Delaware	Weekly	Weekly	"Important"	Pledge to county	
Idaho	Frequent	Frequent	(Not stated)	(Not stated)	
Indiana	Frequent	Frequent	"Some bills"	"Action of caucus"	
Massachusetts	D.—Frequent R.—Irreg.	D.—Frequent R.—Irreg.	"Party measures"	Opposition or withdrawal	
Nevada	Biweekly	Biweekly	None	(Not stated)	
New Jersey	Daily	Daily	Controls program	Not bound	
New York	Three or four times a session		"Important bills"	Notice; Non-attendance	
Pennsylvania	Weekly	Weekly	"Some issues"	Rarely bound	
Rhode Island	Frequent	Frequent	(Not stated)	(Not stated)	
Washington	Several times a session		None	Not bound	
Wyoming	Daily	As needed	"Party measures"	Statement in caucus	

party caucuses are of no vital significance. Factional caucuses within the majority party were reported in seven states where the minority party is quite weak or nonexistent.[11]

Standing Committees

Ten states reported no minority party representation on standing committees, [12] and three others reported that such representation was not invariable.[13] Regardless of formal methods of appointing standing committee members, the agencies set forth in Table 13 were indicated as having the effective power to select majority members in the forty-six states where partisanship in the legislature is recognized.

TABLE 13

Choice of Standing Committees

Chosen by:	Senate	House
Presiding officers	20	33
Committee on committees (formal or informal)	12	3
Party oligarchy	6	4
Caucus	3	3
Governor	1	1
Governor and presiding officers	1	1
Administrative and legislative leaders	1	1
Committee on rules	1	0
Majority leader	1	0

In the choice of standing committee chairmen seniority figures prominently in 14 senates and 12 houses and is not a factor in 23 senates and 36 houses. Where seniority is not a consideration, a wide variety of factors in the selection of chairman was indicated— personal ability or experience, favoritism of presiding officers, party prestige, administrative choice, members' preference, and others.

---

[11] Arizona, Arkansas, Florida, Georgia, Kansas, New Mexico, North Dakota.
[12] Eight one-party states and two nonpartisan states.
[13] Oregon, South Dakota, and Tennessee, in which the majority party holds a large proportion of the legislative seats.

Ten states indicated that committee chairmen tend to dominate their committees, 11 that the committee majority usually has the upper hand, 10 that the relationship varies from one to the other, and 13 that the majority oligarchy controlling the chamber exerted over-all authority over committees and their chairmen. Although many legislative houses have discharge rules or procedures, in at least half the houses such rules were reported as either ineffective or used very infrequently.

Administrative Leadership

Although legislative leadership by the chief executive varies greatly from governor to governor and from time to time in most states, the replies indicated that at least within the biennium studied the governor's leadership was weak in nineteen states. Twenty-nine states reported that leadership of the majority party was a significant factor in the governor's legislative leadership. Eighteen states stressed the governor's personal qualities as an additional or independent factor. Leadership of a dominant faction of his party was mentioned as a primary source of the governor's leadership in 14 states, and 5 indicated ability to control cross-party blocs as a principal basis of the governor's legislative power.

A wide variety of political techniques employed by governors was indicated, among which control of the patronage and ability to maintain a working liaison with the legislature were most frequently mentioned. Administrative power, financial control, use of propaganda, framing the party program, appointment or control of legislative party or factional leaders, and use of the veto and the message were also indicated by a number of states. Senatorial courtesy was reported as unimportant in more than half the states, and several states indicated that senate opposition to gubernatorial nominations was exceptional.

Independent legislative activities on the part of administrative agencies do not figure prominently in twenty-five states, many of them states in which the governor has been made the effective head of the administration or in which he exerts strong political leadership or both. Eighteen states reported that the governor's office served as an effective clearing house for administrative proposals of legislation,[14] 14 that it was partly effective, and 14 that it was ineffective. The departments or agencies most frequently mentioned as engaging in independent legislative activity were those concerned with highways, education, welfare, and health. From state to state, many other varying agencies were named.

PARTY SYSTEMS

Variety of Party Systems

Many of the data secured through the questionnaire take on additional significance if related to the types of party systems found in different states. First, there are the two-party states where the Democratic and Republican parties are fairly evenly matched. In the bienniums of 1949-1951 and 1951-1953 these states numbered 19 (Table 14).[15] Second, there were 9 states in which one of the major parties was in a dominant position, but in which the minority party held a sizable number of seats in one or both of the legislative houses (Table 15). In all 9 the governorship and both houses were in the hands of a single party, 4 being Democratic and 5 Republican.[16] Strong factionalism within the majority party seemingly exists in 5 of the 9;[17] in the remaining 4, factions are more fluid and shifting in character.

Into a third class fall the one-party states in which the dominant party holds the governorship and all or an overwhelming majority of the legislative seats (Table 16). Of these there were 18—the

[14] Arizona, Connecticut, Delaware, Georgia, Illinois, Indiana, Kentucky, Louisiana, Minnesota, New Jersey, New Mexico, New York, Pennsylvania, Rhode Island, South Dakota, Tennessee, Virginia, Washington. In Alabama and Mississippi—appointive agencies only. Idaho reported the attorney general's office as the clearing agency.

[15] California, Colorado, Connecticut, Delaware, Idaho, Illinois, Indiana, Massachusetts, Michigan, Missouri, Montana, Nevada, New York, Ohio, Pennsylvania, Rhode Island, Utah, Washington, and Wyoming.

[16] *Democratic:* Kentucky, Maryland, New Mexico, and West Virginia; *Republican:* Iowa, New Hampshire, New Jersey, Oregon, and Wisconsin. In 1950 the smaller party was able to capture the governorships in Maryland and New Mexico.

[17] Iowa, Kentucky, Maryland, New Hampshire, New Mexico.

TABLE 14

Two-Party States (19)*

PARTY CONTROL AND DIVISIONS OF LEGISLATURE

State	Governor 1949	Governor 1951	Senate Seats 1949-1951	Senate Seats 1951-1953	House Seats 1949-1951	House Seats 1951-1953
California	R	R	R—26; D—14	R—27; D—13	R—45; D—35	R—47; D—33
Colorado	D	R	R—21; D—13	R—20; D—15	D—41; R—24	R—47; D—18
Connecticut	D	R	D—23; R—13	D—19; R—17	R—180; D—92	R—190; D—87
Delaware	D	D	R—9; D—8	D—9; R—8	R—18; D—17	R—19; D—16
Idaho	R	R	D—24; R—20	R—29; D—15	R—35; D—24	R—36; D—23
Illinois	D	D	R—32; D—18	R—31; D—20	D—81; R—72	R—84; D—69
Indiana	D	D	R—28; D—21	R—26; D—24	D—60; R—40	R—69; D—31
Massachusetts	D	D	T—20-20	R—22; D—18	D—122; R—118	D—124; R—116
Michigan	D	D	R—23; D—9	R—25; D—7	R—61; D—39	R—66; D—34
Missouri	D	D	D—19; R—15	D—21; R—13	D—94; R—60	D—86; R—68
Montana	D	D	R—31; D—23	R—28; D—26	D—55; R—35	R—49; D—41
Nevada	D	R	R—11; D—6	R—11; D—6	D—25; R—18	D—23; R—20
New York	R	R	R—31; D—25	R—33; D—23	R—87; D—63	R—87; D—63
Ohio	D	D	R—32; D—4	R—26; D—7	R—123; D—16	R—98; D—36
Pennsylvania	R	R	R—35; D—15	R—30; D—20	R—116; D—90	R—120; D—87
Rhode Island	D	D	T—22-22	T—22-22	D—64; R—35	D—67; R—32
Utah	R	R	D—12; R—11	D—15; R—8	D—41; R—19	T—30-30
Washington	R	R	R—27; D—19	D—25; R—21	D—67; R—32	D—67; R—32
Wyoming	R	R	R—18; D—9	R—17; D—10	R—39; D—17

R—Republican; D—Democratic; T—Tied.

* This and subsequent tables showing party control in state legislatures are based on the tables in *The Book of the States,* *1950-51* (Chicago: The Council of State Governments, 1950), p. 112; and *1952-53,* p. 96.

TABLE 15

States with Weak Minority Parties (9)

| | Governor | | PARTY CONTROL AND DIVISIONS OF LEGISLATURE | | | |
| | | | Senate Seats | | House Seats | |
State	1949	1951	1949-1951	1951-1953	1949-1951	1951-1953
Iowa	R	R	R—43; D—7	R—41; D—9	R—79; D—29	R—93; D—15
Kentucky	D	D	D—29; R—9	D—28; R—10	D—75; R—25	D—73; R—27
Maryland	D	R	D—18; R—11	D—18; R—11	D—87; R—36	D—88; R—35
New Hampshire	R	R	R—17; D—7	R—18; D—6	R—254; D—145	R—263; D—133
New Jersey	R	R	R—15; D—6	R—14; D—7	R—44; D—16	R—38; D—22
New Mexico	D	R	D—18; R—6	D—18; R—6	D—30; R—19	D—46; R—9
Oregon	R	R	R—20; D—10	R—21; D—9	R—49; D—11	R—51; D—9
West Virginia	D	D	D—20; R—12	D—23; R—9	D—78; R—16	D—67; R—27
Wisconsin	R	R	R—28; D—4	R—26; D—7	R—74; D—25	R—76; D—23

R—Republican; D—Democratic.

TABLE 16

One-Party States (18)

State	Governor		PARTY CONTROL AND DIVISIONS OF LEGISLATURE			
			Senate Seats		House Seats	
	1949	1951	1949-1951	1951-1953	1949-1951	1951-1953
Alabama	D	D	D—35; R—0	D—35; R—0	D—105; R—0	D—105; R—1
Arizona	D	D	D—19; R—0	D—19; R—0	D—51; R—7	D—62; R—10
Arkansas	D	D	D—35; R—0	D—35; R—0	D—99; R—1	D—98; R—2
Florida	D	D	D—38; R—0	D—38; R—0	D—95; R—0	D—92; R—3
Georgia	D	D	D—54; R—0	D—53; R—1	D—204; R—1	D—204; R—1
Kansas	R	R	R—34; D—6	R—34; D—6	R—95; D—30	R—105; D—20
Louisiana	D	D	D—39; R—0	D—39; R—0	D—100; R—0	D—100; R—0
Maine	R	R	R—28; D—5	R—31; D—2	R—125; D—26	R—126; D—24
Mississippi	D	D	D—49; R—0	D—49; R—0	D—140; R—0	D—140; R—0
North Carolina	D	D	D—48; R—2	D—47; R—2	D—107; R—13	D—111; R—9
North Dakota	R	R	R—47; D—2	R—48; D—1	R—111; D—2	R—112; D—1
Oklahoma	D	D	D—38; R—6	D—40; R—4	D—95; R—23	D—99; R—19
South Carolina	D	D	D—46; R—0	D—46; R—0	D—124; R—0	D—124; R—0
South Dakota	R	R	R—29; D—6	R—29; D—6	R—64; D—11	R—66; D—8
Tennessee	D	D	D—28; R—4	D—29; R—4	D—80; R—19	D—80; R—19
Texas	D	D	D—31; R—0	D—31; R—0	D—150; R—0	D—149; R—1
Vermont	R	R	R—27; D—3	R—29; D—1	R—219; D—24	R—216; D—22
Virginia	D	D	D—38; R—2	D—38; R—2	D—93; R—7	D—91; R—7; I—2

R—Republican; D—Democratic; I—Independent.

eleven southern states[18] together with Arizona, Kansas, Maine, North Dakota, Oklahoma, South Dakota, and Vermont. In 6 of the 11 southern states the Democrats held every seat in both houses;[19] in 5 additional states the number of minority party seats was almost microscopic;[20] in the remaining 6 one-party states the minority party was discernible with the naked eye, but the percentage of seats held was quite small.[21] Factionalism of a more or less permanent character exists in 9 states;[22] in the remaining 9 factional divisions are definitely fluid and shifting in character.[23] Lastly, Minnesota and Nebraska must be noted as states in which legislative elections are nonpartisan and political parties receive no recognition as such in the organization and functioning of the legislatures. Factionalism, however, plays an important role in the Minnesota legislature. These four classes of states may now be analyzed in some detail.

Two-Party States

Table 14 lists the two-party states and indicates a variety of political situations obtaining in them for the bienniums of 1949-1951 and 1951-1953. It should be emphasized with respect to some of these states that changes of party control occur with frequency and that the picture presented should not be regarded as static. It will be noted that during 1949-1951 only 4 of these 19 states had the governorship and both houses of the legislature under the control of one party—Republican: California, New York, and Pennsylvania; Democratic: Missouri. Colorado, Idaho, and Wyoming were added to the Republican list in 1951-1953. In 8 states the legislatures were di-

---

[18] Alabama, Arkansas, Florida, Georgia, Louisiana, Mississippi, North Carolina, South Carolina, Tennessee, Texas, Virginia, as classified by V. O. Key, Jr., *Southern Politics* (Knopf, 1949).

[19] Alabama, Florida, Louisiana, Mississippi, South Carolina, Texas. In the election of 1950 the Republicans captured three house seats in Florida and one each in Alabama and Texas.

[20] *Democratic:* Arizona, Arkansas, Georgia, North Carolina; *Republican:* North Dakota.

[21] *Democratic:* Oklahoma, Virginia; *Republican:* Kansas, Maine, South Dakota, Vermont.

[22] Arizona, Arkansas, Georgia, Kansas, Louisana, North Dakota, Oklahoma, Tennessee, Virginia.

[23] Alabama, Florida, Maine, Mississippi, North Carolina, South Carolina, South Dakota, Texas, Vermont.

vided between the two parties, the Democrats controlling two senates and six houses and the Republicans six senates and two houses.[24] Ties between the two parties existed in the senates of Massachusetts and Rhode Island and in the Wyoming house. The Rhode Island senate and the Utah house were tied during 1951-1953. In Delaware, Michigan, and Ohio both houses of the legislatures were Republican with Democratic governors; in Utah both houses were Democratic with a Republican governor. In 1951-1953 Illinois, Indiana, Michigan, Montana, and Ohio had Democratic governors and Republican legislatures, and Washington was in the opposite situation. "Party government" in the sense of control of all three political branches could therefore be said to have existed in only 4 of the two-party states during 1949-1951 and in only 7 during 1951-1953. In California, however, where complete control by one party obtained for both bienniums, party ties in both major parties are very weak, both because of traditional attitudes toward party allegiance and the system of cross-filing in the primaries of that state.[25]

Party spirit and cohesion in terms of a reasonable degree of regularity in party voting on important measures and effective party organization within the legislature were indicated as strong in 12 of the 19 two-party states,[26] as moderately strong in 4,[27] and as relatively weak in 3.[28] In the 12 states reporting strong party cohesion and organization it is noteworthy that pressure politics and localism play a less important role than party politics in half of them[29] and a strong but not predominating part in the other half.[30] In all 12

---

[24] Colorado, Connecticut, Idaho, Illinois, Indiana, Montana, Nevada, Washington. Connecticut, Delaware, Massachusetts, and Nevada were in this situation during 1951-1953. Because of the "rotten borough" system the lower house of Connecticut is always Republican; in Rhode Island the governorship and the lower house are normally Democratic and the senate usually Republican.

[25] Consult Dean E. McHenry, "The Pattern of California Politics," *Western Political Science Quarterly,* I (March, 1948), 53.

[26] Colorado, Connecticut, Delaware, Idaho, Indiana, Massachusetts, Michigan, Nevada, New York, Pennsylvania, Rhode Island, Wyoming.

[27] Illinois, Missouri, Utah, Washington.

[28] California, Montana, Ohio. Somewhat stronger in the lower houses of California and Ohio. The cohesion of the minority party is stronger in Ohio.

[29] Colorado, Connecticut, Indiana, Pennsylvania, Rhode Island, Wyoming.

[30] Delaware, Idaho, Massachusetts, Michigan, Nevada, New York.

majority and minority party caucuses function, and majority caucuses meet frequently and more or less effectively bind their members on important measures except in Michigan. In most of the states in which caucus votes are supposed to be binding, however, such votes apply only to a relatively few important bills, and releases of individual members are readily secured by announcement of contrary pledges, notice, or nonattendance at caucus meetings.[31] In 9 of the 12 states the role of the governor as a party leader was described as usually strong; in Michigan, Nevada, and Wyoming as weak.

In the 4 two-party states—Illinois, Missouri, Utah, and Washington—where party cohesion is less marked, pressure and local politics seem to overshadow party politics only in Washington, where party ties are weak and sectional antagonisms are strong. Although majority and minority party caucuses function in all 4 states, they meet infrequently in all but Washington; little attempt to bind members is made except in Utah, and there only with respect to organizational decisions and occasional appropriation measures.

In the 3 two-party states in which party cohesion is weakest—California, Montana, and Ohio—pressure and local politics are of major importance. In California the "third house" is reported to be very strong, and party caucuses assume the form of mere factional meetings except for the Democrats in the lower house. In Montana and Ohio caucuses meet very infrequently and make little attempt to control their members. The political leadership of the governor over the legislature was described as weak in Montana and Ohio.

In general it may be said that the agencies of majority party organization in addition to the caucus are more highly developed and complex in the 19 two-party states than in most of the states not in that category. The speaker exercises a powerful party role in at least 12 states; majority floor leaders are prominent in 11; and potent rules, steering, or sifting committees function in both houses of most of the 19. The governor is mentioned as having considerable control over the internal legislative agencies of his party, particularly in Illinois, New York, and Massachusetts. Fifteen two-party states assigned party leadership as the principal basis of the governor's

[31] See above, Table 12.

influence with the legislature; 8 mentioned factional leadership within his party and 5 personal qualities as additional factors. The governor was characterized as weak in legislative leadership at present in California, Michigan, Nevada, Ohio, and Wyoming.

States with a Large Majority Party

The second general group of states includes those in which one of the major parties is in a dominant position but in which the minority party holds a sizable number of seats in one or both of the legislative houses. These states are 9 in number and appear in Table 15. It may be repeated that 4 of these states during 1949-1951 were controlled by the Democrats and 5 by the Republicans. The party cohesion of both parties was reported as strong in New Jersey and as recently less weak in Oregon.[32] Majority party cohesion is fairly strong and minority party unity weak in Iowa and Maryland, a dominant faction in the majority party in both states somewhat tending to fill the role of a majority party. In Kentucky, New Hampshire, and New Mexico neither party as a whole is well-knit, and factionalism in the majority party is most important. In Oregon and Wisconsin recent conditions within the majority party have been more fluid. With the return of many former Progressives in Wisconsin to the Republican party after 1946 a shifting factionalism has tended to become the pattern of politics in the legislature. In all 9 states in this group except New Jersey, pressure politics seems to play a major role, and localism is strong.

Majority party caucuses are found in the legislatures of all of these states except Oregon; in Wisconsin the joint caucus is the exclusive form. In none of these states except New Jersey do majority caucuses meet regularly, and except in that state they seem to function only for organizational purposes. Decisions binding on members are occasionally but futilely attempted in Kentucky, West Virginia, and Wisconsin. In New Jersey, on the other hand, majority caucuses in

---

[32] Factionalism within the Republican party in Oregon was prevalent until 1948, when Democratic gains in the senate resulted in "forcing the Republicans to reorganize their party legislative groups in the legislature which will be more effective in 1951."

both houses meet daily and exert a tight control over the legislative program, but majority caucus decisions are not considered binding on individual members. The Republican caucus in the New Jersey senate, however, is without doubt the most powerful majority party caucus in any state legislative chamber. Until 1952 no bill or nomination could be reported to the senate unless released by a majority of eleven Republican senators.[33] The number has since been reduced to nine, still an extraordinarily large majority of the caucus.

Minority party caucuses meet in Iowa and Kentucky for organizational purposes only. Occasional minority caucuses are held in New Hampshire, New Jersey, and the upper house of Oregon. In Wisconsin joint minority caucuses are assembled for discussion purposes. Town caucuses are held in New Hampshire and factional caucuses in New Mexico.

Presiding officers exercise considerable power in the lower houses of Iowa, Kentucky, and Wisconsin and in both houses in Maryland and New Hampshire. Floor leaders are found in Iowa, Kentucky, Maryland, New Hampshire, New Jersey, and Wisconsin. Steering, rules, or sifting committees figure prominently in Iowa, Kentucky, Oregon, and Wisconsin. Governors exert considerable political control over the legislatures of Kentucky, Maryland, and New Mexico. Administrative reorganization has been a major factor in Kentucky, although at present the governor exerts strong political leadership over the legislature. In Maryland governors have generally assumed strong legislative leadership. The governor of New Mexico is described as maintaining a continuous control over the legislature through patronage and other political means. The political power of the governor was reported as weak in Iowa, Oregon, and Wisconsin.

One-Party States

It will be noted that 13 of the 18 one-party states set forth in Table 16 are Democratic and include the 11 Southern states, Arizona, and Oklahoma. The remaining 5, which are controlled by the Re-

---

[33] "Where Caucus Is Still King," *National Municipal Review*, 39 (March, 1950), 119-20. The twenty-one members of the New Jersey senate are elected, one from each county, regardless of population. Newly elected Governor Meyner, a former state senator, made the caucus rule a principal issue in the 1953 election.

publicans, are Kansas, Maine, North Dakota, South Dakota, and Vermont. In all 18 the monopolistic majorities of the large single parties are usually so unwieldy as to render party cohesion and leadership difficult. The minority party, which is almost nonexistent in 6 legislatures,[34] is so weak in the others as to be practically without organization except in Kansas and Maine. Here and in Virginia and Tennessee the minority party may very occasionally find itself in a pivotal position as between the factions of the majority party.

A more or less permanent and well-organized dual factionalism is characteristic of half of the one-party states and provides something of a substitute for a two-party system.[35] This situation is most pronounced in North Dakota within the dominant Republican party and in Virginia within the Democratic party. In North Dakota the two factions are known as the Republican Organizing Committee (ROC), which is more or less conservative, and the Non-Partisan League (NPL), which is more or less progressive. The latter is mainly backed by the Farmers Union, a powerful pressure group. The ROC controls the governorship, shares the other state elective offices and the congressional representation with the NLP, and has a narrow majority in the state senate. Democrats and "Independent" Republicans occupy a pivotal position in both houses. Factional caucuses exercise little discipline and recently have played little part. In Virginia, the dominant division of the Democratic party is the Byrd faction, characterized as a "suave dictatorship,"[36] which maintains a system of close cooperation between the governor and the legislative leaders and committee chairmen. This control of the legislature is aided by the formidable powers of the governor affecting legislation.[37]

---

[34] Alabama, Florida, Louisiana, Mississippi, South Carolina, Texas.

[35] Arizona, Arkansas, Georgia, Kansas, Louisiana, North Dakota, Oklahoma, Tennessee, Virginia.

[36] Consult Key, *op. cit.*, ch. 2.

[37] "Item veto; power to return bill to house of origin with specific amendments, which is then voted as a privileged measure, and the vote actually taken on the Governor's amendments; power to refer questions to Advisory Legislative Council; power to name members to interim commissions; responsibility for preparation of budget and budget bill; participation of the Budget Director as the Governor's personal representative at every stage of consideration of finance measures in committees and on floor of House and Senate."—Rowland A. Egger, Director, Bureau of Public Administration, University of Virginia, in reply to questionnaire.

It may be added that the few Republicans usually vote with the Byrd faction, because it has been anti-New Deal and anti-Truman.

To a less pronounced degree factionalism operates in Georgia, Kansas, Louisiana, Oklahoma, and Tennessee. In these states the major bases of division have been administration versus anti-administration, machine versus anti-machine, or a combination of the two. In Georgia and Louisiana factional leadership has strengthened the control of the governor over the legislature, and in Tennessee administrative reorganization has been a contributing factor to such control. In Arkansas differences in attitudes toward the administration are of some importance, but other equally significant causes of division also present themselves.[38]

Factionalism in the other half of the one-party states is of a much more shifting, fluid, and ephemeral character. In some of these states several conflicting and overlapping patterns of division follow each other in confusing succession. In Alabama and Florida the rural versus urban, north versus south, and administration versus anti-administration groupings compete with each other in the legislatures. In Texas section versus section, conservative versus liberal, local versus state-wide, rural versus urban, and administration versus anti-administration alignments are all responsible for temporary combinations on particular issues. In Mississippi and Vermont personal followings are responsible for some lineups. Pressure politics was reported to be exceedingly strong in 14[39] of the one-party states, and logrolling combinations on local bills frequently form in 9.[40] Strong gubernatorial or factional leadership may help to subordinate localism in Kansas, Louisiana, North Carolina, North Dakota, and Virginia.

Majority party caucuses are unknown in all but 5 of the one-party

---

[38] Consult Key, *op. cit.*, pt. 1, for analyses of factionalism in the southern states. See also Alexander Heard, *A Two-Party South* (Chapel Hill: University of North Carolina Press, 1952).

[39] Alabama, Arizona, Arkansas, Florida, Georgia, Louisiana, Maine, North Carolina, Oklahoma, South Carolina, South Dakota, Tennessee, Texas, Vermont. In North Dakota pressure groups are definitely identified with factions. For a study of politics in the Texas legislature, see Rae Files Still, *The Gilmer-Aikin Bills* (Austin, Texas: Steck Co., 1950).

[40] Alabama, Arkansas, Florida, Georgia, Maine, Mississippi, Oklahoma, South Carolina, Texas.

states.[41]   Obviously, where such party meetings may occasionally occur they can perform no functions comparable to those exercised by majority caucuses in two-party states.   Minority party caucuses are very rare.   Factional caucuses within the majority party are held intermittently in 6 of the states in which some degree of permanent factionalism exists.[42]

Internal legislative political machinery in one-party states is organized around the personal or factional leadership of presiding officers, floor leaders, steering committees, and/or the leadership of the governor because of his control of a well-defined faction, his control of patronage, his personality, his executive powers, or his direct control and influence in the choice of legislative officers.   Presiding officers exert considerable control in both houses of 5 one-party legislatures[43] and in the lower house of 3 more.[44]   Steering, rules, or sifting committees function in 5 states[45] and floor leaders in 11.[46]   The governors of only 6 of the 18 one-party states were characterized as weak in political leadership.[47]   Factional leadership is exerted by 6 governors.[48]   Close liaison exists between the governor and the legislature in 6 states[49] and takes the extreme form of actual selection or strong political control of legislative officers or legislative political leaders in Alabama, Georgia, Louisiana, and Tennessee.   Administrative reorganization in Tennessee and Virginia was stressed as an important source of the governor's legislative control.   Exceptional legislative powers of the governor in Virginia have been mentioned.[50]   The patronage powers of the governor are important in 5 states.[51]   It is thus apparent that governors of one-party states who exert considerable influence over the legislatures do so as majority leaders rather

---

[41] Florida, Kansas, Louisiana, Oklahoma, South Dakota.   In Virginia a joint caucus functions to nominate judges.

[42] Arizona, Arkansas, Florida, Georgia, Kansas, North Dakota.

[43] Florida, Maine, North Carolina, Oklahoma, Texas.

[44] Kansas, South Carolina, Virginia.

[45] Arizona, Kansas, Maine, Oklahoma, Vermont.

[46] Arizona, Georgia, Kansas, Louisiana, Maine, North Dakota, Oklahoma, South Dakota, Tennessee, Texas, Virginia.

[47] Florida, Maine, Mississippi, North Dakota, South Carolina, Vermont.

[48] Arkansas, Georgia, Louisiana, South Dakota, Tennessee, Virginia.

[49] Alabama, Georgia, Louisiana, North Carolina, Tennessee, Texas.

[50] See above, footnote 37.

[51] Alabama, Georgia, Oklahoma, Tennessee, and Texas.

than as majority party leaders, in some cases with greater difficulty and in others with greater ease than is experienced by governors who exert genuine party leadership in two-party states.

Nonpartisan Legislatures

Two state legislatures—those of Minnesota and Nebraska—are technically nonpartisan, since candidates for legislative seats are elected on the ballot without party designation. In both states the gubernatorial election remains partisan and, nominally at least, the majority of voters in both states are traditionally Republican. In the Minnesota legislature, however, a strong "conservative-liberal" factionalism exists. Among the "conservatives" are to be found many Republicans and some Democrats. The "liberals" are more or less identical with the Democratic-Farmer-Labor party in the state. Since the adoption of the so-called nonpartisan legislature in 1913 the "conservatives" have always overwhelmingly controlled the senate and have been in power in the house in every session except two; the state has had Republican governors for all but eight years. During the 1930's the governorship was held by the Democratic-Farmer-Labor party.

Factional or group cohesion within the Minnesota legislature has been strongest among the "liberals" in the house, but in general has been overshadowed by pressure politics and occasionally by local blocs. Factional or group caucuses operate in both houses, but only for organizational purposes, except in the case of the "liberal" minority caucus in the house. Caucus decisions are not binding, although the house minority caucus meets frequently and exerts great influence on the votes of its members in the house. In both houses presiding officers, majority floor leaders, rules committees, and standing committees exercise considerable control over legislative business and procedure along with factional oligarchies. The governor is a legislative leader in a factional and bloc sense. Although a partisan, his approach to the legislature is bipartisan or nonpartisan. The governor usually controls the legislative activities of administrative agencies; his office serves as a clearing house for financial proposals.

The situation in Minnesota is well summarized in the following

statement by a competent observer who appended it to his answers
to the questionnaire:

> The Minnesota legislature is elected without party designation. The
> parties in the past have taken a hands-off position in legislative races, but
> recently the minority party, the Democratic-Farmer-Labor party, has
> moved into the legislative picture with an organization program. As a
> result, the Republican organizations at the local level, particularly the
> young Republicans, are doing the same, openly sponsoring candidates who
> take a party stand, and in some cases opposing fellow conservatives who
> they think are too conservative. There is a general feeling that the non-
> partisan (in fiction) legislature leads to irresponsible legislation, and con-
> tributes to undue influence by special interest groups. The lack of party
> designation, as indicated above, places the governor in the position where
> he has to bear the whole responsibility and burden of getting the party
> platform adopted. He is helped by some of his friends in the legislature
> of both parties and groups, and opposed by persons in his own party as
> well as by persons from the other party or minority group.

In Nebraska the political situation in the unicameral legislature is
less partisan and less complex and is summed up as follows by one
closely connected with the legislature:

> The members of our legislature are elected on a non-partisan ballot,
> and there is no party organization whatever in the legislature. The party
> affiliation of each member is usually known, but it is not always the
> case. . . . For some years, the Republicans have had an overwhelming
> majority in our legislature, but that apparently has no effect upon the
> organization or procedure. At least twice, the man elected speaker was
> known to be a Democrat, and during the last session of the legislature,
> several of the most powerful committee chairmanships, including the one
> on budget and finance, went to Democrats. I could not say that a spirit
> of partisanship has never appeared in the legislature, but I can say that
> there has been amazingly little partisanship.[52]

CONCLUSIONS

Various conclusions with respect to party organization and control
in the state legislatures may be drawn from the factual information

---

[52] See Charles R. Adrian, "Some General Characteristics of Nonpartisan
Elections," *American Political Science Review,* 46 (September, 1952), 766-76.

resulting from the questionnaire. Most important is the variety of patterns into which such organization and control fall. Even though it is possible to group the states into four major categories with respect to general types of party or political organization, it is still true that the party system—or its virtual absence—in each state, as reflected in the legislature and in that body's relationship to the governor, is unusual when compared to that in the Congress. It is also evident, except in a few of the two-party states, that no state legislature comes near having the kind of party system found in Congress. Politically speaking, most of these state lawmaking bodies are not little Congresses. They present too many contrasting pictures of political leadership, partisanship, and factionalism.

The fundamental basis of all legislative improvement in the United States, both national and state, is no doubt a root-and-branch reform in our system of party politics with a view to creating more responsible party government.[53] Obviously, party systems and political leadership inside or outside of legislative bodies cannot readily be created or made over by constitutional amendment or legislative enactment. Perhaps it is impossible, therefore, to suggest much that will serve to strengthen party control and responsibility in the states where they are not strongly established. Certain reforms can be proposed, but their realization can do no more than create a better atmosphere in which to effect political improvements. Certainly, few general suggestions can be made that would fit the wide variety of political situations obtaining in the forty-eight state legislatures. However, a joint legislative policy committee composed solely of the recognized legislative party leaders and chairmen of ranking committees, where comparable committees do not exist, might be encouraged. Whether policy committees should divide into majority and minority party policy committees would depend on the strength of formal party organizations in any particular state.[54]

---

[53] James MacGregor Burns, *Congress on Trial* (Harper, 1949), ch. 11; *Toward a More Responsible Two-Party System,* Report of the Committee on Political Parties of the American Political Science Association (Rinehart, 1950).

[54] See recommendations at close of Chapter 11.

Pressure Group Influences
and Their Control

LOBBIES AND PRESSURE GROUPS representing almost every conceivable aspect of human endeavor are extremely active at the state level. In appraising the effectiveness of the existing state lobby regulations at mid-twentieth century it is necessary to acknowledge that lobbying is not a sinister practice but constitutes a legitimate and indispensable part of the legislative process. Pressure groups frequently constitute invaluable sources of information in making public policy. In one sense they represent the public functioning in organized groups. To a certain extent, any pressure group that exerts influence on public policy is clothed with a public interest. Therefore, the public in general and those governmental agencies upon whom this influence is exerted are entitled to full information concerning the activities of such groups. Such regulation does not curtail the constitutional rights of free speech, free press, or petition. It denies to no one the right of appeal for the purpose of influencing legislation. However, some pressure groups, acting as organized minorities, attempt to thwart the public will and act generally in a manner detrimental to the general welfare. Therefore, some degree of government control can be justified to reflect both this positive and negative role of pressure groups in our democratic framework of government.

"THE INDIRECT LOBBY"

In determining what form government control of lobbies should take, it must be emphasized that channels of mass communications serve as powerful informational and educational media that are effectively used by pressure groups in influencing the formulation of public policy. Effective lobbying today is not confined to "buttonholing" of legislators by paid agents in the corridors of the capitol or in their private offices. Modern effective techniques are directed primarily to the grass roots, where large numbers of influential and rank-and-file citizens are reached. A specific piece of proposed legislation may be debated in a campaign involving mass pamphleteering, high volume sale of low-priced books, editorial newspaper advertising, mass letter writing, sponsored and unsponsored radio and television programs. This "indirect lobby" at the state level attains important proportions, first because of the enormous expansion of power at the state and local level in recent decades. Secondly, the growing interest of national organizations in state and local legislation due to the increased meshing of national with state and local legislative proposals in certain areas, as rent control, unemployment, and old-age insurance, makes the "indirect" approach indispensable. To what extent the states have failed to take cognizance of the modern "indirect" lobbying techniques can be established after an analysis of the states' lobbying regulations.

The problem of lobby regulation and control has been given very serious attention by a number of state legislative bodies in recent years. This concern is evidenced not only by the number of bills and resolutions introduced, but also by actual statutory enactments and by the adoption of legislative rules on this subject. The wide publicity given to the activities of lobbies and pressure groups at the nation's capitol, particularly since the enactment of the first general congressional lobbying statute in 1946, followed by the enforcement program of the Department of Justice and the activities of the House Select Committee on Lobbying Activities in 1950, undoubtedly has contributed to the growing interest and action by the states.[1]

The federal lobby law is now being restudied by the United States Senate Committee on Government Operations with a view toward revision after having been challenged several times in the courts where crucial sections of the law were held unconstitutional. On March 17, 1952, in a case brought by the National Association of Manufacturers, the Federal District Court declared sections 303-307 of the federal law unconstitutional as contravening the due process clause of the Fifth Amendment in failing to define the offense with sufficient precision and to set forth an ascertainable standard of guilt.[2] From this decision the government appealed to the United States Supreme Court, and on October 13, 1952, this court dismissed the case as moot without passing on the constitutional questions involved. In *United States* v. *Harriss,* on January 30, 1953, the District Court held Section 308 of the lobby law unconstitutional in that the penalty "in addition to a fine or imprisonment, or both, [it] proscribes any person connected with the statute from attempting to influence the passage or defeat of legislation for a period of three years—a violation of the constitutional right of every citizen to petition Congress."[3] From this decision the Government has appealed to the United States Supreme Court.

None of the state lobby laws have been declared unconstitutional on substantive grounds. However, it is well to note that should the United States Supreme Court agree with the recent decisions of the district courts on the constitutional issues raised, the federal law

---

[1] See United States Senate Committee on Expenditures in the Executive Departments, *Hearings,* February 17, 1948, pp. 88-116, June 12, 1951, pp. 220-27; House Select Committee on Lobbying Activities, *Hearings and Reports,* 81st Cong., 2d sess. (Washington, 1950). Also Belle Zeller, "The Federal Regulation of Lobbying Act," *American Political Science Review,* 42 (April, 1948), 239-71; W. Brooke Graves, "Administration of the Lobby Registration Provision of the Legislative Reorganization Act of 1946" (The Library of Congress, February, 1950).

[2] *National Association of Manufacturers of United States* v. *McGrath,* 103 F. Supp. 510 (1952).

[3] 109 F. Supp. 641 (1953).

would become inoperative.[4] A number of the state lobby laws have sections very similar to the federal law. Not only is the California statute modeled after the federal law, but eight states and Alaska provide for the disbarment of lobbyists for a period of three years after conviction. This provision has been unequivocally declared unconstitutional by the Federal District Court. Apparently the United States Senate has begun its task of revision none too soon.

FEATURES OF LOBBY LEGISLATION

A survey in 1953 showed that thirty-eight states and Alaska regulate lobbying in some way exclusive of prohibitions against bribery, which are found in all states. The survey results appear in Table 17.

Few statutes provide clear, specific, and meaningful definitions of what constitutes legitimate lobbying. In Louisiana and Texas a person is guilty of lobbying who privately or secretly attempts to influence a legislator "except by appealing to his reason." The statutes of Kansas, Kentucky, North Carolina, North Dakota, Rhode Island, South Carolina, and South Dakota apply to those who promote or oppose legislation "affecting the pecuniary interest of any individual, association or corporation as distinct from those of the whole people of the state." In Oklahoma a person employed for a valuable consideration is guilty of lobbying when he *privately* attempts to influence the act or vote of any member of the legislature on measures before that body. Georgia and Tennessee define lobbying as "any personal solicitation of any member of the general assembly . . . not addressed solely to the judgment."

Some states do not define lobbying as such but merely explain the meaning of the term "legislative agent" and "legislative counsel" as one who, for compensation, promotes or opposes directly or indirectly the enactment of laws or resolutions by the legislature or executive. In addition, actual practice in Georgia and California is

---

[4] On March 9, 1953, the Supreme Court held Dr. Edward A. Rumely of the Committee for Constitutional Government not guilty of contempt of Congress when he refused the request of the Buchanan Committee inquiry into "indirect lobbying" to divulge the names of purchasers of large quantities of a book distributed by Rumely's organization.

TABLE 17

State Regulation of Lobbying

State	Laws Limited to Improper Lobbying Practices[a]	Registration Required	Legal Distinction "Counsel" and "Agent"	Financial Report Required	Contingent Payments Prohibited	Penalties for Violations		
						Fines	Imprisonment	Three Years Disbarment after Conviction
Alabama	X	...	...	...	...	Not less than $500 and	1-2 yrs.	...
Arizona	X	...	...	...	...	...	Not over 5 yrs.	...
Arkansas	...	...	...	X	X	...	...	...
California	...	X	...	X	X	Not over $5,000 and/or	Not over 1 yr.	X
Colorado	...	X[b]	...	...	...	...	...	...
Connecticut	...	X	...	X	X	Not over $1,000[c] and/or	Not over 1 yr.	...
Delaware	...	...	...	...	...	...	...	...
Florida	...	X	...	X	...	...	Not over 20 yrs.[d]	...
Georgia	...	X	...	X	X	Not over $1,000 and/or	Not over 6 mos.	...
Idaho	...	X	...	...	...	Not over $200 and	Not over 6 mos.	...
Illinois	...	...	...	...	...	...	...	...
Indiana	...	X	X	X	X	$200-$1,000 or	3 mos.-1 yr.	...
Iowa	...	X[b]	...	...	...	...	...	...

State						Fine	Imprisonment	
Kansas	...	X	X	...	X	Not over $5,000 and/or	Not over 1 yr.	X
Kentucky	...	X	...	X	X	Not over $5,000 and/or Not over $1,000[e]	Not over 5 yrs.	...
Louisiana	X	...	...	...	...	$200-$2,000 and	6 mos.-2 yrs.[f]	...
Maine	...	X	X	...	X	$100-$500		...
Maryland	...	X	X	X	X	$100-$1,000		X
Massachusetts	...	X	X	X	X	$100-$1,000		X[g]
Michigan	...	X	...	X[h]	X	$200-$1,000 or	3 mos.-1 yr.	...
Minnesota	...	...	...	...	...			...
Mississippi	...	X	...	X	X	Not over $1,000 and/or	Not over 3 yrs. / Not over 6 mos.[i]	...
Missouri	X	...	...	...	...	$100-$500 and	10 da.-1 yr.	...
Montana	X	...	...	...	...		Not over 5 yrs.	...
Nebraska	...	X	...	X	X	Not over $1,000[c] and/or	Not over 1 yr.	...
Nevada	...	...	...	...	...			...
New Hampshire	...	X	...	X	...	Not over $1,000	Not over 5 yrs.[d]	...
New Jersey	...	...	...	...	...			...
New Mexico	...	...	...	...	...			...
New York	...	X	...	X	X	Not over $1,000[e] and/or	Not over 1 yr.	...
North Carolina	...	X	...	X	X	$50-$1,000 and/or	Not over 2 yrs.	...

TABLE 17—continued

State Regulation of Lobbying

State	Laws Limited to Improper Lobbying Practices[a]	Registration Required	Legal Distinction "Counsel" and "Agent"	Financial Report Required	Contingent Payments Prohibited	Penalties for Violations		
						Fines	Imprisonment	Three Years Disbarment after Conviction
North Dakota	...	X	...	...	X	$100-$1,000[j]	....	X
Ohio	...	X	...	X	X	$200-$5,000[e]	1-2 yrs.	...
Oklahoma	...	X[m]	...	...	...	$200-$5,000 and/or	10 da.-1 yr.	...
Oregon	X	...	...	...	...	$200-$1,000 or	3 mos.-1 yr.	...
Pennsylvania	...	...	...	...	X	$50-$500 or	....	...
Rhode Island	...	X	X	X	X	$100-$1,000 $200-$5,000[e]	....	X
South Carolina	...	X	...	X	X	$25-$100 or	Not over 30 da.	...
South Dakota	...	X	X	X	X	$100-$1,000 $200-$5,000[e]	....	X
Tennessee	X	...	...	...	...	....	2-5 yrs.	...
Texas	...	X[b]	...	...	...	$200-$2,000 and	6 mos.-2 yrs.[t]	...
Utah	X	...	...	...	...	$500-$10,000[k]	Not over 5 yrs.	...
Vermont	...	X	X	...	X	$100-$500	....	...

220

				Not over 1 yr.	$50-$1,000 and/or
Virginia	....	X	....	X	Not over 1 yr.
Washington	....	....	....	....	....
West Virginia	X	....	X	10 da.-6 mos.	$50-$200 and
Wisconsin	....	X	....	X	$100-$1,000[i] / $200-$5,000[e]
Wyoming	....	....	....	....	....
Alaska	X	X	X	Not over 1 yr.	$100-$1,000[n] or / $200-$1,000 or

a Exclusive of bribery. Provisions may also be found in the constitutions of the following states: Alabama, Arizona, Arkansas, California, Colorado, Delaware, Georgia, Kentucky, Louisiana, Maryland, Montana, New Mexico, North Dakota, Oklahoma, Pennsylvania, South Dakota, Texas, Washington, West Virginia, Wyoming.

b Required by the rules of the Colorado house of representatives and senate, the Iowa house, and the Texas house. No punishment by fine and/or imprisonment is provided in the rules. In Colorado lobbyists must register with chief clerk of the house and the secretary of the senate before appearing before committees. In Iowa (1949) all lobbyists must register with chief clerk of the house. In Texas sworn statements must be filed with house committee on representation before the legislature in advance of committee appearances.

c In addition, a corporation or association must file a statement of legislative expenses within the time required or forfeit $100 for each day thereafter until filed.

d In Florida offense for swearing falsely is perjury with penalty of imprisonment for not more than twenty years. In New Hampshire prison term is provided for filing false statement.

e Applies to individual (other than legislative counsel or agent), corporation, or association. In Kentucky fine up to $5,000 for second and each subsequent offense, and, if a corporation, its charter may be revoked by court.

f Prison term may be added at discretion of the court or jury. In Louisiana fine not to exceed $100 may be imposed for unlawfully going upon floor of legislature while in session. In Texas penalties imposed for illegal practices as defined by statute.

g Massachusetts provides that disbarment run until the termination of the third regular (annual) session.

h Expense statements kept in custody of legislative agent or his employer for a period of six years.

i Longer term in state prison or penitentiary, shorter term with or without the fine in county jail. If corporation or association, a fine of not more than $5,000.

j Compensation on a contingent basis and failure to make known an interest in legislation is punished by imprisonment of not more than one year or by fine not exceeding $200.

k Fine imposed on corporation or association only.

l Applies to lobbyist only. Lobbyist who *fails* to file expense statement may be punished by fine not exceeding $500 and/or imprisonment not exceeding six months; lobbyist who files *false* statement may be punished by fine of $500-$1,000, or by imprisonment of from thirty days to one year. In 1933 Wisconsin provided a fine of not less than $500 and not more than $5,000 for violations of a law regulating the use of money for published articles in newspapers and other periodicals on matters pending before the legislature.

m The senate of Oklahoma also provides in its rules (rule 57 adopted in 1949) that application to lobby shall be filed with the secretary of the senate, approval by a majority of senate members necessary for permission to lobby.

n Applies to legislative agent or counsel. An association or corporation may be fined not less than $200 nor more than $5,000.

in direct contradiction to their constitutions, which still contain the obsolete language that lobbying "is declared to be a crime" (Georgia) or that the lobbyist seeks "to influence the vote of a member of the legislature by bribery, promise of reward, intimidation or any other dishonest means" (California).

Twenty-nine states and Alaska now provide for publicity in the form of registration of legislative agents and legislative counsel who are employed in such capacities *for compensation*. In three—Colorado, Iowa, Texas—registration is required exclusively by the rules of one or both houses of the legislature (see Table 17).[5]

The required information usually includes the name and address of the legislative agent or counsel, by whom employed, date of employment, duration of employment if it can be determined, and the special subject of legislation to which the employment relates. In most states the secretary of state has the responsibility of providing the docket for filing such information and making it available for public inspection. In Kentucky this responsibility resides with the attorney general, in Oklahoma the presiding officers of the senate and house, in Florida the secretary of the senate and the clerk of the house.

In Indiana, Michigan, Mississippi, New Hampshire, Ohio, and Wisconsin certificates are issued upon the payment of a fee of one to ten dollars—attesting to the fact that the legislative agent or counsel has filed his name with the person authorized to receive it. Georgia goes to the extreme of requiring payment by the registered legislative agent of "$250 for every person, firm, or corporation represented by said agent," with the result that there have been no registrations since 1941.

The Oklahoma statute provides that the written application of the legislative agent or counsel must be approved by a majority of either house before the agent or counsel may appear before any committee Most of the laws require that the registration of legislative counsel or agent take place at a specific time—usually one week after the date of employment—whereas others simply state that before any

---

[5] In addition, Arkansas, by resolution of the house of representatives in 1951, required visitors to the house chamber to register with the chief clerk and to state their occupations and the interests they represent.

service is entered upon, such registration provisions must be complied with. Written authorization signed by the employer within ten days after entry of appearance is a common requirement. Some statutes also provide that if employment is terminated, such fact may be entered opposite the name of the legislative agent or counsel by him or his employer.

Some states attempt to discourage personal solicitation of legislators. For example, South Dakota limits the scope of the activities of legislative agent or counsel before the legislature to "appearing before the regular committees thereof, when in session, or by newspaper publication or by public addresses, or by written or printed statements, arguments or briefs delivered to each member of the legislature." Louisiana—another state that restricts personal solicitation—even requires that copies of noncircular letters to members of the legislature be simultaneously mailed to the clerks of either house.

Other states require that copies of written statements or briefs be placed on file before delivery to the legislature or committees thereof. In South Dakota twenty-five copies must be filed with the secretary of state; in Oklahoma twenty copies with the chief clerk of the house before which such person desires to appear. The state of Idaho does not follow the usual procedure of asking a legislative counsel or agent to register and file the information required in most of the twenty-nine states, but stresses almost entirely legislative persuasion through appearance before the committees and written statements, two copies of which must first be deposited with the secretary of state.

A large number of statutes exempt duly accredited counsels or agents of cities, counties, towns, villages, public boards, and public institutions from registering under the provisions of the law. The North Dakota law simply states on this point that it does not apply to any municipality or other public corporation. Some states, Kansas and Mississippi, for example, specifically exempt from the provisions of the law persons who appear in response to an invitation from the legislature or any committee thereof.

Twenty-two states prohibit the employment of any person to promote or oppose legislation for compensation contingent in whole or in part upon the passage or defeat of legislative measures (see Table 17). Indiana restricts any "member or employee of the state central committee of any party" from receiving compensation as legislative agent or counsel; Massachusetts extends this prohibition to district as well as state political committees.

As stated earlier, the state laws are particularly weak in covering pressure groups or lobbyists who resort to "indirect" methods of influencing legislation. Nor is this gap filled in those eight states that draw a distinction between a legislative counsel and agent (see Table 17). The compensated legislative counsel's activities center largely around his appearance before legislative committees, whereas the legislative agent "for hire or reward" does any act to promote or oppose legislation except to appear before a committee as legislative counsel. The statute in Maine specifically adds that the term legislative agent includes "all persons who for compensation shall approach individual members of the legislature or members elect thereof with the intent in any manner, directly or indirectly to influence their action upon proposed legislation." The distinction appears to be of little significance except that separate appearance dockets may be kept for agents and counsel. All other provisions of the law apply equally to agent and counsel. The statute of Massachusetts does provide specifically that no legislative committee shall permit a legislative counsel to appear before it on a matter other than that described in the docket of appearance filed by counsel.

Most lobby laws make no reference to representatives of newspapers or other publications, undoubtedly due to the fear that such provisions might be construed as an abridgement of freedom of the press. As the statute of Virginia provides, such legislation should not interfere with the furnishing of information to newspapers, or apply to publishers acting in the regular course of their business. A similar provision may be found in the California statute passed in 1949. Wisconsin might here serve as a model, for since 1933 special provision has been made that persons associated with newspapers or periodicals must register only if they have received money or other thing of value for any material other than paid advertising published favoring or opposing legislation.

Most state statutes apply to those who lobby for compensation. Extensive lobbying is done at state capitals by representatives of groups such as teachers who are not paid for their legislative services and therefore do not come within the purview of the lobbying legislation. In recognition of this the New York State Joint Legislative Committee studying legislative practices recommended in its final report in 1946 that "all representatives of groups interested in legislation except counsel or agents of localities or public agencies should be required to register with the Secretary of State regardless of whether or not they are compensated for legislative appearances."[6]

Nineteen of the twenty-nine states that require registration of legislative agent and counsel also make provision for the filing of statements of all expenses paid, incurred, or promised in connection with the promotion of legislation.[7] Most states charge the agent *or* his employer with this responsibility, although the wording of the law in several states is somewhat vague in not clearly indicating whether one or both is required to file. However, Mississippi, Ohio, and Wisconsin clearly require both to file expense statements. Most states require that the expense statements be filed within thirty days after the adjournment of the legislature—Connecticut, Georgia, and New York within two months. As a check on objectionable lobbying Nebraska amended its statute in 1945 to require that expense statements be filed *"each month during a session* of the Legislature and upon adjournment of such session." In Maryland the governor may require "a full, complete and detailed statement" if he believes improper expenses have been paid or incurred. Fines of $100 per day for late filing are provided in the statutes of Connecticut, Nebraska, and New York.

Expense statements in most of the nineteen states that require them do not disclose large expenditures. Many states are vague on what constitutes expenditures that must be recorded. Others are somewhat more specific. For example, the laws of North Carolina and

---

[6] *Final Report of the New York State Joint Legislative Committee on Legislative Methods, Practices, Procedures and Expenditures,* Legislative Document (1946), No. 31, p. 27.

[7] In addition Michigan requires that expense statements be prepared, but these are to be kept in the custody of the legislative agent or his employer.

South Carolina apply to executive officers of all corporations (except public corporations) who perform services of legislative agent or counsel "regardless of whether they receive additional compensation for such services." These states, at least so far as executive officers of private corporations are concerned, specifically answer the question often raised of whether identification through registration and the filing of expense statements is necessary for persons who are relieved from their regular positions during the legislative session to perform lobbying duties without extra compensation. Massachusetts requires that when expenses of a legislative agent or counsel are included in an employment by annual salary or retainer, the statement must specify the amount of the salary or retainer apportioned therefor. In case such employment is without such apportionment, then the total salary or retainer that includes such services must be stated.

In Massachusetts, for the 1951 session, 299 expense entries were received from persons, associations, or corporations employing legislative counsel or agents. Seven employers who failed to file returns within the time prescribed by law were reported to the attorney general. The total amount reported as paid to legislative counsel or agents was $423,060. Of this amount $77,125 represented apportioned annual salaries or retainers of regular employees and $56,940 unapportioned; $134,065 represented payments in connection with legislation only. Fifteen employers stated they paid nothing. In Massachusetts the largest expenditures reported ranged from $55,000 to $12,000, with the utility companies at the top, then insurance interests, labor groups, banks, and racing interests. For 1953, although the number (329) of expense entries in Massachusetts exceeded the 1951 figure, the total amount reported paid to legislative counsel or agents was $298,967. Of this amount $69,875 represented annual salaries or retainers of regular employees apportioned, $9,100 unapportioned, and $219,992 payments in connection with legislation only. Nine employers stated that they paid nothing, and nine others who failed to file returns within the time prescribed by law were reported to the attorney general. In 1951 lobbyists in Wisconsin reported expenditures of $235,320; in the state of New Hampshire, 118 expense statements, totaling $66,715, were filed by lobbyists; in Nebraska there were 695 financial statements totaling $116,800. In Mississippi in 1952 twenty-three appearance statements were filed, but only one expense statement.

NEW LEGISLATION IN CALIFORNIA, MICHIGAN, AND WISCONSIN

The lobbying laws of Massachusetts and Wisconsin are among the earliest, dating back to the decade before the close of the nineteenth century, and served for several decades as models for other states. Today, California, Michigan, and Wisconsin should be noted as states that have made the most significant recent contributions to the statutory regulation of lobbying.

California

California has made the most radical departure from the pattern set by the other states with lobbying laws. As a result of unfavorable nation-wide publicity concerning the influence of lobbyists in California, the governor called the legislature in extraordinary session shortly before the Christmas holidays in 1949. The legislators were not willing to accept the recommendations in the governor's bill, which, if enacted, would have represented the most forward and realistic step taken in the control of the lobby.[8] Instead they hurriedly passed and the governor signed a lobbying bill modeled almost word for word upon the Federal Regulation of Lobbying Act. The California law therefore presented the identical difficulties and problems as those presented by the federal law.[9] However, at this same session the legislature did authorize the establishment of a joint interim committee investigating lobbying activities to report back on March 20, 1950.[10]

Following the receipt of the joint legislative committee's report, the legislature enacted new lobby legislation, patterned closely on the

---

[8] The governor's recommendations were incorporated in Assembly Bill No. 30 and Senate Bill No. 7. See also governor's message to the legislature in *Senate Daily Journal* of California Legislature, December 12, 1949, pp. 34-35.

[9] See references in footnote 1 for comprehensive discussion of the federal lobbying law.

[10] For report of this joint committee and proposed bill, see *Assembly Daily Journal* of California Legislature, March 20, 1950, pp. 375-97.

committee's recommendations that revised the earlier measures in many important respects. However, the new legislation retained the vague and ambiguous provision of the federal statute, which requires that any individual or organization whose "principal" purpose is the influencing of legislation shall file with the clerk of the assembly and the secretary of the senate monthly sworn statements of contributions of $100 or more, and total expenditures itemizing expenses in excess of $25. This provision undoubtedly represents an attempt, as it did at the national level, to reach those who receive and expend funds for indirect as well as direct methods of influencing legislation.

The California statute also requires that paid lobbyists, known as "legislative advocates," shall register with the clerk and secretary by filing statements of appearance and monthly statements of all expenditures, listing items of more than $25. Exemptions extend to any person who merely communicated with or petitions his own legislative representative or who appears before legislative committees, to public officials acting in their official capacity, to newspapers and periodicals engaged in the ordinary activities of publication, and to representatives of churches. The lobbyist must identify any persons with whom he splits his compensation or fee. If the lobbyist or his employer employs "any Member of the Legislature, or any full-time state employee, in any capacity whatsoever, he shall file a statement under oath. . . ." Particular attention should be called to the enforcement provisions, which authorize the legislature to establish committees on legislative representation with power to grant certificates of registration to "legislative advocates," to revoke or suspend these certificates, to investigate the activities of lobbyists, to hold hearings and subpoena witnesses, to recommend amendments to the lobbying law, and to report violations of the lobbying provisions to appropriate enforcement officers. The California statute provides a very unique feature by setting up the following standards of conduct for lobbyists:[11]

1. Not to engage in any activity as a legislative advocate unless he be registered as a legislative advocate, and not to accept compensation for acting as a legislative advocate except upon condition that he forthwith register as a legislative advocate.

---

[11] Sec. 9910 of the Government Code, ch. 66, Laws of 1950.

2. To abstain from doing any act with the express purpose and intent of placing any Member of the Legislature under personal obligation to him or to his employer.

3. Never to deceive or attempt to deceive any Member of the Legislature of any material fact pertinent to any pending or proposed legislation.

4. Never to cause or influence the introduction of any bill or amendment thereto for the purpose of thereafter being employed to secure its passage or defeat.

5. To abstain from soliciting any employment as a legislative advocate except on the basis of his experience, or knowledge of the business or field of activity in which his proposed employer is engaged or is interested.

6. To abstain from any attempt to create a fictitious appearance of public favor or disfavor of any legislative proposal or to cause any communication to be sent to any Member of the Legislature, the Lieutenant Governor, or the Governor, in the name of any fictitious person or in the name of any real person, except with the consent of such real person.

7. Not to encourage the activities of or to have any business dealings relating to legislation or the Legislature with any person whose registration to act as a legislative advocate has been suspended or revoked.

8. Not to represent, either directly or indirectly, through word of mouth or otherwise, that he can control or obtain the vote or action of any Member or committee of the Legislature, or the approval or veto of any legislation by the Governor of California.

9. Not to represent an interest adverse to his employer nor to represent employers whose interests are known to him to be adverse.

10. To retain all books, papers, and documents necessary to substantiate the financial reports required to be made under this chapter for a period of two years.

The California special senate and assembly committees on legislative representation have been established as continuing bodies to act both during and between sessions of the legislature. Each is composed of five members, not more than three from any one political party. Each committee has adopted an identical formal set of rules for guidance in the issuance of certificates.[12]   Under these rules the committee is required to submit a report of preliminary determination, which is printed in the legislative journal.   Within five days the cer-

---

[12] See California *Senate Daily Journal,* March 26, 1951, and *Assembly Daily Journal,* April 5, 1951.

tificate is issued to each registrant named in the report, unless there has been filed with the committee a verified complaint with a statement of charges. Opportunity for a hearing is afforded to the applicant denied a certificate.

Under the California lobbying act the filing duties of the chief clerk of the assembly and the secretary of the senate have been assigned to the legislative auditor. The auditor's reports are reproduced photostatically in the journals of the two houses and show all documents pertaining to registrations, employer authorization, and monthly expense statements required under the lobbying act. The copies of the journals containing these statements are bulky indeed.[13]

In 1953 the California Special Senate Committee on Legislative Representation, in accordance with the mandate of the lobby statute enacted in 1950, examined the administration of the law. This senate committee reviewed all the registration papers, letters of authorization, and evidence of good moral character submitted by the "legislative advocates" for the sessions of 1951 and 1952. The committee indicated that it had issued certificates of registration to 363 persons during the general session of 1951 and to 23 more persons during the budget session of 1952. Certificates were denied to three persons against whom complaints had been issued—in all, eleven persons were denied certificates for the two sessions.

From January 1, 1951, to April 30, 1952, 422 persons in all had registered and some 2,100 monthly expense reports were filed. Eighty-six filed no monthly expense report; some 49 were active for less than two months during this sixteen-month period, with expenses less than $1,000. An additional 147 spent less than $500 during this period, and 32 others reported expenses between $500 and $1,000. It was the belief of the committee that from 75 to 85 per cent of the expenses reported were for personal living and traveling.

The California senate committee concluded its report with a list of nine recommendations for revision of the lobby law, practically all of which were incorporated in three bills.[14] These bills—the princi-

---

[13] For expense statements filed during the legislative session of 1953 see report of legislative auditor in the *Journal*, May 8, 1953, and June 10, 1953.

[14] Senate bills Nos. 791, 795, 796 (1953). See report of the California Special Committee on Legislative Representation, 1953 regular session, page 15.

pal one would no longer require lobbyists to list living, traveling, or office expenses—were all pocket vetoed by Governor Earl Warren, who stated:

> Lobbying has become a tremendous business. . . . In California there are about three or four lobbyists for every legislator. Most of them represent legitimate interests and present their views fairly and through proper channels.
>
> But there are many who don't believe in going through the front door. They want to do things in smoke-filled rooms, bars, and other places.
>
> They literally have hundreds of devices for influencing legislation and putting legislators under obligation to them.
>
> The purpose of the lobbying regulatory law is to compel these people to show the amount of money they spend and who they are employed by.
>
> I believe these bills passed by the recent session of the legislature would weaken the existing lobbying regulatory law, I don't believe these bills are in the public interest and therefore I don't intend to sign them.

Michigan

Since 1947 Michigan has required that legislative agents register with the secretary of state, who is responsible for the issuance of certificates upon the payment of a $5 fee good for a legislative biennium. Michigan joins an increasing number of states and the federal government in exempting from the registration provision of the law agents who confine their lobbying activities to appearance before legislative committees. A further exemption is made of those "whose contact with the legislature is limited to furnishing information at the request of any legislator or legislative committee regarding any matter pending before either house of the legislature or any committee thereof."

Unlike the customary procedure for filing expense statements Michigan requires the legislative agent or his employer, or an agent appointed by either, to keep *in his custody for a period of six years,* at an office within the state, the address of which shall be filed with the secretary of state, a record of all expenses incurred or paid together with records of all compensation payments to the agent for his legislative services. Such records "shall be produced . . . upon subpoena issued by a court of competent jurisdiction or by a legislative committee created or authorized by a concurrent resolution of the legislature."

In 1945 Michigan, agitated over the activities of lawyer-legislators in their transactions with private clients dealing with the state, enacted legislation making it a felony for legislators to be employed by persons interested in pending bills at higher compensation than non-legislators would receive, or to accept payment for services in connection with the passage or defeat of bills. There now appears in the new lobbying statute the additional unique regulation that

. . . any legislative agent, who, in his capacity as such, has any financial transaction, with any member of the legislature, shall within 5 days from the date thereof, file a sworn statement with the secretary of state giving in detail the nature of the transaction together with the name of the member of the legislature. If he fails to file such affidavit he shall be guilty of a felony. Upon receipt of any sworn statement, it shall be the duty of the secretary of state to forthwith furnish a copy of said statement to the member of the legislature mentioned therein.

Wisconsin

In the much-revised Wisconsin statute (1947 c. 609) the legislative purpose is stated to be the promotion of "a high standard of ethics in the practice of lobbying, to prevent unfair and unethical practices and to provide for the licensing of lobbyists and the suspension or revocation of such licenses." A hired lobbyist (one who is paid a regular salary or retainer fee) must now apply to the secretary of state for a license at a fee of $10. However, no license is required if the lobbyist is restricted to the following activities: (1) appearance before legislative committees when in session; (2) newspaper publications; (3) public addresses to persons other than legislators; (4) preparation and delivery of briefs to legislators. Licenses may be issued to "any person of full age and good moral character who is a citizen of the United States," and expire December 31 of each even-numbered year. If the license is denied, the applicant is afforded a hearing with a decision within ten days. A license may be revoked after trial in a civil action brought by the county district attorney against the holder of a license after a verified complaint in

writing charging him "with having been guilty of unprofessional conduct or with having procured his license by fraud or perjury or
through error." If the court finds for the plaintiff (the state), costs
will be paid by the county, "but if the court shall determine that
the complaint made to the district attorney was without proper cause,
it shall enter judgment against the person making the complaint for
the costs of the action. . . ."

Wisconsin provides that both the principal who employs the lobbyist and the lobbyist himself must register with the secretary of state,
but it is the responsibility of the employer to keep the records up
to date "so that the docket will show at all times the legislation in
relation to which the lobbyist is employed." The employers of both
licensed and nonlicensed lobbyists must also file within 30 days after
sine die adjournment a sworn statement of expenses paid or incurred.
The lobbyist, too, is required to file with the secretary of state a
sworn statement of expenses made or obligations incurred (except
personal living expenses or traveling expenses) within ten days after
the end of each month. The law specifically states that the lobbyist
must record any expenditures made by him in behalf of or for the
entertainment of any state official or employee if pending or proposed
legislative matters are under consideration.

Number Registered under Lobby Laws

The number of lobbyists registered under the Wisconsin law no
longer holds the record of exceeding by a large margin the number
registered in other states. This situation is undoubtedly due to the
recent revision of the Wisconsin statute requiring no license for a
person whose lobbying activities are limited solely to appearing before
legislative committees.

However, in California the fixing of responsibility for the periodic
checkup of the administration of the law is undoubtedly one factor
in the large number of persons (422) registered, even for a sixteen-
month period (during 1951-1952). In Kansas 365 legislative agents
and 125 counsel registered in 1953. For other states the range
varies widely. For the regular session in 1953 there were none in
Georgia; 3 in Idaho; 11 in South Carolina; in Oklahoma, 61 (house)

and 54 (senate); in New Hampshire, 61 lobbyists and 73 employers; in South Dakota, 64 lobbyists and 101 employers; in Vermont, 81; in Indiana, 94; in New York, 113; in Maryland, 119; in North Dakota, 137; in Iowa, 143; in North Carolina, 152; in Wisconsin, 254 lobbyists represented 373 employers; in Florida, 303 lobbyists represented 299 employers; in Michigan, 310 (lobbyists do not re-register each year if retained by the same employer); in Maine, 342 lobbyists and 187 employers.   During the legislative session of 1952, 69 registered in Kentucky, in Virginia 88 lobbyists and 109 employers; in Massachusetts 295.   The number of lobbyists registered is, of course, not necessarily a barometer of the strictness with which the law or rule is enforced or of the general effectiveness of the regulatory provisions.

APPEARANCE BEFORE ADMINISTRATIVE BOARDS

Because of the recommendation that has been made repeatedly in recent years that the regulatory provisions of the lobby laws be extended to cover persons appearing before administrative agencies, it is well to call attention in this connection to practices in the states of Louisiana and Wisconsin.   In Louisiana registration is not required for lobbyists appearing before legislative bodies.   However, registration is required by persons "retained or employed for compensation" who promote or oppose, directly or indirectly, "the passage of any resolution or other matter then pending" before the Board of Liquidation of the State Debt, State Board of Appraisers, State Board of Equalization, State Board of Education, or any state board that performs any of the duties of these boards "or attempt to dictate any policy or disposition of matters coming before these boards, shall at each and every meeting of the boards before any service is entered upon, file in the office of the Secretary of State a declaration . . . stating the name or names of the person, firm, corporation or association, by whom or on whose behalf he is retained or employed, together with a brief description of the matter in reference to which service is to be rendered."   Compensation contingent upon the passage or defeat of any matter before these boards for consideration is prohibited.   The statute also requires the filing of itemized expense statements with the secretary of state by the agent or counsel and his employer within thirty days after the final adjournment of each session of the board before which an appearance was filed.[15]

In 1951 the Wisconsin legislature after passage of a bill establishing an advisory committee to be appointed by the governor to assist the department of agriculture in establishing food definitions and standards stated that "whoever practices promoting or opposing the making of regulations . . . before the department . . . or the advisory committee . . . shall be deemed a lobbyist" and be subject to the provisions pertaining to restrictions on practice of lobbying. The secretary of state is required to prepare a docket for registration similar to the one for other lobbying registrations. The reports and statements shall be made within ten days after the end of each calendar half year and shall cover the preceding half year period.[16]

ENFORCEMENT OF LOBBY LAWS

The penalties for violations of the lobbying laws, consisting for the most part of light prison terms and/or the payment of fines, are listed in Table 17. Attention is called in particular to those eight states and Alaska that also provide for the disbarment of the guilty legislative counsel or agent.[17] In all but Massachusetts the disbarment is for a period of three years from the date of conviction. In Massachusetts this disqualification runs until the termination of the third regular annual legislative session. The Maryland statute states specifically that a hearing be granted and that cause be shown for such disbarment.

Publicity continues to be recognized by the state legislatures as an important weapon in the enforcement of lobbying laws. To this

---

[15] Louisiana Revised Statutes 1950, 49: 71-76.

[16] Ch. 713 of the Laws of 1951. In Wisconsin, life insurance companies, as a condition precedent to transacting business, must file with the commissioner a statement showing in detail bills opposed or promoted during preceding years, the state in which such legislation was pending, names of counsel, their compensation and expenses.

[17] A similar provision in the federal lobbying law has been declared unconstitutional by the federal district court on two occasions (see pages 216-17).

end the new Michigan statute directs the secretary of state to immediately record and index the information supplied by the legislative agents and to furnish copies to all members of the legislature. The revised Wisconsin measure goes even further by requiring the secretary of state to report *weekly* to each house the names of the lobbyists registered, the names of the persons they represent, and the subjects of legislation in which they are interested. Such reports are to be incorporated in the journals of each house. In Wisconsin the secretary must also forward to each house a copy of the expense statements, which, although open to public inspection, do not have to be incorporated in the journal unless the house so orders. In 1950 Virginia directed by legislative statute that copies of the lists of registered lobbyists be furnished weekly by the secretary of the commonwealth to the clerks of the house and senate, and Kansas, in 1949, provided that the lists be supplied weekly to each member of the legislature. In California since 1949 the clerk and the secretary acting jointly have been required to compile the registration data monthly for printing in the journals of the two houses.

Recent lobbying legislation continues to provide specifically that it is the "duty of the attorney general to prosecute all violations of this act" (Michigan, 1947), or the "secretary of state shall promptly notify the attorney general of any violations of this section of which he may have knowledge" (Connecticut, 1947). However, a number of states have not had a single prosecution under the lobbying laws. In fact, outside of the state of Wisconsin, where enforcement of lobby legislation has been the most energetic, there are only three reported decisions relating to the state lobbying registration laws—two in Kentucky (no convictions), one in Missouri (lobbying act was held to violate a constitutional provision that no bill should contain more than one subject expressed in its title).[18]

In Wisconsin, attempts to prosecute alleged violations led in 1947 to the imposition of fines on two lobbyists and their disbarment from lobbying for three years. In 1949 charges were filed against six lobbyists by the district attorney of Dane County, Wisconsin, four

---

[18] See House Select Committee on Lobbying Activities, *Hearings,* 81st Cong., 2d sess. (March 28, 1950), pt. I, pp. 76, 96-97.

of whom were discharged, one died, and one turned in his lobby license at the end of the 1949 legislative session; the charge was dismissed. In addition a charge against the Wisconsin Wholesale Beer Distributors Association resulted in the payment of a $300 fine for failure to report on expenditure. In 1952 charges were dismissed against two former legislators turned lobbyists for alleged acceptance, in violation of the lobby law, of contingent fees for the passage of a bill. Again in 1953 the charge that the Petco Corporation had paid contingent fees to lobbyists was dismissed.[19]

The Kansas lobby law was a matter of wide public attention in 1953. Wes Roberts, former chairman of the Republican National Committee, was accused in a report of a select committee of the Kansas legislature of failure to register as legislative agent during the 1951 session for his part in arranging the sale of a building of the A.O.U.W., a fraternal benefit association of Norton, Kansas, to the state by act of the legislature. The committee stated that "while there is a doubt that there was a violation of the letter of the law, the committee is firmly convinced that there has been a violation of the spirit of the law, and the protection which it was designed to afford to the people of this state was deliberately and intentionally frustrated." The committee recommended that the Kansas lobby law "be revised and amended to include an attempt to influence, in any manner, the act or vote of any member of the legislature, directly or indirectly."[20]

CONCLUSIONS AND RECOMMENDATIONS

Popular reference to pressure groups as the "third house," "government by pressure," "government by special interests and organized minorities" indicates the extent to which they are intimately associated with the decisions of governmental institutions at all levels and in all branches. Effective lobby regulations should subject pressure groups in their relations to government to crystal bowl exposure—

---

[19] See *Wisconsin State Journal*, March 21, 1952, and *The Capitol Times*, July 29 and 31, 1953.

[20] See *Kansas Journal of the House*, March 27, 1953, pp. 12-13.

without prohibiting or unduly hindering them in their legitimate activities.

1. Every state should provide for a lobby regulatory and publicity statute that takes full cognizance of the role pressure groups play in present-day society.   Paid and unpaid lobbyists, whether known as legislative agents, legislative counsel, or legislative advocates, should be required to register before each legislative session or appearance before administrative bodies.   Periodic statements of expenses incurred by appearance before legislative agencies should be filed during the legislative session (biweekly at least during short legislative sessions) and a final expense statement one month after the close of the legislative session.   A single statement showing expenses incurred by appearance before administrative agencies should be filed within ten days after such appearance.

2. Employers of pressure agents and those who resort to the "indirect lobby," influencing legislative or administrative action by appeals to the public through the use of channels of mass communication, should also be required to file at stated intervals statements of sources of income and itemized expenditures.   All registration and expense statements should be filed in duplicate—one copy to be left with the designated legislative official who keeps the docket, and the other with the enforcement agency.   Summaries of these records should be made periodically by the designated legislative official for inclusion in the journal or other appropriate legislative record.

3. Publicity is powerful in the control of the lobby.   An enforcement agency should be established, either as a special joint committee of the legislature or as a special division in the office of the state attorney general.   This enforcement agency should have the power to suspend or revoke lobbyists' certificates of registration, to hold hearings on complaints, to report violations of the law, to examine periodically the administration of the law, and to recommend revisions.   The usual rules restricting admission of outsiders to the floor should be tightened and more rigidly enforced.

4. It must be recognized that corrupt practices legislation and lobby laws are interrelated.   Any remodeling of the one should,

therefore, be undertaken with due consideration for its impact on the other.

5. Effective regulation of the lobby is also directly linked with the modernization of legislative machinery, the effective use of permanent research facilities, and the assignment of professional and clerical assistants to state legislative committees and individual state legislators.

APPENDIX A

Unicameral Lawmaking in Nebraska

ENOUGH EXPERIENCE has accumulated since the unicameral legislature of Nebraska first met in 1937 that some observations may be offered with a reasonable degree of sureness for the benefit of states that may undertake renovation of their own legislative establishments.

The constitutional amendment approved by Nebraska voters in 1934 affected the legislature only. Constitutional provisions concerning the governor, lieutenant governor, and other elective state officials remained unchanged. The members of the new legislature were to be elected in a nonpartisan manner from single-member districts, with the number to be fixed by law at not fewer than thirty nor more than fifty. The aggregate salary would not exceed $37,500 per annum, an amount low enough to have been a consideration in determining the number of members and districts—the larger the legislature, the lower the individual compensation. The number was fixed by statute at 43 by the last bicameral legislature in 1935.[1]

Two-year terms and biennial sessions remain, but special sessions can be called by the governor as before, or, as provided in law, by the legislature itself. A petition by two thirds of the members may

---

[1] Franklin L. Burdette described the process in the *National Municipal Review*, 24 (June, 1935), 348-49.

require the governor to call a session. The length of the regular session is not limited.

The lieutenant governor is president of the legislature, members of which have designated themselves "senators." The legislature itself elects a member as speaker, but he presides pro tempore. The governor retains the power of veto over legislative measures, subject to possible repassage by a three-fifths vote. The legislature confirms gubernatorial appointments in the place of the former senate. Thus, wisely or not, all the aspects of the separation of powers between the legislature and the executive branch have been retained. Any faults of governmental operation attributable to the separation of powers should not, in an unbiased look at unicameralism, be laid at the door of unicameralism alone. However, since the number of governmental organs is reduced, one may be entitled to look for simplified and somewhat clearer relations between the legislative and executive branches of the state. This has in fact been the Nebraska experience, for the one house has done all that two houses could possibly do, seems to have done it more smoothly, and the product is better.

REPRESENTATION AND ELECTIONS

To be successful a legislature must command the interest of the voters and the confidence of the public in its representative character. To date, at least, this goal has been fairly well achieved in Nebraska. The present legislative districts were laid out in 1935, on the basis of the 1930 census, with an admirable degree of equality. Most districts contain one or more counties, and boundaries follow county lines except for the seven districts in Douglas County (Omaha) and three in Lancaster County (Lincoln). The population of the state was still fairly equally distributed among the 43 districts after the 1940 census. With an average of something over 30,000 inhabitants per representative, no district outside the two metropolitan counties was overrepresented by more than about a fifth. Contrary to the usual legislative membership accorded metropolitan areas in other states, Douglas and Lancaster counties, although slightly below average of representation for all districts in the state, did not have quite so low a ratio as a few other counties. The 1950 population census, however, shows these two counties somewhat further out of line than in 1940. It probably would have been difficult to have arranged these districts with greater accuracy; but, as in other single-member district systems, when population shifts, redistricting could result in a gerrymander. The principal defense against this practice in Nebraska at present is the nonpartisan form of legislative election. A long uncorrected representation for Douglas and Lancaster counties could, as experience of other states shows, amount to a gerrymander in favor of rural counties.

The direct primary election, so far as the legislature is concerned, is an elimination contest. The two candidates, without party designation, receiving the highest primary vote become the only rivals at the general election in their district; and, as a rule, the candidate highest in the primary wins the final election. But exceptions occur, several of them in 1949. Except in a few of the districts in metropolitan areas, the nomination at the direct primary appears to be of little value. In four elections studied, 1942-1948, from 19 to 28 districts have seen no contest in the primary for places on the general election ballot, because no more than two names were on the primary ballot. Districts in which there were no contests whatever ranged from 6 to 13. Conceivably, petition nominations for places on the final ballot would suffice; but, of course, use of the primary machinery may be innocuous.

Perhaps because legislative districts for a 43-member house must be larger generally than small local governmental units, successful candidates usually are persons who have won some local recognition or distinction otherwise and thus attract voter attention. It may be also that the voter sees a more direct contact between his ballot marking and legislative policy in a one-house system. Whatever the cause, a sufficient number of candidacies develop in most districts and most elections to induce rivalry for voter support at either the primary or the general election, and voter response is reasonably lively. An average of 123 candidates sought nomination to the 43 seats in the last four primary elections, 1942-1948, varying from 112 in 1944 to

133 in 1946.[2] The metropolitan areas had the largest number of aspirants. In fourteen instances in the last four elections one district or another had from six to eleven names on the primary ballot, which may be some indication of the attraction of legislative office. Although a number of districts have but a single candidate in some elections, no legislative member, even one of long legislative service, seems to have sewed up his constituency so completely as not to face a rival in the primary, in one election year or another.

VOTER INTEREST

Election statistics indicate that Nebraska voters are interested in their legislators. The number of votes cast may be used as a criterion because the ballot form, having no device or column for straight party voting, does not inflate the vote cast for legislators. Although the legislative section is located about two thirds of the way down the ballot, a position normally attracting fewer votes, more than four fifths of the voters at each of the past four elections have cast votes for legislative candidates. The percentage is slightly higher in congressional than in presidential years, being 84 per cent in 1946, when the total vote otherwise at the election was much lower. Again, although only half as many voters turn out to the primaries as to general elections, of those who do turn out, 80 to 88 per cent in the past four primaries have voted for the "nonpolitical" legislative candidates.

EXPERIENCED MEMBERSHIP

Each legislature has had a sufficient number of former members present to lend the weight of experience and the "know-how" of political and technical procedure and intralegislative leadership. In the 1949 session 28 of the 43 members had been former members, 26 of them in the previous term. Some members had had a long

---

[2] This is, of course, far from the 283 aspirants for the first unicameral election as reported by L. E. Aylsworth, *National Municipal Review*, 26 (February, 1937), 78.

period of continuous service, one of them (from the Omaha area) for seven prior terms. Two members had served in five previous legislatures, four in four, two in three, ten in two, and nine in only one. As late as 1949 four members had had part of their prior experience in the former bicameral legislature, and three had been members of the first unicameral legislature.

In some respects the legislature of 1945 was even more impressive in experienced membership than that of 1949. Thirty could point to previous membership, nineteen of them for two or more terms. One of its members had seven prior terms to his credit, six of them in the bicameral legislature. In fact, nine members in that legislature had served in one or the other of the bicameral houses. Nebraska laws are not made by inexperienced legislators.

The quality of membership, other than evidenced by previous legislative experience, was reported for the first two or three of the unicameral sessions to be reasonably high, and better than in the bicameral legislature.[3] This record seems to have been maintained. Many members have had some form of local recognition or distinction prior to election. Sixteen in 1945 had served on local school boards, some of them for many years. Four had been city attorneys, and several had held some county office, including commissioner, attorney, clerk, and judge. Still others had service on city or village councils, charter commissions, and fair boards. One had been a mayor, another a United States district marshal, and one a member of a state constitutional convention. Several had held local or state-wide office in one of the major political parties. Five members had been presidents of their local chambers of commerce. It is difficult to present this sort of experience in measurable form, but at least two thirds of the members could boast some such distinction.

PROCEDURE AND SAFEGUARDS

The procedure adopted in Nebraska has very well compensated for any lack of safeguards allegedly inherent in a bicameral system,

---

[3] Lane W. Lancaster, *University of Kansas City Law Review,* 11 (December, 1942), 27-28.

where one chamber is expected to review bills passed by the other. The result of this procedure is that bills in the unicameral legislature appear to be better prepared before introduction, and are more adequately considered and more likely to be technically correct than are bills in most American legislatures.

Most bills, or proposed bills, are submitted to the official bill drafters or to the staff of the Legislative Council ahead of the opening, or during the first twenty days, of the session. Few bills are introduced without first having been thus carefully scrutinized as to form and expression. The perfunctory examination observable in some states does not exist in Nebraska. Some members have sought advice of the drafters as to feasibility, or probable constitutionality, of their proposals. Some ask if any other member is contemplating a similar proposal. The drafters, particularly on the Legislative Council staff, must be careful to attend to such a member's wishes and also to protect the privacy of other members' plans. Nevertheless, through their advice and by inviting consultation among members of the legislature, these staff members probably have done much to keep the number of bills somewhere within reasonable limits. This preliminary advice and scrutiny, when coupled with the later review stage in procedure, has no doubt improved the quality of bills.

A bill must take a specified minimum number of steps before becoming law. This procedure is quite deliberate, and some of the oldtimers in the first session or two of the unicameral legislature complained that it was too slow. There is the usual introduction and first reading by title and then reference to committee. The committee, only after a public hearing at a scheduled time announced five days in advance, reports the bill to the general file (first general debate calendar) of the house itself. There it is taken up either in its chronological order, if within the first twenty legislative days, or, thereafter, in the order established by a committee on order and arrangement. After this debate, if favorably considered, and very likely amended, it is referred to the committee on enrollment and review for technical scrutiny. The check-up may amount to rewriting. The bill then returns to the house on select file (a preferred calendar) where, after it has been further considered, it may be sent back to general file, to committee, or back for further review, or, if acceptable, be at once advanced to engrossment by the review committee. After engrossment a bill goes on the final reading (highly preferred) calendar for passage, signature, enrollment, and submittal for executive approval.

Final passage is safeguarded against trickery or precipitable action by the rule that five legislative days must intervene between the technical review of a bill and its consideration on final reading and passage. Further, that final action can come only after the bill has been on final reading file for two legislative days and on a member's desk in reprinted form at least one legislative day.

The bill that is sent back to the standing committee after general file debate may thereafter be indefinitely postponed, but it may be so returned without losing its priority, and then be considered again on general file. A number of such bills have ultimately passed. Various retracings of steps, even to re-engrossment, are possible in order to assure an acceptable bill. However, in the 1949 session for which an analysis has been made in some detail, of the 318 bills that ultimately became law, 224, or 74 per cent, went through without any retracing of steps. Conversely, about a fourth of the bills passed went through some of these added steps, a few of them retracing some steps several times over.

Committees meet and hold bill hearings on a regular schedule, in specified rooms, beginning at two o'clock, unless ordered otherwise by the legislature itself. These rules are adhered to. An apparent attempt at evasion late in the 1949 session was quashed. A committee chairman tried to report to general file a bill to exempt chiropractors from the state's science examination, as though it had the backing of his committee. The legality of the purported committee meeting, not at the scheduled hour and place, and the accuracy of the committee vote, were readily and successfully challenged. Bills are reported by committees, either favorably or recommending indefinite postponement. Some bills held too long in committee have been forced out and passed.

Members of the legislature are provided with adequate information about the progress of bills and amendments. Bills are printed and distributed after introduction and reference. Proposed and adopted amendments are inserted in member's bill books, and bills are entirely reprinted before final reading and passage. A summary of the status of bills is distributed daily, and after the first twenty-day period, the general debate agenda likewise.

BILLS HANDLED

The bulk of materials that a legislator has to handle in Nebraska has been greatly reduced by the unicameral change. Frequently under the bicameral legislature the number of bills ran well over a thousand, some of them, of course, duplicate or companion bills. For the last eleven regular sessions of the bicameral legislature an average of 970 bills was introduced. This average dropped to 511, or by 47 per cent, for the seven regular sessions of the unicameral. Of course, a count of bills gives no inkling of the nature of the measures handled, one-paragraph or two-hundred-page, unopposed or highly controversial, but it is significant in the measurement of the bulk to be dealt with.

In contrast to the bill record, the number of laws passed has increased over the same period from an average of 226 to 246, or 9 per cent. To put it another way, a larger proportion of the bills introduced is considered favorably and passed, an increase from 23 to 48 per cent. Modern conditions call for more and more lawmaking in Nebraska as elsewhere. Also, as elsewhere, most of the measures are not new law, but merely corrections or amendments to statutes already long in force. The improvement in quality over that of earlier enactments cannot, of course, be stated precisely, but persons most intimately concerned are confident of considerable improvement. A review of the sessional procedure and flow of work reveals that this improvement in product is not surprising.

THE FLOW OF SESSIONAL WORK

After the first twenty legislative days of a session bills may be introduced only on recommendation of the governor or by majority vote of a standing committee and consent of a majority of the membership of the legislature. Late introduction by a seldom-withheld unanimous consent, so common elsewhere, does not take place in Nebraska. Only a handful of bills, 17 out of 546 in 1949, were introduced after the deadline, so that a program of the session can to some extent be prepared after the close of the initial period.

Beginning in the second or third week, a steady stream of committee reports brings bills to debate files, with the peak production reached about the middle of the session. Likewise, the peak of bills ultimately disposed of comes at about the middle of the session. Three fourths of the bills of the 1947 session were reported out of committee at about midsession. In 1949, 55 per cent of the bills destined to be defeated had already been indefinitely postponed by the end of the eleventh week of the twenty-one week session, and 53 per cent of the bills to pass had already been enacted. Many of these, of course, were what a critical member described in 1937 as "chicken feed" bills.[4]

Sessional progress is well illustrated in the chart on page 249. At the end of the fourteenth week in 1949, when the session was two thirds of the way along, 87 per cent of the defeated bills had been disposed of, and so had 71 per cent of those ultimately passed. The latter part of the session had a declining number of bills to be handled, most of them, of course, the toughest nuts to crack. The number of bills to be handled declined until only eight bills were dealt with in the last week. The governor had on his desk after the close of the session only thirteen bills, the number usually being under twenty. In 1947 the number left with the governor was forty-five, but even this is a small number compared with that of most state legislatures.

Regular legislative sessions now last a little longer than the earlier bicameral sessions. Special sessions are no more frequent nor any longer. The more deliberate procedure seems to have caused the lengthening of the regular session, though by less than 14 per cent, or an average of twelve legislative days, from 88 to 100.

---

[4] *State Government,* 10 (July, 1937), 132-33.

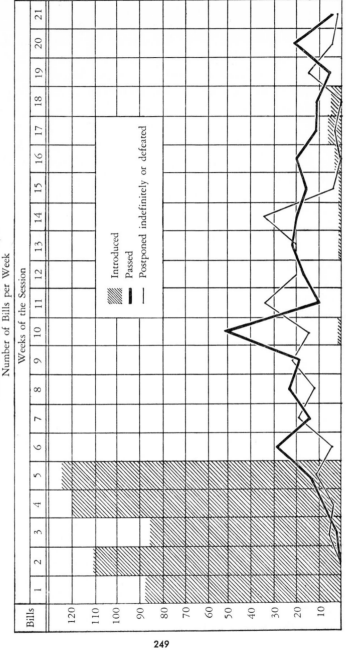

FLOW OF LEGISLATIVE WORK
Nebraska Unicameral Legislature, 1949
Number of Bills per Week

COORDINATION AND LEADERSHIP

Leadership, direction, and coordination of effort are necessary to get the work done, even in 100 days. Several factors contribute to program direction, but political party leadership is ruled out, at least on the surface. The fact that the Republicans outnumber the Democrats in Nebraska by about three to one, coupled with the nonpartisan primary and ballot features, probably means that the larger party does not fear the smaller. Members are not always acquainted with each other's party affiliations. Earlier sessions of the unicameral house experienced elections to offices, or to important committee posts, across party lines, and this continues.[5] The powerful chairmanship of appropriations (budget) in both 1947 and 1949 was entrusted to a Democrat.

Without party labels for members, the governor is of help largely on a business and logical basis varying with the subject in hand. His influence is important but not decisive. Some bills become law without his signature, and three bills were passed over his veto in 1949. The fact that heads of departments, who are more or less independent of the governor, have to deal through the governor on budget requests to a single-chamber legislature, however, seems to have simplified relations between administration and legislature, and the public seems to be better aware of these relations than formerly.

Sessional coordination or leadership comes from within the legislative organization itself, because a program evolves and members do not adjourn until the work is done. Seniority plays a part. At least, an experienced member always heads each committee; and usually the more important committees, especially budget, have few first-term members. The lieutenant governor sometimes seems to hesitate to relinquish the chair to the speaker, but his and the speaker's influence is largely personal.

The pyramidal committee structure aids coordination. There are only eleven subject-matter committees. A committee on committees, composed of a chairman elected at large and three members nomi-

---

[5] For first three sessions see Lancaster, *op. cit.*, pages 25-26.

COMMITTEE ORGANIZATION
Nebraska Unicameral Legislature

Lieutenant Governor

Speaker

Chairman

Reference Committee
Lieutenant Governor
Speaker
Chairman, Committee
on Committees
Assigns bills to
Committees

Committee on Committees
Chairman elected by Legislature at large.
3 members nominated by fellow members from
each of the 4 congressional districts, elected
by the Legislature.
Nominates other standing and select committee
memberships, including chairmen, for election
by Legislature.
Refers governor's appointments to committee.
Schedules bill-committee hearings.

Committee on Order and Arrangement
Chairman, Committee on Committees.
Chairman of bill committees and of
Enrollment and Review.
Determines agenda, after first 20
legislative days, for full legisla-
tive consideration of bills.

Line of participation in agenda making
Line of nomination and hearing scheduling

Agriculture
9 Members

Banking,
Commerce,
Insurance
9 Members

Education
9 Members

Miscellaneous
Appropriations,
Claims
7 Members

Public Works
9 Members

Labor,
Public Welfare
9 Members

Public Health,
Miscellaneous
7 Members

Revenue,
Salaries
9 Members

Budget,
State Institutions
9 Members

Government
9 Members

Judiciary
9 Members

Enrollment
and Review
Chairman only

Technical drafting service

nated by their fellows from each of the four congressional districts of the state and approved by the house early in the session, serves as a nominating committee for other committees, including the designation of their chairmen. The committee on committees serves also as the reference committee for the governor's nominations. The chairman of the committee on committees, the lieutenant governor, and the speaker constitute the reference committee for the assignment of bills and resolutions to standing committees.

Beginning after the twentieth legislative day, after the great bulk of the bills have been introduced, a committee on order and arrangement operates as a program or agenda committee in determining the order in which bills are debated on general file, select file, and final reading file. This committee does not, and seems to have no reason to, assume the functions of the powerful, perhaps self-appointed, and thoroughly hated sifting committees found in so many other legislatures, because in Nebraska all bills have had an opportunity to be considered anyway. The composition of the committee on order and arrangement fits its function, being composed of the chairmen of the subject-matter committees and the chairman of the committee on enrollment and review.

Some committees by the nature of their subject matter, or by traditional pre-eminence, have greater influence than others, and their work greatly affects the others. First in this respect undoubtedly is the budget committee, followed probably by either judiciary or government (handling state and local government bills), or, at times, revenue. In general, the bills appear to be distributed fairly well among the eleven subject-matter or bill-considering committees, but judiciary usually gets by far the greatest number and the widest variety of bills, and occasionally has been thought by some observers to be a little aggressive in its reach for bills.

The appropriations procedure is, of course, an instrument of coordination. The budget committee's general appropriation bill was reported to general file in 1949 on the first legislative day in May, which was the first of the eighteenth week of the twenty-one week session, after nearly nine tenths of the bills of the session had been disposed of and some of the most difficult ones left. It was the last bill passed, the only bill passed on the last day of the session. If the budget chairman had failed to use his strategic position to influence the course of some of the other work of the session, he probably would not have been so readily identified as the most powerful figure in the legislature.

PRESSURES AND OBJECTIVE OPERATION

Leadership or domination cannot, apparently, be attributed to lobby pressures in Nebraska, even though powerful influences are present, because the spotlight of publicity is on them in a single-house legislature as much as on the legislature itself. Although the reported expenditures of several prominent lobbying interests for the last month of the 1949 session ran from several hundred to well over a thousand dollars, lobbyists have been reduced, it is said, merely to the role of the good fellow.

Pressures from local or district sources seem to be much more prominent than other lobby pressures, except, of course, as pressure interests manage to siphon their influence through local channels. Local forces naturally tend to be more disruptive than integrative to a sessional program. This situation was apparent in connection with a few bills in the 1949 session, particularly when, as the legislature elevated four state teachers' colleges to full degree-granting status, some people were able to claim that by vote-trading the state was saddled with the expense of five state universities so that Omaha would not lose gas tax money. These practices do not seem to have caused undue alarm, for everyone knew what the others were doing when it came to formal and official action. The public could also know, because newspaper reporters are barred from nothing, not even executive committee sessions.

The fact that the office of the clerk of the legislature was put on a permanent, year-round basis, and the Legislative Council with research and reference facilities was created should not be overlooked as having a bearing on effective legislative operation. The council and its committees, with the director of research assisting, have gained an enviable reputation for fair hearings and careful preparation of reports and bills in the interim between sessions and for assistance during sessions. Instead of charging the council members and the director of research with being aggressive, legislators have sought council positions and finally, in 1949, passed an act placing all members of the legislature on the council so that the work of committees could be spread further. The staff of the council was also strengthened for the study of state administration and the possibility of amending the constitution. The fact that such an agency can be trusted and utilized so effectively speaks well for the legislature.

CRITICISMS AND PROSPECTS

Unicameralism appears to have come to Nebraska to stay; most people now take it for granted. Some of the earlier opponents of the change were converted, as was a former lieutenant governor who served as the new legislature's president.[6] Others are now seldom heard from, so that today no one of any prominence suggests a return to two houses. Numerous politicians of both major parties have repeatedly urged partisan elections, but no one seems to be eager enough to make a serious proposal for that change. Even gubernatorial predilection for leadership through partisan labels is said to be softening with time. The part played by political parties in state lawmaking is probably exaggerated in most states because of partisan fervor, as was apparently true of Nebraska under bicameralism.[7]

Many local political interests want the legislature increased in size. If this is done, the disintegrative effects of localism would no doubt be increased, and the legislative positions could become merely "local" offices at the disposal of election-managing cliques. Legislative salaries are admittedly very low, but members hesitate to fight very hard for an increase when they are unwilling to increase the compensation of administrative offices. Longer legislative terms of office and annual sessions have also had their persistent advocates.

The legislature in 1949 proposed a constitutional amendment that

---

[6] *State Government,* 12 (November, 1939), 197-98, 207. Apparently some attempt to restore bicameralism will be made in 1954.—*National Municipal Review,* 42 (December, 1953), 563-64.

[7] Ralph S. Boots, *National Municipal Review,* 13 (February, 1924), 115-18.

called for four-year terms, half the members to be elected every two years, for either annual or biennial sessions, and for the power to fix legislative salaries by statute. If annual sessions were provided, the even-year session would be limited to consideration of budgetary appropriations and confirmation of appointments. A petition for an initiative proposal was also started in 1949. It would have increased the membership to not fewer than 75 nor more than 85. It would also have increased salaries somewhat but retained a constitutional limit on the amount. If this measure had appeared on the ballot with the legislative proposal the voter could have had some difficulty in making a choice. Neither proposal affected the essential character of unicameralism. Neither provided for partisan elections. However, the latter failed to reach the ballot, and the legislature's own proposal was voted down.

In conclusion, it may be suggested that legislators are not rendered infallible or virtuous by being confined to a single chamber. No session can please everyone. Pressures, lobbies, local influence, and personal ambition are not eliminated. They are merely obliged to operate in a fairly simple structure where procedure can be observed and reported to the public currently, understandably, and more accurately than is possible among the cross currents of two houses and their various standing and conference committees. Informed Nebraskans are not inclined to dispute the testimony of a veteran Lincoln newspaper reporter: "Having observed the old way and the new, I unequivocally say that the new way is immeasurably the better."[8]

---

[8] *National Municipal Review*, 30 (September, 1941), 514. See also findings of Professor John P. Senning, "Unicameralism Passes Test," *National Municipal Review*, 33 (February, 1944), 60-65. Dr. Roger V. Shumate, writing after the close of the 1951 session, presents a summary of "The Nebraska Unicameral Legislature" in the *Western Political Quarterly*, 5 (September, 1952), 504. He lays some stress on the greater degree of consideration given all bills in the unicameral than has been the experience in the bicameral system, and states that this procedural improvement may reduce somewhat the need for special sessions.

APPENDIX B

The Use of Joint Committees in Massachusetts, Maine, and Connecticut

THE JOINT COMMITTEE, or the system of committees in which members of both houses of the legislature are represented jointly, is frequently cited as a device that will improve legislative deliberation, permit maximum consideration at hearings, save time for both the legislature and the public, and expedite the legislative process. It is surprising indeed that only three states—Massachusetts, Maine, and Connecticut—have adopted a system of joint committees for consideration of legislation. Twenty additional states have one or more joint committees for limited and special purposes.[1] A few states have a joint committee on finance.

At one time or another all New England legislatures utilized a system of joint committees. Vermont is reported to have abandoned the system in 1917 because of the feeling that it nullified to a degree

---

[1] A number of states have some of the features of the joint committee system. California, Washington, Utah, Vermont, and Wisconsin make it possible for committees of both houses to hold meetings jointly for hearings. Arkansas, Mississippi, and Maryland provide for joint investigatory committees, and California, Illinois, Indiana, Iowa, Mississippi, New Hampshire, New Jersey, Rhode Island, Vermont, Virginia, West Virginia, and Wyoming employ the joint committee on strictly procedural matters, such as enrollment or engrossment of bills, printing, revision, and rules. C. I. Winslow, *State Legislative Committees: A Study in Procedure* (Johns Hopkins University Press, 1931), pp. 32-37. See study made by State Law Section, Library of Congress, 1947, entitled "Provisions in the Joint Rules of the State Legislatures for Joint Standing Committees."

the principle of bicameralism.[2] There is a great deal of interest in the experience of Connecticut, Maine, and Massachusetts with the joint committee system as a device for streamlining state legislatures. These three states follow essentially the same pattern with slight variations.[3]

In all three states the chairman of a joint committee is always a senator and the vice-chairman a representative. Because of frequent conflicts among committee meetings, the chairman is often absent and the vice-chairman presides. If both should be absent, the ranking senator presides. There never has been any rivalry between the house and senate members over the chairmanship of committees. The chairman of the committee does not wield such influence over legislation as is common in most legislative bodies. In Massachusetts the position of the chairman is greatly weakened by the requirement that a report must be given on all bills each session. This requirement eliminates any tendency for a committee or its chairman to be arbitrary in reporting on bills assigned.[4] Bills may be reported to either house by joint committees, but more of them are reported to the house than to the senate. This may be explained by the fact that the house has more members on each committee than the senate, and hence is more likely to have a member who is anxious to push the bill. Furthermore, the house tends to handle bills more expeditiously than the senate.

Although representatives predominate on the joint committees in these three New England states, there has not been a marked division of the vote by house membership. If there is a division, it is more likely to follow party lines. Maine and Massachusetts have been

---

[2] Robert Luce, *Legislative Procedure* (Houghton Mifflin, 1922), p. 137.

[3] Connecticut has 32 joint committees concerned with both legislative and procedural matters plus 5 joint committees concerned with procedures: Contingent Expenses, Manual and Roll, Rules, Public Information, and Engrossed Bills. Maine has joint committees for legislative matters and one for procedure, the Committee on Reference of Bills, which assigns bills to committees. Massachusetts has 29 joint committees with a membership of 15 each (4 senators and 11 representatives). The Committee on the Judiciary has 5 senators and 12 representatives; the Committee on Water Supply has 3 senators and 8 representatives.

[4] See John W. Plaisted, *Legislative Procedure in the General Court of Massachusetts* (Boston: Wright and Potter Printing Co., 1948), pp. 29-33.

one-party states, and concurrence on reports is the rule.[5] However,
in Connecticut, where political control has been divided at times
between the Democrats in the senate and Republicans in the house,
the joint committee has not always succeeded in synthesizing differences. When the vote in joint committee is split to any degree, it has
not been uncommon for both majority and minority reports to be
filed. In Connecticut the two houses have often received separate
reports, but in Massachusetts and Maine, where party control has
not been by houses, minority reports accompany the majority reports.[6]

In New England the use of joint committees has not eliminated
the necessity for conference committees. Conference committees are
created during or following deliberation by the two houses, and their
operation and conduct is not unlike that of conference committees in
other states. In conference committees the membership seems to be
more conscious of particular chamber connections, and the members
act more as agents of their respective houses than do those of joint
committees. It has been impossible to eliminate the conference committee because frequently a bill may be assigned to several joint com-

[5] This remains the rule in Massachusetts even though the Democrats got
control of the legislature in 1949. They gained such complete control of the
house and of half of the senate that the practice was not changed. Edith L.
Hary, Law and Legislative Reference Librarian of the Maine State Library,
observed that: "In Maine the Republican Party so far outnumbers the Democratic in the Legislature that on any one committee the Democratic membership
is so small or non-existent that it is almost immaterial. Generally speaking,
therefore, if a Democratic measure is under consideration the vote will be
along party lines; if it is a strictly Republican measure, the Democratic committee members may disapprove, but on the bulk of the bills discussed, the
vote will represent the individual judgments of the members." Letter to L. G.
Harvey, September 6, 1949.

[6] Thomas J. Wood found in an analysis of 7,400 joint committee reports for
four sessions (1941-46) in Massachusetts that there was a surprising degree of
unanimity. Of these reports, 86.5 per cent were without formal dissenting
vote, and another 6 per cent had only one dissenting vote. Only 1.6 per cent
of the reports demonstrated any great divergency or split votes. Wood noted
that when committees reported upon legislation favorably there was even
greater unanimity. Of these reports, 92.5 per cent were by unanimous vote.
However, he observed that even in reporting adversely on measures 80.9 per
cent of the reports carried no dissenting vote. Probably one reason there is
less rivalry in Massachusetts between the representatives and senators is that
the same interests are represented. The urban-rural cleavage is not as marked
as in Connecticut. Thomas J. Wood, *Distinctive Practices of the Massachusetts General Court* (Ph.D. dissertation, Harvard University, 1947), p. 44.

mittees. Disagreement on reports of these committees often makes it necessary for conference committees to be established.

The success of the joint committee in New England is not entirely due to its joint character. Until recent years the legislatures have consisted of members representing the same interests and political party (Republican).[7]

ADVANTAGES OF THE JOINT COMMITTEE

Marked Saving of Time

Joint committees are almost always able to have a quorum at their meetings, mainly because members of the lower house, who constitute a large majority of the membership of each committee, have fewer conflicting committee assignments than the senators. This feature in itself is an important factor in the success of the joint committee. The committee meetings are regular and certain. The petitioner and interested person find it much easier to attend one hearing than two conducted by separate committees.

Fewer Companion Bills

The use of companion bills is cut to the minimum by employing joint committees. To be sure, at times companion bills appear in the two houses in Connecticut, Maine, and Massachusetts, especially if they are for measures attracting popular attention; legislators frequently want the publicity that may come from supporting certain measures. But in these three states companion bills are a minor

---

[7] In Connecticut, where there has been the greatest cleavage between the house and senate because of the split in party control, the joint character of the committees has at times been severely challenged. In 1941 the legislature abolished joint committees and resorted to individual committees in each house. Fortunately, the names of the committees were not changed except to be preceded with "Senate" or "Representative." Soon they were meeting jointly, as if by habit, in order to handle hearings more expeditiously, although they did make separate reports to the two chambers.—*Annual Report of the Legislative Council* (Hartford, 1944), p. 17. In 1949 many bills were reported by one wing of the committee only and were referred back to committee for reconsideration when there was disagreement between the two wings of the committee. Even though the joint committee does not work so well in Connecticut as it does in Maine and Massachusetts, it is preferred to single committees in each house. The experiment of 1941 lasted for only one session.

problem. In New York, on the other hand, they were found to constitute more than three fifths of the bills before the assembly and more than two thirds of those before the senate.[8] And in California companion bills have presented an acute problem, for hundreds of bills are passed twice by both houses, and the governor is frequently in a quandary as to which bill to sign and which to veto.[9]

Companion bills are usually considered separately by the two houses of the legislature, with no attempt at concurrence on either their amendment or the scheduling of hearings. This situation is markedly improved by joint committees, which dispose of companion bills in short order. Although no bills can be pigeonholed in Massachusetts—all must be reported upon—companion bills can easily be reported together by cross reference.

Use of Single Reports

In Maine and Massachusetts differences are ironed out in committee session of joint committees, and a single report is given both houses in practically all cases. Minority reports may be attached, but in Massachusetts they are usually reports of the opposition party.

Less Use of Conference Committees

It is difficult to determine to what extent the joint committees reduce the reference of bills to conference committees. Thomas J. Wood discovered that for the years 1941-1946, 2 per cent of the bills that passed both houses in Massachusetts and 10 per cent of the bills amended by one house were assigned to conference committees.[10] Franklin L. Burdette found that for a comparable period in Nebraska (1921-1933) 10.9 per cent of the bills that passed both houses and 27.2 per cent of the bills amended by one house were subject to conference.[11]

---

[8] *Final Report of the New York State Joint Legislative Committee on Legislative Methods, Practices, Procedures and Expenditures,* Legislative Document (1946), No. 31, pp. 64-65.

[9] *Ibid.,* p. 67.

[10] Wood, *op. cit.,* p. 49.

[11] "Conference Committees in the Nebraska Legislature," *American Political Science Review,* 30 (December, 1936), 1115.

Reduction of Committee Meetings and Conflicts

Use of joint legislative committees reduces the number of committees needed and thus can eliminate many of the conflicts in committee meetings. However, in the three states now using joint committees lack of attention to advance scheduling has caused frequent conflict. In fact, the record of these three states on this point is not as good as that of some legislatures not using joint committees that have exercised greater care.[12]

CONDITIONS FOR SUCCESS OF JOINT COMMITTEES

The success of the joint committee depends upon a number of factors:

1. Joint committees must be relatively few in number to permit a good distribution of membership of the two houses.

2. Both senators and representatives must be limited in committee assignments.

3. Committee meetings must be carefully scheduled to eliminate conflicts and assure a maximum attendance. They must also be scheduled early enough in the sessions to assure adequate deliberation.

4. Bills must be filed early enough to permit adequate consideration by committees. In Massachusetts, where any adult may file a petition if a member of the legislature will agree to sign it, such petitions must be filed by December first for January sessions.[13]

5. The joint committee system works more smoothly where there is an overwhelming majority of one party.

---

[12] Wood (*op. cit.*, p. 50) found that there were fewer conflicts in committee meetings in the California legislature with its separate committees than in the Massachusetts legislature, which uses joint committees.

[13] This early time limit has been necessary in Massachusetts, which continues the practice from colonial days of granting to every adult the right to petition the legislature, a heritage of the British practice of the right to petition Parliament. These petitions may be introduced as bills if signed by a member of either house. The legislator in signing does not endorse the measure. John Adams objected to this practice, but it continues. The great volume of such petitions, running into the thousands each session, has made it necessary to require that they be filed a month in advance of the date for convening the legislature in order to permit their being printed before the legislature assembles.

APPENDIX C

Provisions of Retirement Plans That Include State Legislators

State, Date Law Enacted, Administrative Agency*	No. Legs.*	Basis of Inclusion	Optional	Minimum Age	Minimum Service	Contributions by— Leg.	Contributions by— State	Withdrawal of Funds upon Discontinuance of Service Leg. Cont.	Int.	Retirement Benefits
California, 1949, Bd. of State Emp. Ret. Sys.	121	Special system: legislators and constitutionally elected officials	Yes	63	None	4.82-11.61%	7.20%	Yes	Yes (2½%)	5% final compensation per yr. of service; maximum 75% final salary
Florida, 1949, State Off. and Emp. Sys.	133	Elected officials	Yes	60	10	5%	⅗ leg. cont.	Yes	No	2% salary per yr. of service; 40% 20 yrs. service
Illinois, 1947, Bd. of Tr. General Assembly Ret. Sys.	204	Special system	May elect not to participate	60	8	7%	Actuarial needs	Yes	No	2½% final annual salary per yr. of eligible service, or 20% for 8 yrs.; maximum 50% for 20 yrs. Disability after 10 yrs. Widow's annuity ⅔ amount.
Maryland, 1953, Bd. of Tr. Emp. Ret. Sys.	152	Elected officials	Yes	60	None	4.15-7.15% Women: 4.3-8%	2.58%	Yes	Yes	1/70 annual average salary per yr. of service

System	No.	Coverage		Age	Yrs.			Pub.		Retirement allowance
Mississippi, SB 273, Laws 1952, Emp. Ret. Sys.	189	Members of 1952 legislature and subsequent legislators	No	65	None	1¼% (3¼% by 1970)	1¼% (3¼% by 1970)	Yes	Yes	55% of first $100 average monthly salary since 1951 plus 15% of amount over $100
Montana, 1947, Bd. of Adm. Pub. Emp. Ret. Sys.	146	Elected officials	Yes	60	10	3–8.2% Women: 3.5–9.6%	3.6% (3–7% before 7/1/47)	Yes	2½%	Actuarial equivalent of contributions since 7/1/45; % average salary last 3 yrs. before 1945 (age 65, 35 yrs. service—50% final salary)
New Jersey, 1947, 1953, Bd. of Tr.	81	Elected officials	Yes	60	None	4.12–8.27% Women: 4.14–8.65%	1.37–6.37%	Yes	4%	1/60 average annual salary per yr. of service; after 25 yrs. service retirement as actuarial yr. 60
New Mexico, 1947, Pub. Emp. Ret. Bd.	73	Elected officials	Yes	65 or 70	15 / 5	3½%	3½%	Yes	2½%	1½% highest annual salary in preceding 10 yrs. per yr. of service; maximum $150 per month
New York, 1947, Emp. Ret. Sys.	206	Legislators	Yes	60	None	Actuarial basis	Actuarial basis	Yes	Yes	1/140 average annual salary per yr. of service plus annuity
Ohio, 1947, Pub. Emp. Sys.	175	Elected officials	Yes	60	5	5%	3%	Yes	1½%	Actuarial equivalent of contributions; $400 credit for service before 1935

263

Provisions of Retirement Plans—continued

State, Law Enacted, Date, Administrative Agency*	No. Legs.*	Basis of Inclusion	Optional	Minimum—Age	Service	Contributions by— Leg.	State	Withdrawal of Funds upon Discontinuance of Service Leg. Cont.	Int.	Retirement Benefits
Pennsylvania, 1947, 1949, State Ret. Bd.	258	Employees	Yes	60	None	5.08–9.77%	Amount to meet needs	Yes	4%	2% annual salary per yr. of service; 50% final salary maximum for state annuity, exclusive of member's annuity
Rhode Island, 1947, Emp. Ret. Bd.	144	Employees	Yes	60	10	5%	4½%	Yes	No	1/60 average salary per yr. of service
South Carolina, 1945, Ret. Bd.	170	Employees	No	60	10	4%	5.1%	Yes	4%	Actuarial equivalent of contributions
Washington, 1949, Ret. Bd.	145	Elected officials	Yes	60	10	5%	4%	Yes	Yes	Actuarial plan plus $100 plus 1/140 average annual salary; maximum $800 per yr.

* Bd.—Board   Emp.—Employees   Ret.—Retirement   Sys.—System   Off.—Officials   Tr.—Trustees   Pub.—Public   Adm.—Administration
Leg.—Legislator

Bibliography

GENERAL

Alabama Legislative Reference Service, *General Laws with Local Application* (1950).

Bartley, Ernest R., *The Legislative Process in Florida* (University of Florida, Public Administration Clearing Service, 1950).

Bebout, John E., *The Making of the New Jersey Constitution* (Trenton, N. J.: MacCrellish & Quigley, 1945).

Benton, Wilbourn E., *Population Bracket Bills in Texas: A Study of Local and Special Legislation* (Unpublished dissertation, University of Texas, 1948).

Brake, Hale D., "Practical Suggestions and Prospects for Legislative Reform," *State Government,* 20 (June, 1947), 161-64, 178-79.

Bromage, Arthur W., "Restrictions on Financial Powers of the Legislature in Michigan," *State Government,* 20 (May, 1947), 141-43, 153.

Buck, A. E., *Modernizing Our State Legislatures* (Philadelphia: American Academy of Political and Social Science, 1936).

Caldwell, Lynton K., "Strengthening State Legislatures," *American Political Science Review,* 41 (April, 1947), 281-89.

Catterson, Lorace E., "The Legislative Process in Florida," Florida State University Studies, *History and Political Science,* No. 4 (Tallahassee: Florida State University, 1951), 61-136.

Chamberlain, Joseph P., *Legislative Processes: National and State* (Appleton-Century, 1936).

Chase, Fred I., *How Michigan Makes Her Laws* (Michigan Public Expenditure Survey, 1946).

Coigne, Armand B., *Statute Making: A Treatise on the Means and Methods for the Enactment of Statute Law in the United States* (Chicago: Commerce Clearing House, 1948).

Cooper, Charles M., *General Laws with Local Application, 1940-1950* (Alabama Legislative Reference Service, 1950).

Corrick, Franklin, *Report on the Validity of Special Legislation in Kansas* (Topeka: Revisor of Statutes, 1945).

The Council of State Governments, *The Book of the States* (biennial editions, Chicago).

————, *Our State Legislatures* (rev. ed., Chicago, 1948).

————, *State-Local Relations* (Chicago, 1946).

Dority, Ione E., *General Constitutional Revision in the States: A Selected List of References Covering the Period 1937-1947* (University of Michigan, Bureau of Government, 1948).

Evans, Alvin E., "The Nature of Municipal Legislation," *Kentucky Law Journal*, 40 (May, 1952), 384-99.

Everstine, Carl N., "The Establishment of Legislative Power in Maryland," *Maryland Law Review*, 12 (Spring, 1951), 99-121.

Farmer, Hallie, *The Legislative Process in Alabama* (University of Alabama, Bureau of Public Administration, 1949).

Geary, T. C., *Law Making in South Dakota* (rev. ed., University of South Dakota, Governmental Research Bureau, Report No. 19, 1949).

Graves, W. Brooke, *American State Government* (4th ed., Heath, 1953).

————(ed), "Our State Legislators," *The Annals* of the American Academy of Political and Social Science, vol. 195 (January, 1938).

————, "Writing a New Constitution," *National Municipal Review*, 31 (February, 1942), 92-99.

Gregorie, Anne K., "Legislators Usurp Counties," *National Municipal Review*, 37 (July, 1948), 361-63, 376.

Harkey, Paul, "Televising the Legislature in Oklahoma," *State Government*, 24 (October, 1951), 249-50.

Harris, Joseph P., "Modernizing the Legislature," *National Municipal Review*, 36 (March, 1947), 142-46.

Hawaii Legislative Reference Bureau, *Manual on State Constitutional Provisions* (1950).

————,*Territorial Legislative Organization and Procedure* (1949).

Hindman, Wilbert L., "Road Blocks to Conventions," *National Municipal Review*, 37 (March, 1948), 129-32, 144.

Hounshell, Charles D., *The Legislative Process in Virginia* (University of Virginia, Extension Division, 1951).

Johnson, Claudius O., *State and Local Government* (Crowell, 1950).

Jones, Chester, *Statute Law-Making in the United States* (Boston Book Company, 1912).

Kammerer, Gladys M., "Kentucky's Legislature under the Spotlight," *Kentucky Law Journal*, 39 (November, 1950), 45-63.

Keith, John P., *Methods of Constitutional Revision* (University of Texas, Bureau of Municipal Research, 1949).

Kentucky Legislative Research Commission, *Kentucky's General Assembly, a Working Legislature* (1952).

League of Women Voters of Minnesota, *Ninety Days of Lawmaking in Minnesota* (rev. ed., University of Minnesota Press, 1949).

Lederle, John W., "State Legislative Reorganization," *Marquette Law Review*, 31 (February, 1948), 272-80.

Luce, Robert, *Legislative Assemblies* (Houghton Mifflin, 1924).

McHenry, Dean E., *A New Legislature for Modern California* (Los Angeles: Haynes Foundation, 1949).

Mallison, W. T., Jr., "General versus Special Statutes in Ohio," *Ohio State Law Journal*, 11 (Autumn, 1950), 462-94.

Maryland Commission on Administrative Organization of the State, *Local Legislation in Maryland* (1952).

Minnesota, Constitutional Commission of, *Reports* (1948).

Napier, Milton F., *The Legislative Process in Missouri and How It Works* (St. Louis: 1950).

National Municipal League, Committee on State Government, *Model State Constitution, with Explanatory Articles* (5th ed., 1948).

Neuberger, Richard L., "The Decay of State Governments," *Harper's*, 207 (October, 1953), 34-41.

New York State Joint Legislative Committee on Legislative Methods, Practices, Procedures and Expenditures, *Interim Report* (Leg. Doc. 35, 1945); *Final Report* (Leg. Doc. 31, 1946).

Nixon, Clarence H., "The Southern Legislatures and Legislation," *Journal of Politics*, 10 (May, 1948), 410-17.

Nokes, George O., Jr., "Constitution and Legislature in Texas," *State Government*, 21 (July, 1948) 149-53.

North Carolina Commission on Public-Local and Private Legislation Authorized by the 1947 General Assembly, "Report," *Popular Government* (February-March, 1949), entire issue.

Ohm, Howard F., "Legislative Reference in Wisconsin," *State Government*, 21 (December, 1948), 240-43, 253.

Oklahoma State Legislative Council, *Oklahoma Constitutional Studies* (1950).

———, *Strengthening the Legislative Process* (1948).

O'Rourke, Vernon A., and Campbell, D. W., *Constitution-Making in a Democracy: Theory and Practice in New York State* (Johns Hopkins Press, 1943).

Perkins, John A., "State Legislative Reorganization," *American Political Science Review,* 40 (June, 1946), 510-21.

————, "The Legislatures and the Future of the States," *State Government,* 19 (October, 1946), 254-57, 266.

Philbrick, Frederick A., *Language and the Law; the Semantics of Forensic English* (Macmillan, 1949).

Porter, Kirk H., "The Administrative Process and the Quasi-legislative Process," *Iowa Law Review,* 37 (Fall, 1951), 21-35.

Powell, Alden L., "Constitutional Growth and Revision in the South," *Journal of Politics,* 10 (May, 1948), 354-84.

Prendergast, William B., "State Legislatures and Communism: the Current Scene," *American Political Science Review,* 44 (September, 1950), 556-74.

Read, Horace E., and MacDonald, John W., *Cases and Other Materials on Legislation* (Foundation Press, 1948).

Reed, Thomas H. (ed.), *Legislatures and Legislative Problems* (University of Chicago Press, 1933).

"Record of 1949-50 Massachusetts Legislature Indicates Need for Reform," *Taxtalk* (Massachusetts Federation of Taxpayers Association), July-August, 1950.

Short, Lloyd M., "Constitutional Revision in Minnesota," *State Government,* 23 (May, 1950), 97-99.

Siffin, Catherine F., *Shadow Over the City: Special Legislation for Tennessee Municipalities* (University of Tennessee Record, June, 1951).

Smith, Dick, *How Bills Become Law in Texas* (University of Texas, Bureau of Municipal Research, 1945).

Smith, Rhoten A., *The Life of a Bill* (University of Kansas, Governmental Research Bureau, 1947).

Smith, Thomas V., *The Legislative Way of Life* (University of Chicago Press, 1940).

South Carolina Joint Committee on Reorganization, *Legislative Reorganization Findings and Recommendations* (1949).

Sutherland, Jabez G., *Statutes and Statutory Construction* (3 vols., Callaghan, 1943).

Toepel, M. G., "The Legislative Reference Library: Serving Wisconsin," *Wisconsin Law Review,* 1951 (January, 1951), 114-24.

Underwood, Cecil H., *The Legislative Process in West Virginia* (West Virginia Bureau for Government Research, 1953).

Walker, Harvey, *The Legislative Process: Law Making in the United States* (Ronald, 1948).

Webster, Donald H., and others, *The Legislature and Legislative Process in the State of Washington* (1948).

Weeks, O. Douglas., *Research in the American State Legislative Process* (Ann Arbor: J. W. Edwards, 1947).

Weiner, Minnie (comp.), *Schedule of Latest Editions of Federal, State and Territorial Statutory Compilations with Supplements and Subsequent Session Laws to Date* (Office of the General Counsel, Federal Works Agency, 1948).

Young, C. C., *The Legislature of California: Its Membership, Procedure, and Work* (San Francisco: The Commonwealth Club of California, 1943).

REPRESENTATION

Asseff, Emmett, *Legislative Apportionment in Louisiana* (Louisiana State University, Bureau of Government Research, 1950).

Barclay, Thomas S., "Reapportionment in California," *Pacific Historical Review*, 5 (June, 1936), 93-129.

————, "The Reapportionment Struggle in California," *Western Political Quarterly*, 4 (June, 1951), 313-24.

Bemis, George W., "Sectionalism in State Politics," *The Annals* of the American Academy of Political and Social Science, 248 (November, 1946), 232-35.

Birkhead, Guthrie S., "Legislatures Continue to Be Unrepresentative," *National Municipal Review*, 41 (November, 1952), 523-25.

Blair, George S., "Cumulative Voting in Illinois," *National Municipal Review*, 42 (September, 1953), 410-14.

Bone, Hugh A., "States Attempting to Comply with Reapportionment Requirements," *Law and Contemporary Problems*, 17 (Spring, 1952), 387-416.

Brannon, Victor D., "Missouri's Apportionment Key," *National Municipal Review*, 35 (April, 1946), 177-82.

Breckenridge, Adam C., "The Mockery of Classification," *National Municipal Review*, 36 (November, 1947), 571-73.

California State Chamber of Commerce, *Initiative and Referendum in California* (San Francisco, 1940).

Callender, Clarence N., and Charlesworth, James C. (eds.), "Ethical Standards in American Public Life," *The Annals* of the American

Academy of Political and Social Science, 280 (March, 1952)

Christie, Mrs. Ronald, *Problems of Legislative Apportionment* (League of Women Voters of Illinois, 1951).

Colorado Legislative Reference Office, *The Initiative and Referendum in Colorado* (Denver, 1940).

Collings, R. A., Jr., "California's New Lobby Control Act," *California Law Review*, 38 (August, 1950), 478-97.

Commonwealth Club of California, *Direct Legislation* (San Francisco, 1931).

Cottrell, Edwin A., "Twenty-five Years of Direct Legislation in California," *Public Opinion Quarterly*, 3 (January, 1939), 30-45.

Crouch, Winston W., "The Constitutional Initiative in Operation," *American Political Science Review*, 33 (August, 1939), 634-45.

——, *The Initiative and Referendum in California* (Los Angeles: Haynes Foundation, 1950).

Csontos, Mildred B., *History of Legislative Apportionment in New York State, 1777-1940* (New York State Library, 1941).

De Grazia, Alfred, *Public and Republic* (Knopf, 1951).

Dorweiler, Louis C., Jr., "Minnesota Farmers Rule Cities," *National Municipal Review*, 35 (March, 1946), 115-20.

Douglas, Paul H., *Ethics in Government* (Harvard University Press, 1952).

Dowell, J. E., "Apportionment in State Legislatures: The Practice in Florida," *Economic Leaflets* (University of Florida) February, 1948, entire issue.

Durfee, Elizabeth, "Apportionment of Representation in the Legislature: A Study of State Constitutions," *Michigan Law Review*, 43 (June, 1945), 1091-1112.

Echternach, Betty June, *Retirement Systems for Legislators* (Hawaii Legislative Reference Bureau, 1949).

Fairlie, John A., "The Nature of Political Representation," *American Political Science Review*, 34 (April-June, 1940), 236-48, 456-66.

Farmer, Hallie, "Legislative Apportionment" (University of Alabama, Bureau of Public Administration, 1944).

Fifth Annual Statement of the Board of Trustees, General Retirement System of Illinois, June 30, 1948.

Gibbs, Clayton R., *State Regulation of Lobbying, Constitutional and Statutory Provisions of the States*, 9 (The Council of State Governments, 1951).

Greenfield, Margaret, *Legislative Reapportionment* (Berkeley: University of California, Bureau of Public Administration, 1951).

Harris, Joseph P., "Modernizing the Legislature," *National Municipal Review*, 36 (March, 1947), 142-46.

Harvey, Lashley G., "Reapportionment of State Legislatures—Legal Requirements," *Law and Contemporary Problems*, 17 (Spring, 1952), 364-76.

———, "Some Problems of Representation in State Legislatures," *Western Political Quarterly*, 2 (June, 1949), 265-71.

Hawaii Legislative Reference Bureau, *Constitutional Provisions for Legislative Apportionment and Reapportionment* (1948).

Hyneman, Charles H., "Tenure and Turnover of Legislative Personnel," *The Annals* of the American Academy of Political and Social Science, 195 (January, 1938), 21-31.

Illinois Legislative Council, *Reapportionment in Illinois* (1945).

———, *Legislative Apportionment in Illinois* (1952).

Johnson, Claudius O., "The Initiative and Referendum in Washington," *Proceedings* of the Public Affairs Conference, July, 1949.

Kansas Legislative Council, *Annual Legislative Sessions* (1953).

Key, V. O., "Procedures in State Legislative Apportionment," *American Political Science Review*, 26 (December, 1932), 1050-58.

Killpartrick, E. W., "Bay State Lobbyists Toe Mark," *National Municipal Review*, 34 (December, 1945), 536-39, 543.

Korsak, T. Z., and DiSalle, Richard, "Legislative Apportionment in Pennsylvania," *University of Pittsburgh Law Review*, 12 (Winter, 1951), 215-43.

Kramer, Robert (ed.), "Legislative Reapportionment," *Law and Comtemporary Problems*, 17 (Spring, 1952). Entire issue.

Lancaster, Lane W., "Rotten Boroughs and the Connecticut Legislature," *National Municipal Review*, 13 (December, 1924), 678-83.

League of Women Voters of Wisconsin, *Reapportionment* (1952).

Lederle, John W., "Legislative Personnel Given Careful Study," *Michigan State Bar Journal*, 28 (July, 1949), 23-27.

McClain, Robert H., Jr., "Compulsory Reapportionment," *National Municipal Review*, 40 (June, 1951), 305-7, 324.

McConaughy, John B., "Certain Personality Factors of State Legislators in South Carolina," *American Political Science Review*, 44 (December, 1950), 897-903.

McHenry, Dean E., "Urban v. Rural in California," *National Municipal Review*, 35 (July, 1946), 350-54, 388.

McKean, Dayton D., *Pressures on the Legislature of New Jersey* (Columbia University Press, 1938).

MacNeil, Douglas H., "Urban Representation in State Legislatures," *State Government*, 18 (April, 1945), 59-61.

McNickle, R. K., "Legislative Apportionment," *Editorial Research Reports,* 1 (January 3, 1950), 3-19.

Macrae, Duncan, Jr., "The Relation Between Roll Call Votes and Constituencies in the Massachusetts House of Representatives," *American Political Science Review,* 46 (December, 1952), 1046-55.

Mather, W. W., "Geographic Basis for a Unicameral Legislature," *The Annals* of the American Academy of Political and Social Science, 248 (November, 1946), 236-38.

Nebraska Legislative Council, *Report of Committee on Annual Legislative Sessions* (October, 1952).

Neuberger, Richard L., "I Am a $5-a-Day Senator," *This Week Magazine,* January 30, 1949.

———, "Government by the People," *The Survey,* 86 (November, 1950), 490-93.

———, "Our Rotten Borough Legislatures," *The Survey,* 86 (February, 1950), 53-57.

———, "The Country Slicker vs. the City Yokel," *New York Times Magazine,* July 31, 1949, pp. 17, 36 ff.

New Jersey Historical Society, *Study of Apportionment Issue throughout the Legislative History of New Jersey* (1952).

Page, Thomas, *Legislative Apportionment in Kansas* (University of Kansas Bureau of Government Research, 1952).

Pelletier, L. L., "The Initiative and Referendum in Maine," *Bowdoin College Bulletin* (Bureau of Municipal Research, March, 1951).

Pollock, James K., *The Initiative and Referendum in Michigan* (University of Michigan, Bureau of Government, 1940).

Pierce, Melvin, "The 'Third' House in Indiana," *National Municipal Review,* 40 (October, 1951), 473-79.

Radin, Max, "Popular Legislation in California," *Minnesota Law Review,* 23 (April, 1939), 559-84.

Reed, Thomas H. (ed.), "Lobbying," *Legislatures and Legislative Problems* (University of Chicago Press, 1933).

Rutgers University Bureau of Government Research, *Legislative Apportionment in New Jersey: A Survey of Modern Methods Available* (1952).

Schenk, Willis J., *Occupational Profile of the South Dakota Legislature, 1900-1949* (a thesis submitted for the B.A. degree, University of South Dakota, Department of Government, May, 1950).

Schumacher, Waldo, "Reapportionment in Oregon," *Western Political Quarterly,* 3 (September, 1950), 428-34.

————, "Thirty Years of the People's Rule in Oregon," *Political Science Quarterly,* 47 (June, 1932), 242-58.

Scott, E. M., and Zeller, Belle, "State Agencies and Lawmaking," *Public Administration Review,* 2 (Summer, 1942), 205-20.

Sears, Kenneth C., *Methods of Reapportionment* (University of Chicago Law School, 1952).

Short Lloyd M., "States That Have Not Met Their Constitutional Requirements," *Law and Contemporary Problems,* 17 (Spring, 1952), 377-86.

Shull, Charles W., "Political and Partisan Implications of State Legislative Apportionment," *Law and Contemporary Problems,* 17 (Spring, 1952), 417-39.

————, and Leonard, James M., *Reapportionment of the State Legislature in Michigan* (Bureau of Governmental Research, 1941).

————, "Revitalizing Representation," *Social Science,* 25 (October, 1950), 234-38.

Siffin, Catherine Fox, *Shadow over the City* (University of Tennessee, Bureau of Public Administration and Municipal Technical Advisory Service, 1951).

Silverman, Morris, *The Struggle for Reapportionment in New York State* (Yeshiva University, 1949).

Steinbicker, Paul G., and Faust, Martin L., *Manual on the Amending Procedure and the Initiative and Referendum* (Missouri Constitutional Convention of 1943).

Thomas, David Y., "The Initiative and Referendum in Arkansas Comes of Age," *American Political Science Review,* 27 (February, 1933), 66-75.

Tilberry, James H., "Lobbying—A Definition and Recapitulation of Its Practice," *Ohio State Law Journal,* 11 (Autumn, 1950), 557-67.

United States Congress, House Select Committee on Lobbying, *Hearings and Reports* (81st Cong., 2d sess., 1950).

Van der Vries, Bernice T., "Women in Government," *State Government,* 21 (July, 1948), 127-28, 134.

Van Deusen, Glyndon G., *Thurlow Weed: Wizard of the Lobby* (Little, Brown, 1947).

Velie, Lester, "Secret Boss of California," *Collier's,* August 12 and 20, 1949, and reprinted in *Congressional Record,* August 19, 1949, pp. 12096-99.

————, "The Great Unwatched," *The Reader's Digest,* January, 1953.

Walker, Harvey, "Wellsprings of Our Laws," *National Municipal Review,* 28 (October, 1939), 689-93.

Walter, David O., "Reapportionment of State Legislative Districts," *Illinois Law Review*, 37 (1942-43), 20-42.

Weaver, Ellsworth E., *Legislative Apportionment in Utah* (University of Utah, Institute of Government, 1950).

Webster, Donald H., "Voters Take the Law in Hand," *National Municipal Review*, 35 (May, 1946), 240-45.

Weeks, O. Douglas, "Politics in the Legislatures," *National Municipal Review*, 41 (February, 1952), 80-86.

Weinberg, A. A., "Retirement Planning for Public Employees," *State Government*, 20 (January, 1947), 10-19, 32.

"What Congress Pensions Mean," *United States News,* September 6, 1946, pp. 26-27.

Wood, Fred B. (comp.), *Federal and State Laws on Lobbying* (Sacramento, 1949).

Zeller, Belle, *Pressure Politics in New York* (Prentice-Hall, 1937).

————, "State Regulation of Lobbying," *The Book of the States, 1948-49,* and in succeeding editions (Chicago: The Council of State Governments).

ORGANIZATION

Aly, Bower (ed.), *Unicameral Legislatures* (2 vols., Columbia, Mo.: Lucas Brother, 1950).

Arkansas Legislative Council, *Operation Costs of Arkansas General Assembly* (1950).

Asseff, Emmett, *Legislative Apportionment in Louisiana* (Louisiana State University, Bureau of Government Research, 1950).

Brake, Hale D., "Practical Suggestions and Prospects for Legislative Reform," *State Government,* 20 (June, 1947), 161-64, 178-79.

Buehler, E. C. (ed.), *Unicameral Legislatures* (Noble and Noble, 1937).

Burdette, Franklin, "Conference Committees in the Nebraska Legislature," *American Political Science Review,* 30 (December, 1936), 1114-16.

Caldwell, Lynton K., "Strengthening State Legislatures," *American Political Science Review,* 41 (April, 1947), 281-89.

Carroll, Daniel B., *The Unicameral Legislature of Vermont* (Vermont Historical Society, 1933).

Chute, Charlton F., "Meeting a Legislative Crisis," *State Government,* 19 (August, 1946), 199-200.

Cohen, Julius, *Materials and Problems on Legislation* (Bobbs-Merrill, 1949).

Coigne, Armand B., *Statute Making: A Treatise on the Means and Methods for the Enactment of Statute Law in the United States* (Chicago: Commerce Clearing House, 1948).

Colvin, D. L., *The Bicameral Principle in the New York Legislature* (Ph.D. thesis, Columbia University, 1913).

Connecticut Legislative Council, "Joint Committees," *Annual Report* (1944), pp. 15-20.

Culver, Dorothy C., *Legislative Reorganization* (Berkeley: University of California, Bureau of Public Administration, May, 1941).

Faust, Martin L., *Manual on the Legislative Article* (Missouri Constitutional Convention of 1943).

Fletcher, Mona, "Bicameralism as Illustrated by the Nineteenth Assembly of Ohio," *American Political Science Review*, 32 (February, 1938), 80-85.

Griswold, T. I., *Bicameralism in Ohio* (Cleveland: Western Reserve University, 1937).

Hyneman, C. S., and Ricketts, E. F., "Tenure and Turnover of the Iowa Legislature," *Iowa Law Review*, 24 (May, 1939), 673-96.

Illinois Legislative Council, *Annual vs. Biennial Legislative Sessions* (1950).

——, *Committee System of the Illinois General Assembly* (1940).

——, *The Printing of Legislative Bills* (1949).

Johnson, A. W., *The Unicameral Legislature* (Minneapolis: The University of Minnesota Press, 1938).

Kammerer, Gladys M., "Kentucky's Legislature under the Spotlight," *Kentucky Law Journal*, 39 (November, 1950), 45-63.

Lederle, John W., "New York's Legislature under the Microscope," *American Political Science Review*, 40 (June, 1946), 521-27.

——, "State Legislative Reorganization," *Marquette Law Review*, 31 (February, 1948), 272-80.

Lee, Eugene C., *The Presiding Officer and Rules Committee in Legislatures of the United States* (Berkeley: University of California, Bureau of Public Administration, September, 1952).

Lewis, Henry W., *Legislative Committees in North Carolina* (Chapel Hill: University of North Carolina, Institute of Government, 1952).

——, *The General Assembly of North Carolina: Guidebook of Organization and Procedure* (Chapel Hill: University of North Carolina, Institute of Government, 1951).

McHenry, Dean E., *A New Legislature for Modern California* (Los Angeles: Haynes Foundation, 1940).

Michigan State Bar Association, *The Legislative Structure and Procedure of Michigan: A Comprehensive Factual Survey* (1947).

New York State Constitutional Convention Committee, *Problems Relating to Legislative Organization and Powers* (Albany: J. B. Lyon, 1938).

Nixon, Clarence H., "The Southern Legislatures and Legislation," *Journal of Politics*, 10 (August, 1948), 410-17.

Perkins, John A., "State Legislative Reorganization," *American Political Science Review*, 40 (June, 1946), 510-21.

———, "The Legislatures and the Future of the States," *State Government*, 19 (October, 1946), 254-57, 266.

Rossell, Beatrice S., *Working with a Legislature* (Chicago: American Library Association, 1948).

Schaffter, Dorothy, *The Bicameral System in Practice* (University of Iowa Press, 1929).

Senning, John P., "Unicameralism Passes Test," *National Municipal Review*, 33 (July, 1944), 60-65.

———, *The One House Legislature* (McGraw-Hill, 1937).

Shull, C. W., *American Experience with Unicameral Legislatures*, pamphlet (Detroit Bureau of Governmental Research, 1937).

Shumate, Roger V., "The Nebraska Unicameral Legislature," *Western Political Quarterly*, 5 (September, 1952), 504-12.

Sikes, Pressly S., "Special Interim Commissions in the Indiana Legislative Process," *American Political Science Review*, 36 (October, 1942), 906-15.

South Carolina Joint Committee on Reorganization, *Legislative Reorganization: Findings and Recommendations* (1949).

Spencer, Richard C., "Nebraska Idea 15 Years Old," *National Municipal Review*, 39 (February, 1950), 83-86.

Summers, H. B., *Unicameralism in Practice, The Nebraska Legislative System* (New York: H. W. Wilson Co., 1937).

Thornton, Herschel V., *Legislative Organization and Procedure* (Constitutional Survey Committee, Oklahoma Legislative Council, 1948).

Trimble, Bruce R., and Stamps, Norman L., *The Structure of the Legislature: Bicameral or Unicameral* (Missouri Constitutional Convention of 1943).

Unicameral System of Legislation (Symposium), *Congressional Digest*, 16 (August and September, 1937), 197-224.

Washington Legislative Council, *Report of the Subcommittee on Rules, Organization and Procedure of the Legislature* (1948).

———, *The Reorganization of Internal Management Facilities in State Government* (1948).

Webster, Donald H., *The Legislature and Legislative Process in the State of Washington* (University of Washington, Bureau of Governmental Research and Services, 1942).

Weeks, O. Douglas, *Two Legislative Houses or One* (Dallas, Texas: Arnold Foundation Studies, vol. VI, Winter, 1938).

Willoughby, William F., *Principles of Legislative Organization and Administration* (The Brookings Institution, 1934).

Winslow, C. I., *State Legislative Committees: A Study in Procedure* (Johns Hopkins University Press, 1931).

Wood, Thomas J., *Distinctive Practices of the Massachusetts General Court* (unpublished dissertation, Harvard University, 1947).

PROCEDURE

"Action by the Legislatures, 1947," *State Government,* 22 (July, 1949), 168-74, 181-82.

Bennett, C. E., "Yeas and Nays Waste Time," *U. S. A.* (National Association of Manufacturers), April, 1952, pp. 59-63.

Braham, W. Walter, "Reform of Pennsylvania's Legislative Procedure," *Temple Law Quarterly,* 25 (April, 1952), 420-27.

Chichester, Cassius M., *Notes on Draftsmanship of Bills in Virginia* (Division of Statutory Research and Drafting, 1947).

Coigne, Armand B., *Statute Making: A Treatise on the Means and Methods for the Enactment of Statute Law in the United States* (Chicago: Commerce Clearing House, 1948).

Connecticut Public Expenditure Council, *Further Improvements in Legislative Procedure* (1947).

The Council of State Governments, *State Bill Drafting Manuals* (July, 1951, mimeo.).

Dodds, H. W., *Procedure in State Legislatures* (Philadelphia: The American Academy of Political and Social Science, 1918).

Farmer, Hallie, *The Legislative Process in Alabama* (University of Alabama, Bureau of Public Administration, 1949).

Faust, Martin L., *Organization Manual* (Missouri Constitutional Convention of 1943).

Grant, J. A. C., "New Jersey's 'Popular Action' in Rem to Control Legislative Procedure," *Rutgers Law Review,* 3-4 (1950), 391-417.

Guild, Frederic H., and Snider, Clyde F., *Legislative Procedure in Kansas* (rev. ed., Lawrence: University of Kansas, Bureau of Governmental Research, 1946).

Illinois Legislative Council, *Legislative Broadcasting and Recording* (February, 1952).

———, *Scheduling Legislative Workloads* (1952).

Illinois Legislative Reference Bureau, *Notes on Bill Drafting in Illinois* (rev. ed., 1950, mimeo.).

Kennedy, Duncan L., *Drafting Bills for the Minnesota Legislature, Suggestions for Draftsmen in Preparing Bills for Introduti* (West Publishing Company, 1946).

———, "The Legislative Process with Particular Reference to Minnesota," *Minnesota Law Review,* 30 (June, 1946), 653-79.

———, "Legislative Bill Drafting," *Minnesota Law Review,* 31 (December, 1946), 103-20.

Lewis, Henry W., *The General Assembly of North Carolina: Guidebook of Organization and Procedure* (Chapel Hill: University of North Carolina, Institute of Government, 1951).

Louisiana Legislative Council, *The Legislative Process in Louisiana* (1953).

Luce, Robert, *Legislative Procedure* (Houghton Mifflin, 1922).

Marshall, George B., "Life History of a Bill in the Ohio Legislature," *Ohio State Law Journal,* 11 (1950), 447-55.

Metzenbaum, Howard M., "Judicial Interpretation of Constitutional Limitations on Legislative Procedure in Ohio," *Ohio State Law Journal,* 11 (Autumn, 1950), 456-61.

New York State Bill Drafting Commission, *Bill Drafting Manual* (1948).

New York State Joint Legislative Committee on Legislative Methods, Practices, Procedures and Expenditures, *Interim Report* (Leg. Doc. 35, 1945); *Final Report* (Leg. Doc. 31, 1946).

Olmsted, H. M. (ed.), "Massachusetts Body Urges Legislative Changes," *National Municipal Review,* 41 (April, 1952), 198.

Plaisted, John W., *Legislative Procedure in the General Court of Massachusetts* (Boston: Wright and Potter Printing Co., 1948).

Poldervaart, Arie, "Legislative Drafting in New Mexico," *New Mexico Tax Bulletin,* 21 (December, 1942), 177-83.

"Sabotage in the Legislatures," *National Municipal Review,* 42 (July, 1953), 320-21.

Sharkoff, Eugene F., "The Michigan 'Log Jam' Rule," *State Government,* 24 (February, 1951), 34, inside back cover.

Sinclair, Thornton, *Procedural Limitations on the Legislative Process in the New Jersey Constitution* (Governor's Committee on Preparatory Research for the New Jersey Constitutional Convention, 1947).

Sullivan, Rodman, "Some Quantitative Aspects of Legislation in Kentucky," *Kentucky Law Journal,* 34 (January, 1946), 118-37.

Underwood, Cecil H., *The Legislative Process in West Virginia* (West Virginia Bureau for Government Research, 1953).

Walker, Harvey, *The Legislative Process: Law Making in the United States* (Ronald, 1948).

Young, C. C., *The Legislature of California: Its Membership, Procedure, and Work* (San Francisco: The Commonwealth Club of California, 1943).

LEGISLATIVE AIDS

Arkansas University School of Law, *Bill Drafting Handbook for the State of Arkansas* (Arkansas Legislative Council, 1950).

Bubolz, Gordon A., "Improving Government through Legislative Research," *Governmental News,* May, 1952, pp. 7-9, 33.

Campbell, Willard D., "Code Revision in Ohio," *State Government,* 20 (July, 1947), 195-96.

———, "Continuous Code Revision in Ohio," *Ohio State Law Journal,* 11 (Autumn, 1950), 533-50.

Cullen, Robert K., "Revision of the Oregon Statutes," *Oregon Law Review,* 28 (February, 1949), 120-37.

Davey, Harold W., "The Legislative Council Movement in the United States, 1933-1953," *American Political Science Review,* 47 (September, 1953), 785-97.

Farmer, Hallie, "Legislative Planning and Research in Alabama," *Journal of Politics,* 9 (August, 1947), 429-38.

Fortenberry, C. N., "Classes for Mississippi Legislators," *State Government,* 25 (April, 1952), 85, 92-93.

Glosser, Lauren A., "Ohio Legislators Get Help," *National Municipal Review,* 40 (October, 1951), 468-72.

———, "The Ohio Program Commission: A New Approach to Legislative Studies," *State Government,* 24 (February, 1951), 35, 44.

Graves, W. Brooke, "Legislative Reference Service for the Congress of the United States," *American Political Science Review,* 41 (April, 1947), 289-93.

Grove, L. R., "Massachusetts School for Legislators," *State Government,* 25 (April, 1952), 84, 92.

Guild, Frederic H., "Legislative Councils: Objectives and Accomplishments," *State Government,* 22 (September, 1949), 217-19, 226.

———, *Legislative Councils: An Article and a Bibliography* (Kansas Legislative Council, 1944).

Heineman, Ben W., "A Law Revision Commission for Illinois," *Illinois Law Review,* 42 (January-February, 1948), 698-727.

Illinois Legislative Council, *Law Revision Agencies* (1949).

Jones, Harry W., "Bill Drafting Services in Congress and the State Legislatures," *Harvard Law Review,* 65 (January, 1952), 441-51.

Kammerer, Gladys M., "Legislative Research and Planning in Kentucky," *Kentucky Law Journal,* 36 (May, 1948), 379-400.

————, "Right About Face in Kentucky," *National Municipal Review,* 37 (June, 1948), 303-8.

————, "The Development of the Legislative Research Arm," *Journal of Politics,* 12 (November, 1950), 652-67.

Larsen, Christian L., and Ryan, Miles F., Jr., *Aids For State Legislators* (University of South Carolina, Bureau of Public Administration, 1947).

Lindsey, Jim T., "The Texas Legislative Council," *Baylor Law Review,* 2 (Spring, 1950), 303-17.

Meller, Norman, "The Policy Position of Legislative Reference Service Agencies," *Western Political Quarterly,* 5 (March, 1952), 109-23.

Nevada Legislative Counsel Bureau, *Survey of Recodification Problems in Nevada* (1950).

National Education Association, *Aids in Bill Drafting for Use by Legislative Committees of Teachers' Organizations* (1942).

Ohm, Howard F., "Legislative Reference in Wisconsin," *State Government,* 21 (December, 1948), 240-43, 253.

O'Rourke, Lawrence W., *Legislative Assistance* (Los Angeles: University of California, Bureau of Governmental Research, 1951).

Philbrick, Frederick A., *Language and the Law; the Semantics of Forensic English* (Macmillan, 1949).

Pierce, Melvin, "The 'Third' House in Indiana," *National Municipal Review,* 40 (October, 1951), 473-79.

Richards, Allan B., *Legislative Services* (University of New Mexico, Department of Government, Division of Research, 1953).

Rhodes, Jack A., "Legislative Services in the British Parliament," *Southwestern Social Science Quarterly,* 33 (June, 1952), 28-37.

————, "Light for State Legislatures," *National Municipal Review,* 35 (September, 1946), 473-79.

Rossell, Beatrice S., *Working with a Legislature* (Chicago: American Library Association, 1948).

Saltiel, Edward P., "The Illinois Legislative Council," *Public Aid in Illinois,* 15 (October, 1948), 4-6, 15.

Schwartz, Arthur A., "The Ohio Legislative Reference Bureau and Its Place in the Legislative Process," *Ohio State Law Journal,* 11 (Autumn, 1950), 436-46.

Sikes, Pressly S., "Special Interim Commissions in the Indiana Legislative Process," *American Political Science Review,* 36 (October, 1942), 906-15.

Sparlin, Estal E., "Experts for the Lawmakers," *National Municipal Review,* 37 (June, 1948), 299-302, 314.

Sutherland, Jabez G., *Statute and Statutory Construction* (3 vols., Callaghan, 1943).

Toepel, M. G., "The Legislative Reference Library: Serving Wisconsin," *Wisconsin Law Review,* 1951 (January, 1951), 114-24.

Wight, Mark H., *Bill Drafting in Washington* (University of Washington, Bureau of Research and Services, 1950).

Wilcox, Jerome K. (ed.), *Manual on the Use of State Publications* (Chicago: American Library Association, 1940).

Wilkes, James C., "Better Legislation through Cooperation—The Work of the Drafting Committee of the Council of State Governments," *State Government,* 22 (January, 1949), 16-18, 22.

EXECUTIVE-LEGISLATIVE RELATIONS

Bowles, Chester A., "A Governor's Job as Seen by a Governor," *New York Times Magazine,* July 24, 1949, pp. 8, 30 ff.

The Council of State Governments, "Governors' Messages," *State Government,* March issue, 1949 and subsequent years.

Ewing, Cortez A. M., "Southern Governors," *Journal of Politics,* 10 (May, 1948), 385-409.

Farmer, Hallie, *The Legislative Process in Alabama,* ch. 8 (University of Alabama, Bureau of Public Administration, 1949).

Faust, M. L., *Manual of the Executive Article for the Missouri Constitutional Convention of 1943* (1943).

Illinois Legislative Council, *The Veto Power in Illinois* (1943).

Kammerer, Gladys M., "Legislative Oversight of Administration in Kentucky," *Public Administration Review,* 10 (Summer, 1950), 169-75.

Lipson, Leslie, "The Executive Branch in New State Constitutions," *Public Administration Review,* 9 (Winter, 1949), 11-21.

McGeary, M. Nelson, "The Governor's Veto in Pennsylvania," *American Political Science Review,* 41 (October, 1947), 941-46.

Perkins, John A., *The Role of the Governor of Michigan in the Enactment of Appropriations* (University of Michigan, Bureau of Government, 1943).

Prescott, Frank W., "Constitutional Provisions on the Governor's Veto Power," *Tennessee Papers on Constitutional Revision*, 2 (University of Tennessee, 1947), 64-88.

————, "The Executive Veto in American States," *Western Political Quarterly*, 3 (March, 1950), 98-112.

————, "The Executive Veto in the Southern States," *Journal of Politics*, 10 (November, 1948), 659-75.

Prothro, James W., *A Study of Constitutional Developments in the Office of the Governor of Louisiana* (Louisiana State University, mimeo., 1947).

Ransone, Coleman B., *The Office of Governor in the South* (University of Alabama, Bureau of Public Administration, 1951).

Solomon, Samuel R., "The Governor as Legislator," *National Municipal Review*, 40 (November, 1951), 515-20.

Walker, Harvey, "Governors' Messages and the Legislative Product in 1932," *American Political Science Review*, 26 (December, 1932), 1058-75.

White, Leonard D., "Legislative Responsibility for the Public Service," in *New Horizons in Public Administration*, a symposium (University of Alabama Press, 1945).

Index